The American Success Myth on Film

The American Success Myth on Film

Julie Levinson
Babson College, USA

palgrave
macmillan

First published 2012 by
PALGRAVE MACMILLAN

Palgrave Macmillan in the UK is an imprint of Macmillan Publishers Limited, registered in England, company number 785998, of Houndmills, Basingstoke, Hampshire RG21 6XS.

Palgrave Macmillan in the US is a division of St Martin's Press LLC, 175 Fifth Avenue, New York, NY 10010.

Palgrave Macmillan is the global academic imprint of the above companies and has companies and representatives throughout the world.

Palgrave® and Macmillan® are registered trademarks in the United States, the United Kingdom, Europe and other countries.

ISBN 978–0–230–36336–6

This book is printed on paper suitable for recycling and made from fully managed and sustained forest sources. Logging, pulping and manufacturing processes are expected to conform to the environmental regulations of the country of origin.

A catalogue record for this book is available from the British Library.

A catalog record for this book is available from the Library of Congress.

10   9   8   7   6   5   4   3   2   1
21   20   19   18   17   16   15   14   13   12

Printed and bound in Great Britain by
CPI Antony Rowe, Chippenham and Eastbourne

Contents

Figures

Acknowledgments

The American success myth is such vast and varied terrain that it took me a while to map this corner of it and to draw the boundaries of my study. As I navigated my way through the thicket of ideas that inform the myth, I had a good deal of companionship and support.

I am beholden to several people who read portions of the book and whose comments and insights helped to shape my analysis: Pat Aufderheide, George Bluestone, Fritz Fleischmann, Alan Lebowitz, Nan Levinson, Bill Paul, Karen Rosenberg, and Marty Tropp. With characteristic engagement and efficiency, my former students Esha Bawa and John Chartier assisted with the end matter of the book. Janet Silver graciously offered her professional expertise and advice. My employer, Babson College, USA, has been steadfast in its support for this project. Summer stipends from the Babson Faculty Research Fund, along with the bounty of the Leeds Hackett and William F. Glavin Term Chairs, enabled me to bring the book to fruition.

Finally, my family has cheered me on during every step of the journey. Phyllis Levinson, my mother as well as my lifelong lodestar and exemplar, helped me in countless ways. My husband, Al Weinstein, boon companion on all of my excursions and explorations, brought to this one an abundance of love, encouragement, and good humor. This book is dedicated to my daughters, Elena and Molly – the grandest of successes.

I am grateful for permission to reprint the following previously published material:

Chapter 1's epigraph is from 'Myth' by Manfred Beller in Manfred Beller and Joep Leerseen, ed., *Imagology: The Cultural Construction and Literary Representation of National Characters: A Critical Survey* (Amsterdam: Rodopi, 2007), p. 373. Reprinted with permission.
Chapter 2's epigraph is from Leslie Fiedler, *A Fiedler Reader* (New York: Stein and Day, 1977), p. 239. Reprinted with permission.
Chapter 4's first epigraph is from the movie *Possessed* (1931), directed by Clarence Brown. Screenplay by Lenore Coffee, based on the play *The Mirage* by Edgar Selwyn. Used with permission of Warner Bros. Entertainment Inc. on behalf of Turner Entertainment Co.

Chapter 4's second epigraph is from Steven Cohan, *Masked Men: Masculinity and the Movies in the Fifties* (Bloomington, IN: Indiana University Press, 1997), p. 78. Reprinted with permission.

The Conclusion's epigraph is from Morris Dickstein, *Dancing in the Dark: A Cultural History of the Great Depression* (New York: W.W. Norton, 2009), p. 359. Reprinted with permission.

1
Top of the World: Cultural Narratives, Myths, and Movies

> The invention of a myth is the founding act of a community's self-image.
>
> – Manfred Beller, *Imagology*

It is an old story but, in all of its guises, a perennially appealing one. A poor boy makes good. A secretary marries her boss, thereby launching herself from the steno pool to the penthouse. A lowborn young man with a burning ambition and an idea that everyone tells him is crazy becomes a successful entrepreneur. A fresh-off-the-boat immigrant seizes the promise of the new world and reinvents himself as a dyed-in-the-wool American tycoon. These classic – if clichéd – success stories were already deeply etched in the popular consciousness by the time Hollywood put its stamp on them. Scores of self-help manuals, popular novels, religious tracts, and biographies have played their part in the ritual re-enactment of one of our most enduring cultural doctrines: that trading rags for riches is not only possible but is part of our national entitlement. The movies' particular contribution to the American idea of success has been to codify, perpetuate, amplify, and sometimes challenge that idea in notably complex ways.

The myth of success, with its fervid conviction that the opportunity for material attainment and spiritual fulfillment is every individual's birthright and is within each person's power, is central to American national identity. Our public discourse and our cultural artifacts exalt the archetype of the self-made man who, with determination, industriousness, and strategy, propels himself to the pinnacle of achievement. Since the eighteenth century, the success myth has been a key component of American master narratives: those resonant stories that seem to contain the essence of the nation and that get told and retold across

1

generations and genres. The myth's continuity and ubiquity attest to its strong hold on our national imagination and to its definitional role in our ongoing cultural conversation about what it means to be an American.

At its most basic, the success myth enshrines optimism and self-invention. Paradigmatic success myth stories involve ordinary young men who, through individual will and initiative, overcome their humble beginnings and all other hurdles to advancement. The myth tends to deny or downplay innate limitations, social constraints, or systemic obstacles while satisfying the hopeful belief that if an individual remains true to his aspirations, he will receive his just rewards. Just as Jay Gatsby, the most poignant of self-made men, persisted in his faith in 'something commensurate to his capacity for wonder,' the classic success myth hero keeps his eyes firmly fixed on the prize until, at last and inevitably, it becomes his.[1]

The myth is so durable because its promise that individuals can remake themselves and can wield absolute agency over their own fate is so appealing. Americans, the myth insists, are self-authoring and autonomous. It is our personal choices, rather than our social status or conditions, that create our identity and destiny. This cornerstone of American thought is one of the fundamental aspects of our national imaginary: a locution that derives from historian Benedict Anderson's notion of nations as 'imagined communities' whose peoples are bound together by a common sense of experience and set of mores. In suggesting that a country's national imaginary is underpinned by a 'narrative of identity,'[2] he and other scholars of nationhood have argued that national identities are reinforced by a web of discursive practices that selectively distill the reality of our daily existence and that bind us in spite of our differences.[3] Our sense of community and commonality is repeatedly instilled by the traditional stories that we tell ourselves about ourselves: our national myths. These myths are among the representations that acculturate us to a particular sense of the world and our place within it. In this view, national character, rather than being an essentialist predisposition to certain traits, is fostered by cultural constructs, among them rhetorical and narrational conventions which create, as much as they reflect, our collective sense of identity and ideals.

Ancient and contemporary myths

Myths are among the most enduring and resilient of those cultural constructs. In an essay linking the function of contemporary cultural narratives to ancient myth, Bruce Lincoln claims that both are 'the stories through which groups accomplish the task of sociocultural reproduction by inscribing their values and sense of shared identity on those who are its members-in-the-making so that they will come to know and remember just who they are and just where they belong.'[4] Lincoln is among many theorists who insist that the term 'myth' denotes not simply a loose set of cultural beliefs. Rather, by definition, myths are ritually retold consensus narratives that exemplify cultural creeds, and that are marked by recurring conventions of plot, characterization, and causality.[5] The success myth is related to, but distinct from, 'The American Dream,' because it couches the promises of that catchall idiom in specifically narrative form.[6] A myth is differentiated by three essential attributes: its narrative structure, its status as a sacred truth for the culture, and its social function of affirming and relaying cultural norms and practices.

The methods of dissemination for contemporary myths may differ from the oral diffusion of pre-literate myths; rather than telling tales huddled around the light of a fire, we relay our mythic lore by the light of a flickering screen. But although the transmission of modern myth may differ in its formal qualities and its reach, the functions and structures of cultural narratives have much in common with classic myths, since narrative remains the primary way for human consciousness to articulate and make sense of our experiences. Like sacred myths in pre-modern cultures, our master narratives are tales of individuals that purport to explain larger phenomena and to articulate behavioral and aspirational norms, thereby creating social cohesion. And like all sustaining fictions that are deeply etched in a community's collective psyche, they offer a particularly felicitous way to explore how a culture's cherished stories and ideologies interact to consolidate – and perpetuate – a standardized, idealized set of values and self-images.

Many myth theorists have confronted the question of the extent to which contemporary cultural narratives correspond to pre-modern myths. Nearly every scholarly consideration of myth begins by declaring that there is no unified, universally accepted rubric that encompasses all myths. Although comparativist theorists, such as Joseph Campbell, have searched for overarching thematic commonalities across cultures, and structuralist theorists, notably Claude Lévi-Strauss, have sought consistent narrative patterns, there is wide variation in views about the existence of universal mythic norms. Nonetheless, there are a few generally accepted approaches to considering the functions and attributes of myths across cultures and across millennia.

One point of consistency has to do with the fundamental truths that myths contain for a given culture. At their most basic, myths are shared beliefs conveyed in the form of narrative and endowed with cultural authority and validity. In common parlance, a myth is taken to be something that is unbelievable and substantially untrue. Whereas the Greek *logos* refers to language rooted in reason, *mythos* refers to the articulation of the imaginative and the non-rational. But from the perspectives of cultural anthropology and comparative religion, myths are assumed by their hearers to contain essential, often sacred, truths about their experience. Although mythic narratives may seem fantastical, these stories' underlying values have deep validity for those who perceive and perpetuate them. Robert Segal, who has written widely about the history and theory of myth, defines myths, at their most basic, as ritually repeated stories that derive their power and place in a culture through repetition, variation, and adaptability. He insists that for a cultural narrative to qualify as a myth, it needs to be consistently and tenaciously believed by its adherents, even when it seems to contradict lived experience. With myths, Segal explains, 'The conviction remains firm even in the face of its transparent falsity.' Because they are intrinsic to social values, their truth is taken for granted and sanctified by the culture that cherishes them. They are distinguished from legends, folk tales, and historical accounts because, beyond simply telling an engaging, familiar story, they 'accomplish [...] something significant for their adherents.'[7]

That 'something significant' is a cultural consensus about how the world can be made intelligible and morally lucid. When science and rationality reach their limits in explaining natural or social phenomena, myths reassure their hearers that those phenomena are coherent and are containable within a narrative discourse. In ethnologist Bronislaw Malinowski's succinct formation:

Myth fulfills [...] an indispensable function: it expresses, enhances and codifies belief; it safeguards and enforces morality; it vouches for the efficiency of ritual and contains practical rules for the guidance of man. Myth is thus a vital ingredient in human civilization; it is not an idle tale, but a hard-worked active force; it is not an intellectual explanation or an artistic imagery, but a pragmatic charter of primitive faith and moral wisdom.[8]

Malinowski's functional view suggests that myths provide a reassuring narrative framework for understanding a culture's beliefs about how the world works and how individual members of that culture are expected to proceed through that world. They sanction a particular, comprehensible explanation for why things are the way they are.

As such, myths contain an aura of inevitability: what religion scholars Wendy Doniger and Laurie Patton call 'an "always-already given" quality.'[9] Mythic narratives tend to naturalize particular ways of interpreting experience, so that we hold these myths to be self-evident and we barely notice their lingering presence in our cultural discourse. It is this ostensibly timeless, ineluctable aspect of mythic narratives that endows them with such cultural status and resonance. As they mediate our world views, social arrangements, and moral judgments, their contingent qualities go undetected. So stories that are, in actuality, highly inflected with historical, cultural, and ideological assumptions camouflage those assumptions to present a cultural logic that seems incontrovertible. In *The Myth of the State*, his study of the intersection of mythic thinking and political theory, Ernst Cassirer claims that mythic thinking has its own brand of emotion-laden logic: 'A myth is in a sense invulnerable. It is impervious to rational arguments; it cannot be refuted by syllogisms.'[10] He echoes Malinowski in claiming that the 'truth' of myths derives from an emotional attachment to their cosmological outlook. Both theorists have a pragmatic view of myth: to promote harmony and cohesion among cultural constituents who share a deeply emotional response to mythic lore.

Cassirer endows myth with both a psychological and a sociological function. Psychologically, myths fulfill their hearers' needs by providing a reassuring and emotionally satisfying explanation for how things are. Sociologically, they provide a sense of solidarity and affinity for those who absorb and repeat these stories.[11] Such a functional view of mythic narratives suggests that they exist to validate social behaviors and structures, and to supply a clarifying lens through which a culture might communally gaze on its lived experience. Doniger has come up with an apt description of that mythic lens with her metaphor of the microscope and the telescope. In her formulation, myths provide a sort of double vision, focusing simultaneously on the close-up details of individual human lives and the panoramic view of cosmic matters:

> The myth offers a fictive solution to the problem that it raises, but we may carry it back into our lives to make it real.... Myths form a bridge between the terrifying abyss of cosmological ignorance and our comfortable familiarity with our recurrent, if tormenting, human problems. Myths make us reverse the focus, viewing through the telescope of detachment the personal lives that we normally view

through the microscope and viewing the cosmic questions through the microscope of intimate involvement.[12]

So the double lens of myth allows us to perceive, with seeming facility, stories that resonate with personal, communal, and ontological concerns.

Doniger goes on to claim that myths, however deeply encoded and ritually invoked, have no fixity of meaning. Instead they are conventional stories that are capable of being understood and interpreted in any number of ways:

> A myth is a much-retold narrative that is transparent to a variety of constructions of meaning, a neutral structure that allows paradoxical meanings to be held in a charged tension. This transparency – the quality of a lens – allows a myth, more than other forms of narrative, to be shared by a group (who, as individuals, have various points of view) and to survive through time (through different generations with different points of view). The transparency of myth has at least three significant effects: (1) any single telling may incorporate various voices; (2) any myth may generate different retellings, different variants, each with its own voice; and (3) any single telling is subject to various reinterpretations.[13]

Myths endure in a culture precisely because they are able to evolve and adapt to varying circumstances. The basic narrative attributes and cultural ideals remain stable, or at least recognizable, but the meaning derived from those attributes is variable. This is the paradox of mythic narrative: both the familiarity of the stories and their interpretive suppleness are essential to their endurance. Myths, while inflected with social values and meanings, are also organically responsive to social changes. Indeed, they function to mediate those changes as they provide a template for confronting new challenges with old ideals. Particularly for contemporary myths, which appear and reappear in a variety of permutations and representational forms, the interplay between familiar narrative contours and fresh contexts allows for a dynamic tension.

Myth and ideology

Latter-day myths generally function to explain social, rather than physical, phenomena. They are cosmogonies in the sense that they address the culturally inscribed origins of human tendencies and aspirations, rather than the origins of the universe. So instead of helping us to comprehend the mysteries of nature, contemporary myths try to comprehend the workings of human nature. Our mythic stories tend to resonate experientially and ideologically, if not literally; although we may not give absolute credence to the actual events of the narrative in the way that hearers of sacred myths did, we nonetheless subscribe to the normative values and world views contained in that narrative. The root assumptions of contemporary myths have a fundamental ideological validity that taps into a culture's self-image and that is sustained through changing social and historical circumstances.[14] The intersection of cultural myths and national ideologies is the starting point for many considerations of how current myths function and what needs they fulfill. These works have informed my analysis of the American success myth, and my own sense of the extent to which the forms and functions of sacred, pre-modern myths are pertinent to secular cultural narratives in modern times.[15] By transposing classic myth theory to contemporary iterations of myth, these works suggest that the site where myth, social history, and national ideology intersect is fertile ground for mapping the transcendent ideas of American culture. But it is also contested terrain where denotative signposts point in multiple directions. Hence, these cultural artifacts need to be unearthed and examined for the varied meanings they may reveal. Among those cultural artifacts, myths are, by definition, so familiar that the process of analyzing them requires a critical estrangement from formal and thematic norms and a deliberate, evidential excavation of the ideologies contained within them.

In his work on political myths, Christopher G. Flood defines contemporary myth as 'ideology cast in the form of story,' and claims that the delights of narrative help to naturalize and legitimize prevailing ideological assumptions so that they seem inevitable and universally applicable. According to him:

> The narrative discourse carries the imprint of the assumptions, values, and goals associated with a specific ideology or identifiable family of ideologies, and it therefore conveys an explicit or implicit invitation to assent to a particular ideological standpoint.... To be the expression of a *myth* the telling of a given narrative in any particular instance needs to be perceived as being adequately faithful to the most important facts *and* the correct interpretation of a story which a social group already accepts or subsequently comes to accept as true.[16]

In a sense, myths provide good cover for embedded dogma, since their persistently recycled narrative conventions seem to be 'the once-and-forever-known repository of exemplary models.'[17] Both myths and their values-laden assumptions are so much a part of a culture's collective DNA that they seem to be an element of nature rather than of culture. The ideological givens of the American success myth – the credo of individualism, the assumption of universal opportunity for advancement and self-improvement, the unified idea about what success entails – come to us via a set of thematic and formal conventions that are instantly recognizable and seemingly incontestable. They are so deeply implanted in the national mind that we tend to accept them uncritically and forget their status as cultural constructions. So the task of reading contemporary myths involves ferreting out and deciphering how entrenched ideologies are presented, reinforced, and, sometimes, challenged in multiple tellings of the myth.

American myths and contemporary cultural narratives

Two decades ago, film scholar Robert Ray demonstrated one method of employing myth theory to illuminate – and complicate – the ideologies embedded in contemporary cultural narratives in his book *A Certain Tendency of the Hollywood Cinema, 1930–1980*. His analysis of five decades of Hollywood movies was among a few works of film hermeneutics to proceed from Claude Lévi-Strauss' theory of binary oppositions.[18] In arguing that myths across cultures display an 'astounding similarity' and are subject to certain universal structural principles, Lévi-Strauss had identified several antinomies that recur in mythic narratives.[19] In his comparative structural analysis, all myths contain sets of paired forces that pull against one other, as well as forces that then try to mediate or resolve this apparent incompatibility. According to this theory, myth's function in, and appeal to, a given culture involves its attempt to reconcile such oppositions: to imply that both can be accommodated and that their discrepancies can be negotiated or overcome.

Ray's systematic study of American films exposes our own mythology's recurring oppositions: adventure/domesticity, individual/community, and worldly success/ordinary life. The thematic paradigm that he identifies seems to confirm Lévi-Strauss' claim of a reconciliatory pattern in mythic narratives, as these movies repeatedly deny the necessity for choosing between such contradictory desires. Ray suggests that American movies insist on a 'both/and' rather than an 'either/or' ethic. Our cultural narratives adamantly split the difference between competing commitments by suggesting that, as Americans, we can gratify conflicting desires and can thereby avoid irrevocable decisions that exclude other possibilities. This denial of the need to make difficult choices, and the concomitant belief that we can have it all, is, Ray claims, one of the hallmarks of American exceptionalism, which optimistically endorses the notion that we are unbound by limits and exempt from the burdens of history that beset other nations.[20] Lévi-Strauss' theory of binary oppositions is the jumping-off point for Ray's exploration of the ideological implications of these wish-fulfilling resolutions of dialectical forces that appear repeatedly in success myth narratives.

One of the foundational works on American mythology is historian Richard Slotkin's monumental trilogy on the myth of the American frontier.[21] Slotkin echoes anthropological definitions of myths as symbolic formulations which transmit a culture's values and world view from one generation to the next. They do so by renewing their basic narrative qualities but also by adapting them to changing social and historical circumstances.[22] Since myth traffics in well-established beliefs and calls forth predetermined, almost ritualized, responses, it provides a shorthand way of interpreting our material conditions and our lived existence. So we intuitively recognize a myth's contours even when it appears in new forms or eras.

Like Ray, Slotkin sees mythic values as simultaneously appealing and simplistic (or, more to the point, appealing because they are simplistic). 'The moral and political imperatives implicit in the myths are given as if they were the only possible choices for moral and intelligent beings; and, similarly, the set of choices confronted are limited to a few traditional "either/or" decisions.'[23] The stark symbolic dualities that define the frontier myth (east/west, civilization/nature, cowboy/Indian, rancher/homesteader, settler/nomad) or the success myth (material/spiritual success, worldliness/ordinariness, fame/anonymity, ambition/acquiescence, self-interest/civic duty) contain moral valuations that consistently privilege one alternative of each pair over the other. Slotkin labels such mythic discourses as 'a constraining grammar of codified memories and beliefs' that affect both our outlook and our behaviors by enlisting us in their comfortingly oversimplified program.[24] He further claims that once the formal qualities of myth are 'reduced to a set of powerfully evocative and resonant "icons" ... [they] become part of the language, as a deeply encoded set of metaphors that may contain all of the "lessons" we have learned from our history, and all of the essential elements of our world view.'[25]

Slotkin's wide-ranging, broadly diachronic study posits myth as a buffer against the changes wrought by history. As he examines the mythology of the frontier from the seventeenth through the twentieth centuries across discursive forms (literary, political, performative, and cinematic), he demonstrates the ways in which cultural myths condition us to interpret and respond to historical change. Mythic narratives and their attendant ideologies function as cultural ballast, providing stability and assurance as we navigate the upheavals of history. They also stand as a denial of temporality:

> Myth has a paradoxical way of dealing with historical experience: although the materials of myth are historical, myth organizes these materials ahistorically .... What is lost when history is translated into myth is the essential premise of history – the distinction of past and present itself. The past is made metaphorically equivalent to the present; and the present appears simply as a repetition of persistently recurring structures identified with the past. Both past and present are reduced to instances displaying a single 'law' or principle of nature, which is seen as timeless in its relevance, and as transcending all historical contingencies.[26]

The familiarity of mythic beliefs encourages us to view them as eternal verities that provide a ready frame for understanding what is happening to and around us. In this way, mythic narrative functions transhistorically, not only creating national comity but also eliding past and present so that our communal experience is purportedly 'readable' by a few, multipurpose mythic lenses. This idea that myth provides one of our dominant interpretive tools is a large and highly fraught claim. But Slotkin painstakingly demonstrates how, across 400 years of American history, the frontier myth has served as a broadly applied metaphor, used in our public discourse to rationalize and justify everything from America's expansionist policies to our political choices to our role in global affairs. His demonstration of the reciprocity between myth and social history and the ways in which the frontier myth has been subtly responsive to changing social, political, and economic circumstances is applicable to the success myth as well.

Slotkin recognizes the success myth as a variant of the frontier myth in that both associate self-invention with the consolidation of a national identity. Early in our history the frontier myth's protagonist established himself as the embodiment of autonomous individualism by doing battle with hostile elements to make the country safe for civilization. He was later joined in the popular imagination by the self-made man, who exercised his own brand of unfettered individualism in the somewhat less communally minded cause of his own social and material advancement. Like the frontiersman, the success myth hero is a staunch individualist compelled by restless ambition to face down challenges while exploring frontiers of possibility. Both myths often appear as stories of initiation in which the protagonist acquires know-how and grows in wisdom and, sometimes, moral stature through his adventures. But what the success hero often comes to know, as Slotkin points out, is how to exploit his opportunities and, when necessary, his fellow man: 'For these heroes, self-transformation takes the primitive form of learning to be "shifty in a new country," and is consummated by the achievement of upward mobility.'[27]

As America became more urbanized and the actual frontier closed, frontier tales were, indeed, often relocated to other metaphorical settings. However, Slotkin's comparison is illuminating only up to a point. The stories of self-made men were not simply chronicles of rugged individualism transferred from the hostile environment of the American West to the equally hostile urban frontier. Although they tapped in to some of the same ideals, success myth tales distinguished themselves with their own compelling iconography and narrative conventions, not to mention their own stance toward ambition, individualism, and civilization. The self-made man may be the urban twin of the maverick frontiersman; he wields business acumen rather than a six-gun, sports a fedora in place of a ten-gallon hat, and is as loquacious as the frontiersman is laconic. The distinctions are not merely superficial, however. The urban version of the success hero marks a significant change from both the frontiersman, with his rustic authenticity, and the earlier, religiously derived exemplars of success, with their piety and modesty. As the country came to grips with a rapidly industrializing, urbanizing, and diversifying America, the attendant myths became tinged with a greater moral ambiguity and with a deep vein of ambivalence toward the very essence and definition of success.

The American success myth in history

The ideology of the American success myth and its avatar, the self-made man, were implanted in the American mind long before the advent of the movies. By the early decades of the twentieth century, the dream of rags-to-riches, the image of the can-do American, the credo of self-reliance, the doctrine of individual enterprise, and the faith in meritocracy had long since staked a claim on the popular imagination. Success stories' insistence that we are unbound by the past, by social identities, or by economic circumstances was already central to America's self-conception by the time the movies took up the myth.

The development of success literature in the centuries leading up to the birth of the movies has been well documented, so a brief overview of the evolution of success myth lore will suffice.[28] The point of revisiting this material is not simply to recapitulate the copious literary analyses and social histories dealing with the American idea of success. Instead, this précis intends to establish a historical basis for two analytical tacks that will inform the discussion of individual films in the upcoming chapters. First, the ideological dualities that lie at the heart of movie versions of the success myth were present early on and remained central to the myth across changing historical circumstances and narrative forms. The elasticity of the myth allowed it to synthesize and accommodate multiple – and, often, antipodal – impulses and beliefs. Second, the paradigmatic success myth narrative, although crystallized by the mid-nineteenth century, experienced a significant shift in values around the turn of the twentieth century that brought these internal contradictions to the fore. The celebration of entrepreneurial energy and autonomy that had characterized the success myth to that point began to transmute into concern about how the period's corporate capitalism, with its stress on efficiency and hierarchy, altered the formula for success. This ideological rupture roughly coincided with the consolidation of the movie industry's business practices, distribution apparatuses, and formal strategies. So although scores of novels and self-help tracts had imparted the fundamentals of the success myth, it was Hollywood movies that effectively enabled the myth's wider dissemination and, more importantly, its repeated enunciation of deep-seated, albeit contradictory, cultural aspirations and anxieties.

The etiology of the success myth is rooted in the social and religious doctrines of colonial America. In 'A Christian and His Calling,' written in 1701, Cotton Mather inaugurated some of the enduring ideas of the success myth. In his view, economic achievement was both a calling and an indication of God's favor. Economic success was not an end in itself but was, rather, a sign of spiritual attainment and perhaps of the approval of God.[29] If a man fulfilled his covenant with God, he may, in turn, receive his just reward. This spiritual dimension of success, along with the notion that a man's employment served the greater good of the community, formed the basis of the earliest, and arguably simplest, incarnation of the success myth. By conflating material and spiritual success, and individual initiative with the commonweal (not to mention with eternal salvation), Mather laid out what would, in a later, more mobile social order, become competing strands of success myth thought.

Later in the century, the Puritans' insistence on the religious purpose of success gave way to the ethos of economic individualism. Ben Franklin's *The Way to Wealth* became the new secular scripture for aspiring and enterprising Americans. Here Franklin, himself the embodiment of self-making, celebrated the bounty and opportunity of the new world, as land and resources were plentiful and commerce was expanding. In his vision of the new social order, each man could strive to lay claim to the wealth of the new land. Thus, the prototype of the self-made man was born. Accidents of birth no longer dictated a man's fate, in Franklin's view; rather, each individual held his future in his own hands. Through a combination of diligence, temperance, and frugality, a man could succeed in elevating his station in life. Conversely, if he failed to achieve his goals, the fault lay with him since, in theory, neither social class nor social conditions worked against the aspirant.[30] Success was now seen as a matter of personal will. In this vision of meritocracy, talent would win out and social mobility would reward those who strived for it. The belief in the absolute agency of individual Americans was to become an article of faith for success myth narratives; its corollary belief is that disappointed expectations are attributable to individual failings or lack of initiative rather than to any systemic inequities or social forces.[31]

Franklin's early writings offer a largely secular, individualist definition of success. Self-improvement, which the Puritans pursued in order to fulfill their covenant with God and thereby be eligible for divine redemption, was now directed at social mobility and the accumulation of wealth. Although in his posthumously published autobiography he did resurrect the ideals of public responsibility and moral virtue as necessary components of success, his earlier homilies and recipes for achievement had so fired the popular imagination that these later, more reflective musings on the nature of success were overshadowed. His enduring legacy to the generations that followed was a utilitarian individualism that stressed material accomplishment over spiritual salvation and devotion to one's own advancement over obligation to one's community. These competing strands of belief that emerge in Franklin's collected writing would preoccupy success myth narratives from his day forward.[32]

Throughout the first half of the nineteenth century, Franklin's construction of the self-made man gained wide currency.[33] It was furthered by the Jeffersonian ideal of a natural aristocracy that would rise to the top through 'virtue and talents,' as opposed to what Jefferson considered an 'artificial aristocracy founded on wealth and birth.'[34] Abundant economic opportunity and geographic expansion seemed to open the door to success for all who could muster the wherewithal to cross the threshold. The very idea of American democracy implied that opportunity was within grasp for all who reached for it. In the decades leading up to the American Civil War, the myth began to appear in narrative form, as characters, settings, and chains of causality became conventionalized in the didactic and sentimental novels of the period. But most self-improvement literature still appeared in the form of handbooks or readers: the precursors to today's self-help books.[35] Generations of schoolchildren were steeped in Franklin's homilies, which appeared widely in schoolbooks, and in the simplistic formulae of the McGuffey Readers, which were the most widely read primers of the period.[36] With their exhortation to 'Try, try again' and their accompanying promise that 'Time will bring you your reward,' the books' mantra of success based on discipline and virtue was drilled into schoolboys' heads. McGuffey furthered the conventional wisdom that 'The road to wealth, to honor, to usefulness, and happiness is open to all, and all who will, may enter upon it with the almost certain prospect of success. In this free community, there are no privileged orders. Every man finds his level. If he has talents, he will be known and estimated, and rise in respect and confidence of society.'[37]

The inspiration of aspiring young men was further carried out by Horatio Alger's phenomenally popular novels, the first of which was published a year after the end of the Civil War. For the next 30 years until his death in 1899, Alger's output was prodigious. His name is still synonymous with self-made success, and his stories' wide-eyed belief in the surefire formula of 'pluck plus luck' remains a staple of our cultural narratives. Most of Alger's 135 novels told essentially the same story. A young, impoverished boy – often fatherless – manages to pull himself out of his dire circumstances through a combination of hard work, rectitude, and, above all, good fortune.[38] Along the way, he often bests a better-heeled but ethically bankrupt boy, thereby proving his mettle and that of his class. By the end of the story, he is usually installed in a business and, thanks to the benevolence of a patron-*cum*-surrogate father, is on his way to solid standing in the community. Although the phrase 'rags to riches' is frequently applied to Alger's books, in fact his protagonists rarely achieve or, for that matter, aim for great riches. Rather, as John Cawelti points out, they aspire to middle-class respectability earned with strong moral fiber and intelligence (along with, it must be noted, dumb luck). In most of the novels, wealthy characters are villains who have amassed their riches through immoral means or, equally damning, through inheritance. Alger's books are in keeping with earlier success myth wisdom in prescribing an aristocracy of character where social mobility is achieved through the traditional virtues of industriousness, integrity, and thrift. They are terrifically appealing, highly sentimental versions of the success myth where men are governed by virtue more than by naked self-interest, and success is the reward for conscientious and ethical habits of mind. In this, they are in keeping with what came before. But on the threshold of the changing social and economic circumstances of the late nineteenth century, they seem, even for their time, quaint and anachronistic.[39]

The post-Civil War industrial revolution set the stage for a notably different social and vocational landscape from that which had nurtured the original success myth. The earlier myth that tried to reconcile spiritual and material, as well as individual and communal, success was sorely tested by the rapidly industrializing, highly competitive antebellum American economy. Utopian ideals of a society where success was within the reach of anyone who worked hard enough for it had little place in the dynamic environment of late nineteenth-century industrial capitalism.[40] America's burgeoning corporate culture and the rise of a professional/managerial elite signaled a break not just from earlier forms of enterprise but also from the success ethos of the pre-war agrarian society of yeoman farmers, tradesmen, and artisans.[41] As the population began to concentrate in urban areas, class and ethnic distinctions seemed more pronounced and less bridgeable. The conception of America as a land of abundance which offered broad access to its plenitude ceded to a less credulous vision of a tough, competitive urban culture. In the Gilded Age of the late 1800s, a new sort of success narrative took its place alongside the more facile, benign versions of Franklin, Alger, and the earlier proponents of self-making. In its focus on self-determination and individual uplift, there was narrative and ideological continuity from earlier renditions of the success myth. But there was also a distinct shift toward wealth as the primary criterion of success and an insistence that only the fittest could survive and prosper in a social Darwinist world. In his history of success literature of the period, Richard Weiss maintains that 'The traditional association of virtue and success came under increasing ridicule during the Gilded Age.... The assault on the moral equation of the success ideology brought the whole range of assumptions on which it rested into the open.'[42]

Acknowledging the conditions of industrial, corporate America, the updated myth viewed success frankly as something accessible only to the few who were able to rise to the top of the teeming masses. The unprecedented wealth of the robber barons seemed proof positive that the most ingenious and ruthless were rewarded while the rest languished. Success narratives of the period betrayed a creeping suspicion that the hierarchical structure of the corporation and the uneven distribution of the economic bounty were inimical to the truism that every man could and would receive his just reward. The popular literature was still rife with examples of entrepreneurial energy and triumphant individualism. But the new, less sanguine prescription for success in these Gilded Age stories lamented the straitened opportunities of corporate life and counseled a more opportunistic precept. This updated myth implanted in the American imagination the seeds for a character type later found on movie screens: the aggressive urban gangster. That figure encapsulated the tension between the original myth's focus on material wellbeing as the reward for spiritual goodness, the updated myth's celebration of economic self-interest, dog-eat-dog triumph, and the unchecked pursuit of wealth, without regard for how it was gained. The competitive individualism of this mythic strain equated self-worth with net worth; the myth's earlier emphasis on spiritual and communal success seemed outmoded and inapplicable to contemporary circumstances.

Early twentieth-century consumer culture and its accompanying pleasure ethic worked yet another mutation on the original success myth. The instant gratification that consumption provided replaced Franklin's emphasis on thrift, as the culture of commodities encouraged people to spend rather than save, consume rather than produce. The newly established advertising industry touted commodities as the best yardstick for, and demonstration of, one's level of success.[43] Many success narratives of the period pondered the concomitant ascendancy of the personality ethic, characterized by boosterism and self-promotion, over the character ethic celebrated in early success narratives. In *Made in America: Self-Styled Success from Horatio Alger to Oprah Winfrey*, Jeffrey Louis Decker regards *The Great Gatsby* as only the best known of many novels of the period which heralded a broad-based shift – or, as he calls it, a crisis – in the myth. Decker argues that Fitzgerald's novel 'represents the diminishing moral authority of uplift stories. [In it] a story of entrepreneurial corruption, accented by the language of nativism, competes with and ultimately foils the traditional narrative of virtuous ambitions.'[44] *The Great Gatsby* and other tales of self-made men of the period divulge a profound anxiety about the inherent contradictions of the success ethic and about the promise of autonomy, mobility, and wealth. Although that anxiety was present, if more muted, in the myth's earliest incarnations, it had become particularly pronounced by the time American feature films entered their classical era, and began to colonize the cultural landscape and the moral imagination of the American populace.[45]

The myth and the movies

The foregoing digest of success in American thought up to the period when movies engage the myth is not meant to suggest a serial progression of mythic prototypes and values, one neatly replacing the other. If the fundamental features of the myth are present from the start, so, too, are essential questions and anxieties about the nature of success, and about what is gained and what is lost in its pursuit. The mythic oppositions that pull against one another – among them, individual self-interest and communal wellbeing; character and personality ethics; material and spiritual fulfillment; conformity and rebellion; work and leisure – are intrinsic to the success myth throughout its development. At different periods in history, one or the other value may be ascendant but, whatever the era, the success myth is loaded with ideological tensions that define and haunt it from its inception to the present. Lévi-Strauss' claim about the reconciliatory function of myth is qualified by his parenthetical acknowledgment that that function is frequently unrealizable: 'the purpose of myth is to provide a logical model capable of overcoming a contradiction (an impossible achievement if, as it happens, the contradiction is real).'[46] The endurance and apparent irreconcilability of the success myth's contradictions suggest that those contradictions are, indeed, real and all too insoluble. The myth in all of its manifestations remains pertinent and captivating precisely because its dialectics continue to inform our social, vocational, and political lives.

The consolidation of the American film industry as a set of narrational and formal conventions and industrial practices coincided with

the early twentieth century's growing ambiguity about what consti-
tuted success and increasing disillusionment about what was required
to achieve it.[47] Both Benedict Anderson and Richard Slotkin have
pointed to print capitalism as the linchpin for codifying and circulating
national imaginaries. Anderson writes of the novel and the newspaper
in the eighteenth century as 'the technical means for "re-presenting"
the *kind* of imagined community that is the nation.'[48] Slotkin claims
that 'Printed literature has been from the first the most important vehicle of myth in America, which sets it apart from the mythologies of
the past.... Since Americans turned readily to the printed word for the
expression and the resolution of doubts, of problems of faith, of anxiety
and aspiration, literature became the primary vehicle for the commu-
nication of mythic material... [and it] enjoys the advantage of formal
permanence.'[49] But the formal and industrial system that is Hollywood
far outstrips print narratives in its ability to engrave the success myth
and its ideological tensions in the popular imagination. From the 1920s
to the present in film after film, and from genre to genre, American
movies have homed in on, and regularly renegotiated, the cultural
schisms of the success myth.

Given the abundance of Hollywood movies that traffic in the
American idea of success, an exhaustive survey of the success myth's
frequency in film would be encyclopedic. Instead, this study uses a
necessarily delimited, selective framework for tracking the succession
of movie renditions of the drive to succeed. Chapter 2 surveys films
from a variety of eras and genres to establish the primacy of social
and vocational mobility in success myth stories. Chapters 3, 4, and 5
focus on the centrality of work to the promise of social mobility by
analyzing a selection of American cinema's rich and varied contempla-
tions of the success myth's warring ideologies. Rarely do movies address
those ideologies didactically or even knowingly. As Slotkin insists, 'Myth
does not argue its ideology, it exemplifies it.'[50] But in the interstices of
many seemingly simple narratives are roiling subcurrents that reveal a
deep sense of uncertainty about what constitutes success and how it is
achieved.

Part of the mission of comparative mythography is to identify the
most consistent, across-the-board elements of a given myth: to seek
commonalities among pure instances of a particular recurring narrative.
However, it is when a myth deviates from, or complicates, the standard
version that it is most indicative of cracks in the cultural consensus.
To be sure, the history of American movies offers many classic success

stories that trumpet the myth in its simplest essence: a young man on the make confronts and overcomes challenges by pulling himself up by his bootstraps to achieve success. But for every movie that unproblematically conveys and endorses the basic elements of the myth, there are scores more that, in their consideration of human behavior and social institutions, are beset by ambiguities and qualms. It is these films that provide the most intriguing evidence of how narrative forms reflect cultural phenomena.

In some sense, most Hollywood movies incorporate the success myth by celebrating individual enterprise while suggesting that personal shortcomings and societal circumstances can always be overcome by initiative and will. Part of the appeal of many Hollywood endings is their magical ability to submerge any social concerns or systemic problems that may have surfaced by resolving (in however unlikely a fashion) the protagonists' plight, thereby gratifying the audience's foremost desire.[51] Social issues that may have been explicitly or implicitly addressed are handily pre-empted by Hollywood endings that reinstate the story of individual fates at the forefront of the audience's concern. Frederic Jameson calls this sort of closure a 'strategy of containment' in which narratives project an 'internal coherence' by allowing only one foregone conclusion and by posing imaginary solutions to real problems.[52] But, as he and many others have pointed out, often even seemingly triumphant resolutions do not entirely dispel the tensions and apprehensions that have been aroused. The most conventional of happy endings cannot always erase the irreconcilability of the narrative's dialectical inclinations. So many American films – westerns, immigrant sagas, coming-of-age stories, workplace comedies, social issue dramas, gangster movies – contain both the best aspirations and the worst anxieties of the American ethos: ambition and greed, industriousness and relentlessness, ingenuity and guile, generosity and ferocity, optimism and despair. The patness of their endings aside, these films are of interest less because of their resolutions than because of their identification and articulation of those incongruities.

At the climactic moment of the crime drama *White Heat* (1949), the psychotic, mother-fixated gang leader, Cody Jarrett (James Cagney), ascends a gas tower, raises his arms heavenward and, with a cry at once jubilant and plaintive, crows, 'Made it, Ma! Top of the world!' right before the gas explodes and the flames engulf him. The detective who has been pursuing him watches and declares, 'He finally got to the top of the world . . . and it blew right up in his face.' This is one of many movie moments that stand as framing metaphors for our socially inscribed attitude toward success. American culture indoctrinates us to consider it our birthright and our destiny to stake our claim to the top of the world. But our cultural artifacts, movies foremost among them, see success as both a boon and a burden, so we are warned not to climb too far too fast, lest success blows up in our face. The American success myth is both inspirational and cautionary, but even as it contradicts itself it contains multitudes.

2
Moving Up and Moving On: Mobility and the American Success Myth

> But to be an American ... is precisely to *imagine* a destiny rather than to inherit one; since we have always been, insofar as we are Americans at all, inhabitants of myth rather than history ...
> – Leslie Fiedler, *A Fiedler Reader*

At the heart of the American dream and at the center of classic success myth stories lies the promise of mobility and self-making. Americans, these stories tell us, are endowed with the inalienable right to create an adult self out of whole cloth, rather than simply making do with the identity in which we find ourselves clad. We are active subjects rather than compliant objects of our personal destinies. Accidents of birth, rather than being implacable impediments to advancement, are merely challenges to be overcome through hard work. From log cabin to White House, from scruffy music club to arena rock superstardom, from the mailroom to the executive suite, the biographical and fictional heroes of success myth tales accomplish their rise through their single-minded application of the work ethic and their adherence to the individualist credo of competitive advantage. And if they can do it, these stories tell us, anyone and everyone can too if they want to badly enough.

In one of the earliest articles about the success myth on film, Chuck Kleinhans explains how stories of individual success inspire hope, and how they sustain our belief in the possibility of success for anyone:

> The function of the myth in American life is to encourage hope and a belief in individual opportunity. Because of its promise of reward for hard labor, the myth serves to distract people from seeing institutional obstacles to striving, and from considering the small number of wealthy and powerful at the top of the success pyramid

in comparison to the massive base of 'failures.' The myth promises to those who lack money, educational advantages and influence – the vast majority of Americans – that a personality committed to ambition, determination, perseverance, temperance and hard work will earn its appropriate reward.[1]

The conviction that great success is within reach for those who deserve it is sustained by widely disseminated stories, both fact-based and fictional, meant to demonstrate that mobility is largely a matter of individual agency. In biographical accounts, the progression from rags to riches happens just often enough and is trumpeted widely enough to keep hope alive for those to whom it has yet to happen. By encouraging us to identify with those who have made it, standard success myth stories normalize the outliers. In a sort of cultural synecdoche, we extrapolate from the tales of people who have achieved significant social and vocational mobility the conviction that everyone in America can do the same. Although this evidence is highly selective and is offset by a good deal of evidence to the contrary, we continue to subscribe to the credo of self-making, telling these mythic stories in a variety of forms as an incantation designed to make our aspirations come true. This is how myth works; it sustains our belief and it binds us to one another through our shared faith in its verities.

The protagonist's upward progress from one social and vocational level to another defines the basic plot movement of success myth stories. Like many mythic heroes, he is required to perform a series of labors and defeat a succession of challengers in his quest for the holy grail of success. As he advances to the top, he overcomes his origins, overtakes his competitors, and wins over his superiors, whose initial indifference or resistance to his advancement often turns into full-fledged endorsement of his rise through the ranks. At story's end, he is triumphantly ensconced in his new and improved life.

It is striking how little these archetypal success myth tales have varied over the years. The stories' settings and circumstances certainly adapt to changing times and to particular sociocultural moments. But the essential elements and the moral lessons stubbornly endure even, or perhaps especially, when social and economic conditions belie the myth's inspirational homilies. These chronicles of conquering heroes are so familiar and so much a part of the collective unconscious of the American psyche that they function normatively, suggesting a unified, universal definition of success and a strategy for its attainment. They also function allegorically to fulfill our belief in the promise of America, with the hero's individual self-making and accomplishment standing in for national self-determination and exceptionalism: for the fundamental essence of America itself. We extract from these well-publicized inspirational stories a belief in the possibility of success for all, since America rewards professional skill and drive. So we tell them again and again, and find comfort in their formulaic assurance that hard work and virtue reliably yield upward mobility and happiness – social, economic, or systemic handicaps notwithstanding.

The dream defined

An exemplar of the basic success myth narrative could be plucked from any era of film history and it would be much like those from any other. But a recent specimen will effectively illustrate how the myth at its most orthodox endures without evolving, remaining blithely unconcerned with anything that might contradict its articles of faith. *The Pursuit of Happyness* (2006) was a blockbuster at the box office, grossing over $300 million worldwide and starring Will Smith, one of Hollywood's most bankable stars, due to his everyman persona and his crossover appeal to both black and white moviegoers, as well as to both men and women.[2] The film is based on a true story: Hollywood's favorite stamp of approval meant to certify the movie's irrefutable veracity.[3] The film takes place in San Francisco in the early years of the Reagan administration at a moment of soaring inflation, rising unemployment, and sagging confidence in the American economy. Chris Gardner (Will Smith) is a self-employed salesman of medical devices that no one wants. He has a shrewish wife (Thandie Newton) who has no faith in his ability to help support the family, and an adoring and adorable five-year-old son Christopher (Jaden Smith), to whom he is utterly devoted. Chris is clearly smart, as demonstrated by his prowess at solving the Rubik's Cube and as confirmed by the voice-over in which he tells us how smart he is. But he cannot catch a break, and a series of misfortunes early in the movie – his car is ticketed and then towed, one of his machines is stolen, his landlord is hounding him for back rent, his wife is pestering him to put aside his dreams and earn some money – indicate that, in spite of his diligence, intelligence, and charisma, he is going nowhere. At a moment when both his work life and his home life are becoming progressively bleaker, he spies and admires a flashy car parked in front of a midtown skyscraper. He asks its owner two questions: 'What do you do and how do you do it?' When the owner replies that he is a stockbroker and that the job requires only that one be 'good with numbers

Figure 2.1   Chris Gardner (Will Smith) first lays eyes on the sports car that inspires him to set his sights on success. *The Pursuit of Happyness* (2006). Directed by Gabriele Muccino

and good with people,' Chris sets his cap for that career. From that point onward, he is indefatigable and no amount of adversity can deter him.

The amount of adversity that Chris overcomes is daunting indeed. Disgusted over his continuing inability to earn a living, his wife leaves him and, soon after, surrenders their son to his care. After father and son get evicted from their apartment, they bunk at successively seedier lodgings: a squalid motel, a homeless shelter, a subway station men's room, and, for Chris, a one-night stay in a jail cell for non-payment of his parking tickets. But his luck begins to turn when, through persistence and charm, he lands a coveted spot in an internship program for stockbrokers in training. Alas, the internship is unpaid. So Chris continues to hawk his wares in his off-hours and works harder than any of the other interns, since only one of the 20 will be offered a job at the sponsoring firm when the internship ends. *The Pursuit of Happyness* has all of the familiar signposts of a bootstrap story, so it hardly comes as a surprise that Chris' self-discipline is rewarded when he is ultimately selected for that spot. Since Hollywood movies are considerably more enamored of swashbuckling entrepreneurs than of corporate drudges, *The Pursuit of Happyness* strategically vaults over Chris' life as an organization man by cutting directly from the day when he lands the job to the end titles. The on-screen text at the end of the film informs us that the real Chris Gardner eventually set off on his own business venture and went on to become a multi-millionaire.

Like other straightforward success myth tales that celebrate social and occupational mobility, *The Pursuit of Happyness* insists that success is within reach for anyone with the gumption to grab for it. In these fantasies of individual agency, success is simply a matter of unwavering faith, tactical calculation, and indomitable will. The mythic hero is undeterred by social determinants, structural barriers, or personal limitations. Those are merely pesky hurdles over which he needs to leap, propelled by sheer grit. This movie's absolute adherence to that conviction accounts for its erasure of the protagonist's race. That Chris is black, and that his race could conceivably play a part in his circumstances or present a stumbling block on his path to the top, is never addressed. Rather, his race is a seemingly insignificant detail. The creed of the self-made man insists that triumph over adversity means triumph over any social disadvantages or structural inequities that might encumber one's desires. There is no acknowledgment that race or poverty or any other cultural forces and categories of identity might be a countervailing force strong enough to hinder his progress or prevent the realization of his dream.

The movie is not color blind, however. In its insistence that success is an equal opportunity prospect, it is positively color happy. The repeated sidewalk scenes that punctuate the movie consistently foreground professionally dressed, seemingly successful black extras in numbers that, regrettably, are proportionally far greater than in actuality. Chris sells one of his medical devices to a black doctor, and a successful black businessman is among the elite who share box seats at a football game to which Chris wheedles an invitation. In the final shot of the film, a slow motion crowd scene in which Chris joins a walking throng while cheering his bright future, we see a veritable rainbow of ethnically mixed professionals accompanying him on his victory lap. In order to sustain the presumption of universality, the movie's protagonist is deracialized, just as everyone around him is essentially undifferentiated. Chris is just another down-on-his-luck all-American go-getter who won't stop going until he gets what he wants. If the claim of equal opportunity and universality is to prevail in classic success myth stories, the hero needs to be abstracted; hence, ethnic or racial distinctions must be downplayed or displaced in favor of an idealized, generic American identity. In case we miss the point, the mise-en-scène of these exterior shots often prominently features American flags: one more reminder that this is an American dreamscape, heedless of anything that might rouse it from its reverie of success for all.

There are other aspects of *The Pursuit of Happyness* that mark it as a particularly credulous disciple of success myth dogma. In several of the movies discussed in the next chapter, the self-making man makes his way toward his professional goal in spite of the opposition of already established, successful businessmen. The older blocking characters in these Oedipal dramas represent what the young striver has to overcome, not just in their interference with his drive toward success but also in their particular brand of rapacious and ruthless capitalism. Such success myth stories frequently posit a dichotomous view of capitalist enterprise, with the young protagonist representing the honest, well-earned variety of business success and the older, entrenched characters representing a morally tainted version that has to be routed before the central character can take his well-deserved place and thereby restore the rightful order.[4] Those movies rarely go so far as to suggest that institutional changes may be necessary if corporate capitalism is to be equitable and humane. Instead, they tend to localize the problem in the person of an immoral boss; once he is ousted, the self-made man can presumably ply his trade happily ever after from within the corporate apparatus. In other words, what is preventing the protagonist's rise and the ethical practice of business is a flawed individual; there is generally little acknowledgment that systemic flaws might be the source of the problem.

In its wide-eyed awe of the men who have made it in business, this movie goes beyond those that diagnose individual rather than structural defects as the source of the protagonist's problems. Far from having any misgivings about corporate capitalism or those who excel at it, *The Pursuit of Happyness* celebrates the corporation and its guardians as the be-all-and-end-all of happiness and achievement. Here, Chris' would-be bosses and well-heeled clients are consistently benevolent, if oblivious to his plight. Approachable and encouraging, one after another indulges the young man's idiosyncratic behavior: showing up at their homes uninvited, arriving at the office in paint-spattered clothes or wearing only one shoe, madly dashing around town on coffee breaks. The head honcho in the firm that eventually hires him is a benign old coot who speaks to Chris as if he were a dim child. When he offers Chris the job, he sounds like a magnanimous father bestowing on his child a weekly allowance ('Would you like that, Chris? Good ... we couldn't be happier. Was it as easy as it looked? Good luck, Chris'). Unlike many films set in the corporate sphere, this vision of success has no nagging doubts that the prize is worth the slog and that those who win it deserve it.

The Pursuit of Happyness' generous take on its rich and successful characters is countered by a significantly less generous portrait of its poor and failed ones. In a scene straight out of the social Darwinist handbook, a group of homeless men lined up outside a shelter turn on one another as they vie for the limited number of available beds. Chris' friend refuses to repay money owed to Chris, and he weasels out of the loan by suggesting that what Chris took as an act of kindness was actually a *quid pro quo*. Christopher's day care provider is slothful and neglectful (and, to top it off, she cannot spell: hence, the title). The paternalistic munificence of the rich is contrasted with the petty nastiness of the poor, suggesting that people attain the status that they deserve. This whiff of social Darwinism allows the film to sidestep any vexing concerns about how success is achieved, who has a shot at it, or what might preclude it. Success is its own vindication. Those that survive and thrive are those that should; those who cannot pull themselves up and out of poverty belong where they are. Spurning environmental determinism, the logic of this and other classic success stories insists that everyone has the opportunity to succeed but only those individuals that should do. Men earn their own fate and deserve their station.

Several scholars have pointed out that American self-reinvention is often tinged with wistfulness for the self and the life and the class status that are shed. In *Ragged Dicks: Masculinity, Steel, and the Rhetoric of the Self-Made Man*, James Catano offers an extended discussion of self-making as self-erasure and pinpoints the success myth's ideal of masculine agency as 'a willful struggle to separate, leave origins behind, and move toward the places and goods whose possession denotes a place at society's top rather than its bottom.'5 In the many dramas of social mobility that are more nuanced than this one, there is regret at deracination and a marked nostalgia for the protagonist's past milieu, even as he moves on to embrace his new one. While he arches toward his future success, the self-making man in those stories often finds himself yearning for the authenticity and class solidarity of his past. There is ambivalence about the need to forsake one's prior self and community and to don a mask in order to fit in with the striver's new milieu. But Chris unmakes his old self without a trace of regret. He has no sentimentality about leaving his former friends or his old life – and wife – behind. He is willing to do whatever it takes to ingratiate himself with his new professional cohort. As appealing as Will Smith makes this character, there is a lapdog obsequiousness about him as he curries favor with those in whose hands his fate rests. A master of the personality ethic, Chris is a compliant and opportunistic shape shifter who is eager to disguise his class origins and renounce his prior self to achieve his ends. He understands intuitively that no matter what he is selling, he is selling himself. Many success myth heroes share this sense of personality as a performance, rather than an essence. The modernist notion of identity as a fluid construct is very much at the heart of classic American success stories, which posit selfhood as a strategically selected costume that allows its wearer to win the desired role.[6] Both the character and the movie that tells his story downplay race and class origins in an effort to become a generic, salable product.

Along with the movie's breezy treatment of race and class is its equally one-dimensional stance toward gender conventions and relations. Although Chris' devotion to good parenting might appear to be an enlightened, contemporary take on fatherhood, the film's gender politics are a throwback to much earlier ideas about family, gender, and success. Masculine agency and self-sufficiency are definitional characteristics for classic success myth heroes (and, for that matter, for American manhood in general as Leslie Fiedler pointed out long ago[7]). Whatever is feminine or domestic needs to be transcended, abandoned, or kept in its place (its literal place being the home) if the hero is to achieve his dreams. The dependency and mutuality of home life run counter to the freewheeling masculine self-assertion necessary to propel success myth heroes to their goal. In his examination of the cultural rhetoric of success found in both fictions and biographies, Catano relates self-making to a fear of the feminine and the domestic. Self-making is, he claims, 'freedom from determining physical origins – an escape from family, class, or race.' It necessitates a 'departure from the general realm of the feminine with its daily interpersonal concerns and a subsequent movement into the mythical realm of the workplace,' the principal site of masculine self-definition.[8] So success sagas insist on a rigorous separation of home life and work life, of feminine and masculine realms and qualities.[9]

The Pursuit of Happyness accomplishes this separation by making Chris' harpy of a wife easy to dispense with. She is a drag on his hopes and a dream-killer who mocks her husband's grandiose ambitions ('Stockbroker? Why not an astronaut?'). Because she works overtime to compensate for Chris' lack of an income, she is an absentee mother to boot. When she eventually moves away for a work opportunity, abandoning husband and son with a curt, 'I know you'll take good care of him, Chris,' the movie seems to bid her good riddance so that it can get on with its business of ushering its hero to his fate. As the sole caregiver for his son, Chris does need to attend to both working and parenting, but his ability to juggle both under such dire circumstances only adds to the character's superman mystique. In its steadfast focus on the classic trajectory of the self-made man, *The Pursuit of Happyness* refuses to consider that devotion to family and devotion to career may be difficult to reconcile.

The movie's take on the myth of the self-made man also manifests a notably simplistic definition of success and a formulaic notion of how to achieve it. Chris' dream is directly inspired by material desire and his career choice is completely instrumental. In essence: If I can do this, I can buy that and I will then be happy. There is no sense of work being meaningful beyond its economic rewards, and no notion of a commitment to anything other than his own (and, by extension, his son's) advancement and acquisition. Conspicuous consumption is both the prerogative and the reward of success, not to mention the visible marker of self-realization and economic superiority. Material goods are how we declare and telegraph our ascension to a higher, enviable rung. The red sports car that Chris lovingly gazes at early in the movie is one among many commodities that have totemic significance for him. In one scene, he and his son make a pilgrimage to the suburbs so that Chris can try to close a deal with a potential client. As father and son ride on a bus through the upscale streets, they are awestruck by how the other half lives. The music swells and the camera switches to slow motion: the better to ogle the sprawling mansions, manicured lawns, and happy kids enjoying their bounty. Shots of the houses are crosscut with reaction shots of Chris and his son, gaping with longing at the spoils of success. The cloying music track, the slow motion, and the close-ups of their yearning faces evoke an emotional intensity usually reserved for love scenes. Indeed, this is a sort of love story between a man and his materially rewarding future.

The Pursuit of Happyness does evince occasional self-awareness that it is treading a well-worn path. At one point in the first-person voice-over that guides us through the episodes of Chris' life, he says, 'The moral of the story is as trite as they come: don't let anyone convince you to give up on your dreams.' But the movie wears its 'trite as they come' sentiments shamelessly. For instance, after initially chastising his son for having overinflated dreams of basketball glory, he doubles back to say, 'Don't ever let somebody tell you you can't do somethin'.... You got a dream, you gotta protect it.... You want somethin', go get it. Period.' This pep talk is underscored by the maudlin musical theme that has run throughout the movie, as if we need a prod to tell us that this sentiment is significant.

As contrived, formulaic, and emotionally manipulative as the story is, audiences are still suckers for the uplifting message that infuses such fables of mobility. We never tire of their bromides, even as we recognize them as such. In success myth stories, problems of class, race, and gender may get displaced onto the general problem of simply overcoming obstacles, whatever they may be. But that is part of their enduring appeal. The sort of earnest universalizing of *The Pursuit of Happyness* assumes a generic, unproblematic definition of success, not to mention a formula for achieving it. In her *New York Times* review of the movie, Manohla Dargis aptly called *The Pursuit of Happyness* 'a fairy tale in realist drag.'[10] Although it may pretend to offer a frank look at the indignities of homelessness and unemployment as well as the rigors of professional advancement, this feel-good movie *par excellence* is not really interested in the social conditions that weigh Chris down or the practices of the brutally cutthroat business world that he wants to enter. Like a fairy tale or a classical myth, it is designed only to give us the satisfaction of a predictable story of triumph that resolves itself according to our desires and thereby holds in check the tensions that underlie those desires.[11]

This extended discussion of one commonplace, morally uncomplex example of the success myth is intended to provide a baseline from which to explore more wayward success stories. Although archetypal success myth movies such as *The Pursuit of Happyness* have been Hollywood staples for decades (and well before that, staples of popular fiction), they are outnumbered by movies that are less sure-footed in their tour of the landscape of American success.[12] The unambiguous picture of success presented in *The Pursuit of Happyness* and its ilk becomes smudged in films that view the possibility and price of mobility with a more jaundiced eye. American cinema is teeming with characters who, unlike Chris, struggle not just with the pursuit of happiness and success, but with the very definition of those goals. The *idée fixe* of success is, according to the evidence of those movies, less fixed and clear-cut in the American mind than classic versions of the myth suggest.

Support for such a claim abounds across the decades of Hollywood movie production, during which both traditional and variant renditions of the success myth co-exist.[13] Many of our most beloved classics take up the familiar elements of the myth inscribed in movies like *The Pursuit of Happyness*: the erasure of the protagonist's prior self, the flight from the domestic sphere, the individualism and opportunism required for upward mobility, the equation of material gratification with spiritual fulfillment, and the conviction that success accrues to those who deserve it and desire it with enough fervor. But they do so with an awareness of the ideological contradictions and moral complexities of those aspects of the myth, exhibiting what Barbara Klinger once called 'a revelatory rather than a complacent relation to the ideology.'[14] Whereas standard success myth fare has little compunction about what the hero needs to do to rise through the ranks or about the worth of the reward when he makes it to the top, scores of American movies are notably ambivalent about the requisites and perquisites of success. Although less reassuring and inspiring than the more anodyne success myth stories, these demythologizing movies also serve a collective sociocultural need: to present, investigate, and mediate the unresolvable oppositions that strain against one another at the core of the success myth. The uplifting success stories sustain our hope. And the stories that problematize success perform the equally necessary cultural work of addressing the variance between the rhetoric of mythic narratives and the negotiations involving mobility and success that we necessarily perform in our own lives.

The dream deferred

Frank Capra's *It's a Wonderful Life* (1946) is widely adored (and also frequently disparaged) as a sentimental movie about the value in every life, however thwarted or unsung that life may be. But as many film historians have pointed out, it is actually a frank and stark portrait of success *manqué*, and an astute distillation of American culture's deep disquiet about self-making, mobility, and success.[15] Here, the assumptions of conventional success myth tales are unsettled and complicated by a narrative that, on examination, is significantly less mawkish and reassuring than it initially appears to be. In spite of the film's putatively happy ending, *It's a Wonderful Life* is shot through with an awareness of the compromises, disappointments, and irreconcilabilities that lie beneath the cheery certitudes of classic success myth stories. The movie follows George Bailey (James Stewart) from childhood to early middle age, charting his degeneration from a bright, ambitious, and purposeful boy to a neurotic, dissatisfied, and immobile man. His nemesis Henry Potter (Lionel Barrymore), the movie's cartoonishly evil capitalist, accurately sums up George's condition: 'He is an intelligent, smart, ambitious young man who hates his job.... A young man who has been dying to get out on his own ever since he was born' but instead has become 'a warped, frustrated young man.' Or, in film critic James Agee's equally on-target description, George is 'a local boy who stays local, doesn't make good, and becomes at length so unhappy that he wishes he had never been born.'[16] As the movie traces George's deterioration from boundless ambition to suicidal despair, *It's a Wonderful Life* retreats from the dewy-eyed vision of possibility found in *The Pursuit of Happyness* and similarly facile success myth stories to expose that vision as meretricious.[17] What emerges is an aesthetics of failure:

the flip side of the success myth in which those who do not make it languish in the shadow of the looming myth. The movie shows us in vivid detail what happens, in George's case, to a dream deferred; it implodes.

The predicament that drives George to his suicidal state is a crisis of stasis; literally and figuratively he is going nowhere. He has never traveled beyond his boyhood home either geographically or psychically (a point repeatedly made by the ritual childish gestures and code words that he and his lifelong pals continue to perform: 'Hee Haw,' 'I wish I had a million dollars,' etc.). Many Hollywood films conflate physical and social mobility, with the road functioning as one of the most enduring and overdetermined elements of American iconography.[18] In genres ranging from the Western to the gangster film to the road movie, geographic relocation – to another town, a better neighborhood, a sunnier coast – symbolizes progress, self-realization, and renewal.[19] Men uproot themselves not only to seek economic opportunity but to flee the confines of their past, their home, and the feminizing constraints associated with family and domesticity. Migration and starting anew are essential to the American idea of success, just as the spirit of ambition and exploration are central to the ideal American character. Thus, in many quintessentially American stories, physical mobility is equated with individual autonomy and nimbleness, which together comprise the ability to craft one's own identity and will one's own path to suit different circumstances and opportunities.

George's tragedy is that he is immobile. Like *Waiting for Godot,* another late 1940s contemplation of existential stasis, *It's a Wonderful Life* ends each of its acts in George's unfolding biography with his inability to leave the spot to which he is rooted. His father's death, his brother's marriage, a Depression-era run on the Building and Loan business that he has reluctantly inherited all conspire to keep George in his place. In spite of his youthful declaration that 'I'm shakin' the dust of this crummy little town off my feet and I'm gonna see the world . . . and then I'm gonna build things,' George remains in his town, sees the world only in photographs, and builds modest starter homes, rather than the skyscrapers that he intends to build, which are the national emblem of aspiration and achievement. The movie's bifurcated vision of post-war life, contrasting the idyllic town of Bedford Falls with the nightmarish city of Pottersville, seems to suggest that George is perhaps better off for having stayed put. But in spite of its patina of nostalgia for the storybook small-town, the movie presents us with a protagonist who cannot quell his wanderlust or shake the feeling that there is nowhere to go in Bedford Falls. He has imbibed the success myth's insistence that the city is the locus of success, and he longs for the spirit of movement and adventure that defines the American ethos. According to the myth's precepts, an American man who cannot move at will and 'light out for the territory,' as Huck Finn put it, is a blighted man who has to settle for a life of stagnation in a 'crummy little town.'

The analyses of both Robert Ray and Robin Wood focus on the mythic oppositions that *It's a Wonderful Life* grapples with, pointing out, in Ray's words, 'the incompatibility of the dream of exploring and the fact of settling down' in American cultural narratives.[20] Unlike films such as *The Pursuit of Happyness,* where family obligations and domestic life do not hinder the protagonist's drive for success (and if they do, they are handily written off, like the wife in that film), here the central character, at his moment of despair, reveals that he feels saddled with, rather than sustained by, his family. The repeatedly delayed gratification of George's dreams and his suppressed rage at being held back by his obligation to hearth and home come to the surface, as he lashes out at his wife, Mary (Donna Reid), demanding, 'You call this a happy family? Why do we have to have all these kids?' At another point, he displaces his frustrations onto Uncle Billy (Thomas Mitchell), his heretofore endearing business partner and the film's resident lovable eccentric, by calling him a 'silly old fool.' The loyal, selfless helpmeet and adoring children that propel many success myth heroes forward are certainly present in *It's a Wonderful Life.* But the ferocity of George's meltdown reveals how hamstrung his picture perfect family makes him feel.

Ironically, it is George's boundless ambitions that cause his acute discontent. Because he is a dreamer, with his head full of boys' adventure stories and grandiose schemes, his own quotidian life is inevitably disappointing. In his consideration of the director's *oeuvre,* Ray Carney regards Capra's entire body of work as 'the most profound questioning of the whole idealistic mythology of success and the creation of the free and independent self in all of Hollywood.'[21] His reading of George's predicament focuses on the disparity between the character's fertile imagination and his sessile situation:

> George represents an imaginative energy and mobility for which there can be no ultimately adequate expression in the world.... He embodies a principle of imaginative yearning that, no matter where he is or what he is doing, is always gesturing elsewhere, to a possibility than can never be realized in the practical forms of his expressive life.[22]

Carney goes on to call George an 'imaginative exile': spiritually cast out of the placidity of Bedford Falls by his own unquenchable desire for something else and something more.[23] George's capacity to wonder is, to his dismay, not commensurate with his capacity to wander.

The capacity to wonder and the project of individualist self-making that define the success myth are revealed, in this and other movies that probe the myth, to be both an opportunity and a curse. Our national mythology tells us that Americans are blessed with the exhilarating liberty to fashion a self and then to continue to work on and improve upon what we have fashioned. But if the self that we fashion does not measure up to the ideal, we are thrust into a crisis of confidence.[24] Likewise, the promise of mobility is double-edged. Success, in mythic narratives, means never standing still and never being satisfied with the status quo, since there is always a higher rung. The restless American soul requires perpetual motion and continuous betterment. Contentment is complacency. Lack of ambition for something better is downright unpatriotic in the myth's estimation. So we must perpetually uproot ourselves in the name of progress and be literally restless if we are to succeed. In his study of the cult of American restlessness, James M. Jasper notes that,

A range of cultural signals send the same message: that individuals are in control of their lives because they can get up and move. America's famous optimism comes from the confidence that you can always find a new place that is right (or at least better) for you, a place where you can start over on a better track.[25]

Of course, the insistence on continual improvement and movement creates a sort of spiritual motion sickness, since it does not allow us ever to rest on our laurels.

The movie's ending in which George learns to be satisfied with his lot appears, at first glance, to resolve his predicament. He is rescued from Potter's scheming by the eleventh-hour intervention of the family and community members to whom he has devoted his life. He is enlightened by an actual *deus ex machina:* a guardian angel named Clarence (Henry Travers) who reveals to George that his life has, after all, been a rewarding and important one – at least by the constricted terms of small town life. In the last scene, surrounded by family and friends in a cozily crowded mise-en-scène, George is ostensibly reborn. But even though Clarence insists that 'You see George, you've really had a wonderful life,' everything that we have witnessed before this final, reconciliatory scene indicates that George's life is somewhat less wonderful than he had hoped it would be. The ending seems to suggest that in order to be a mature, contented adult we need to scale back our desires, make peace with disappointment, and rein in our imagination and sense of longing. This is why Ray calls this moment of closure a 'nominal happy ending' in which the protagonist's immediate problem is superficially resolved, but the larger questions that gnaw at him – and at us – retain their bite.[26] Interpreting the film in this way does not require a concerted effort to read against the grain. The ambivalence and ruefulness of George's newfound embrace of his life's wonderfulness is embedded in the final scene. A brief series of crosscuts is particularly telling. One by one, the denizens of Bedford Falls repay George's years of selflessness, generosity, and devotion to the community by ponying up their life savings so he can pay off the debt caused by Uncle Billy's forgetfulness. This moment is genuinely touching, although it is difficult to forget that George's bighearted community spirit is what precluded his mobility and the realization of his dreams: the collision of individualist striving and communal wellbeing is among the clashing values that torment George. After the procession of well-wishers have said their piece, someone reads a cable from Sam Wainwright, George's old friend and former romantic rival, who has made it big by profiting handsomely from the post-war boom. His cable announces that he will cover the full amount of George's debt (which, ironically, makes the collective generosity of the townspeople monetarily unnecessary since the largesse of one wealthy benefactor has trumped their penny ante munificence). As the cable is being read, the camera shows first a close-up of Mary's face as she glances at George worriedly. The camera then cuts to George; his face falls and his smile dissolves when he hears the offer. He shoots Mary a look and she returns his gaze with a pasted-on smile of encouragement. Finally, the camera cuts back to George who, still unsmiling, gives his daughter Zuzu what can only be construed as a compensatory cuddle: to wit, he may not have millions but he has this. Yet the pain of not being able to have both domestic fulfillment and worldly success lingers in his eyes. A few minutes later, his brother Harry – who, unlike George, was able to go to college, move out of town, succeed in business, and engage in wartime derring-do – shows up to declare George 'the richest man in town.' This, too, is a bittersweet moment for George; the *noblesse oblige* of the two people who have done what he wished to do is a mixed blessing. For all of the kneejerk populism and 'sentimental hogwash' (to borrow Potter's phrase) at the end of the film, the hard truth is that, according to societal standards, George is not a success. By acting on his communitarian instincts, rather than indulging his individualist self-interest, George has sacrificed his claim to the success myth's promises.

Most of the detailed analyses of *It's a Wonderful Life* agree that the affirmation of the ending is undercut by the undercurrent of despair that has run throughout the film. Wood notes 'the extreme precariousness of [the ending's] basis' and suggests that it is 'a far more potentially subversive film than has been generally recognized.'[27] Ray, too, points out, 'The evident strain involved in achieving the film's happy ending'[28] and claims that the film 'could not entirely allay the anxieties it had invoked.'[29] He maintains:

> The truly subversive point about *It's a Wonderful Life*, then, was its recognition that a man could have so many of the things promised by the American Dream (wife, children, job, friends, house, car) and still be unhappy. For the movie acknowledged that having one thing (domesticity) required giving up its opposite (adventure). George had chosen and was unhappy that he had had to do so – after all, the American myth had suggested that he could have it all.[30]

That audiences generally consider the ending heart-warming and life-affirming, rather than myth-shattering, reveals our desire for mythic fulfillment but also our perplexity about what constitutes success: we may admire George but, in our drive to succeed and to move up and on from where we began, we certainly do not want to emulate his stasis. The ending of *It's a Wonderful Life* might intend to redefine success by insisting that righteousness trumps riches, but it cannot wholly erase George's craving for something else or the culture's assessment regarding who and what is successful. There remains an abiding suspicion that a change in one's individual attitude is not enough to cast out or recast societal criteria for success, let alone institutional barriers to its realization.

Conventional movie endings that handily try to sweep under the rug all of the ideological tensions that the foregoing narrative has revealed are, according to some scholarly stances, not just ambiguous but also pernicious and patronizing. In resolving genuine social problems through a fantasy of individual agency, these endings seem to endorse social stability over collective action and social change. A recurring narrative convention of Hollywood movies valorizes the lower classes while villainizing the rich. Such movies encourage us to root for the little guy and hiss at the machinations of his oppressors, thereby patting us on the back for our right-thinking populist sympathies and patting us on the head for being satisfied with the status quo.[31] There are multiple hypocrisies in this subject position. In *The Hollywood Social*

Problem Film: Madness, Despair, and Politics from the Depression to the Fifties, Peter Roffman and Jim Purdy sum up the problematic stance of this posture:

> The basic question of all these films is not whether success is possible, but whether or not it is desirable. Since to be rich is to be robbed of your humanity, to be left alone and unhappy, the success is of dubious benefit. Correspondingly, economic adversity may be preferable since the poor are allowed to retain a sense of compassion and identity with their fellow man. Attacking the success ethic in this way is really an argument for staying where you are when there are no other alternatives within society. Immobility and stasis are thereby pictured as positive values.[32]

Likewise, in her study of class and social mobility in film, Gwendolyn Audrey Foster points to the 'Capraesque film ideology that seeks to pacify the masses who live in a world where actually achieving the American Dream is increasingly more difficult.' *It's a Wonderful Life* takes pains to point out what George (and, presumably, most of the audience) lacks, only to then do a u-turn and reassure us that he – and we – is alright without those things. The paradoxical impulses in American movies, which sometimes urge us to reach for the top and other times encourage us to be happy with where and what we are, amount to a rather vexed cultural perspective on success and mobility. As Foster says, 'We really do not know whether to demonize millionaires or to worship them.'[33]

Indeed, we don't. The discursive practices of Hollywood accomplish the neat trick of alternately glorifying the conspicuous rewards of competitive capitalism as well as the modest gratifications and essential decency of the 'little people.' Those movies that endorse the success myth without qualification along with those that disturb its simplistic sureties cumulatively represent the inconsistencies inherent in the American idea of success. It's lonely at the top but the bottom is teeming with disappointed nobodies. The rich and successful are materially fulfilled but spiritually, morally, and relationally bereft. The unsung are authentic and ethical, and are graced with family and friends, but they languish in the lower strata of the social and vocational pecking order – professionally unrecognized and materially unrewarded. Family is our sustaining social institution but domestic obligations encumber the drive for success and personal reinvention. The successful keep moving upward and onward, but when a man forgets where he came from and loses touch with his roots, he loses his soul. The push–pull of these contradictory – and, often mutually exclusive – messages allows American success mythology to validate both our ambitions and our insecurities: to grant us the pleasure of identification with the triumphant achiever as well as the reassurance that we are worthy and fulfilled even if we do not stand astride the top of the world.

The rise-and-fall pattern

This double function of success narratives is particularly apparent in the rise-and-fall variant of the myth, which gives us both the thrill of the vertical ride up the trajectory of success along with the sense of moral superiority toward the protagonist as he descends from the heights. The first part of such movies contains the hallmarks of classic success myth stories while the latter part functions as a cautionary tale, highlighting the down side of the character's upward scramble. By following the main character beyond youth, these stories sequentially accommodate the forthright faith in the myth displayed in such films as *The Pursuit of Happyness* as well as the element of doubt betrayed by such films as *It's a Wonderful Life*. A brief discussion of a few representative movies that fit this narrative pattern will demonstrate how it addresses the irresolvable dualities that haunt the success myth.[34]

From their inception, conventional rags-to-riches tales have focused on youthful protagonists. According to these coming-of-age stories, success is a young man's game.[35] Success narratives are firmly in the *bildungsroman* tradition, structuring themselves around the central character's coming-of-age experiences and learning curve. Like *The Pursuit of Happyness*, these stories tend to end at the consummation of desire: the achievement of the character's dream job or promotion or material reward and the accompanying vindication of his industry and morality. Just as the romance genre focuses on, and culminates in, the act of falling in love (and generally treats staying in love in a long-term union as either a joke or an affliction), classic success myth tales are about becoming successful, not living with success.

Those films that follow their characters beyond early adulthood have a hard time sustaining unwavering belief in the myth's assurances. Movies of this sort puncture the myth by moving past the moment when the character dons the mantle of success to the point where his sense of youthful possibility morphs into cynicism or jadedness or greed. In charting the arc of the character's ascension, they focus on what is gained materially; the ensuing downfall deals only sometimes with material loss but, almost always, with spiritual loss (frequently insisting that spiritual loss is a direct result of material attainment). The allure of this particular narrative pattern comes from the double satisfaction of our conflicting views of mobility and success: our own ambitions and consumerist fantasies are vicariously fulfilled by the protagonist's rise – what Alexis de Tocqueville once referred to as 'the charm of anticipated success' – while our sense of pity and moral superiority kicks in at his fall, during which both the character and his fate are significantly less charming.

There are countless Hollywood movies that manifest this reversal of fortune mode, representing a variety of genres and settings. Among the most recurrent specimens of the up-and-down pattern are biopics: those 'based on a true story' tales that provide audiences with a glimpse into the private lives of public figures. The enduring appeal of these biopics suggests that the fascination of the rise-and-fall success saga never exhausts itself.[36] Throughout Hollywood history, the biopic's fealty to the facts has been less crucial than its adherence to reigning cultural truisms about success. Early biopics tend to culminate in an unequivocal celebration of the central figure's success, often concluding at the 'eureka' moment when the protagonist finally realizes his ambitions. Movies from the past few decades, however, generally track their subjects beyond the crest of career achievement, so the conventional bootstrap story is followed by a revelation of the myth's ideological incongruities.[37] Bearing witness as the protagonist hits the down side of success, this narrative progression offers audiences the perverse pleasure of warts-and-all voyeurism as we marvel at how the mighty have fallen.

A substantial number of biopics center on legendary figures from the realm of show business: that all-purpose metaphor for glamour and dissipation.[38] These movies grant us the dual satisfaction of reveling in the fame and material indulgence of the celebrity arriviste while also wallowing in schadenfreude at the spectacle of his or her inevitable comedown. They concomitantly satisfy our desire to believe in the myth's guarantee that hard work and talent yield success as well as our skepticism that success, in turn, yields sustained happiness. This vacillating subject position is apparent in all of the rise-and-fall versions of the success myth, both those that are based on the biographies of actual personages and those that are fictional. In many of these tales of excess, the fanatical focus on self-making and self-realization is carried to its logical extreme: ambition as a sort of pathology that devours its carrier. The farther the protagonist moves from his origins, the more he is a man possessed and consumed by the blandishments of success. The essential moral of these movies boils down to the not particularly original observations that power corrupts and that it is lonely at the top. *A Face in the Crowd* (1957), Elia Kazan's monitory tale about media manipulation and the gullibility of the American populace, exemplifies how the rise-and-fall narrative addresses the success myth's warring values. 'Lonesome' Rhodes (Andy Griffith), a drunken vagrant, is discovered in a jail cell sleeping off a bender. His Pygmalion is Marcia Jeffries (Patricia Neal), a radio producer who is taken in by his good ol' boy southern charm. She launches and then accompanies him on his unlikely journey from small-town radio personality to national television phenomenon, advisor to politicians, and, eventually, self-worshipping demagogue and would-be kingmaker.

Unlike the classic success myth hero, Rhodes has neither a strong ambition nor a good work ethic. What he does have is preternatural self-possession and a streak of opportunism. When Marcia first asks him to perform as she tapes him, he parries, 'What do I get out of this: me, myself, and I?' Although initially he is proudly lazy and consistently disdainful of bourgeois values and acquisitions, as his fame grows he is seduced by the roar of the crowd and his power over them. Rhodes is a savvy self-promoter, happy to collude in his own commodification and to see himself as one more product to be packaged and sold. *A Face in the Crowd* is one of innumerable movies in which the successful mien is presented as a strategically crafted mask. As the character rises, we watch the mask take form; as he falls, it is peeled off to reveal the monster that has been created underneath. Like many such Jekyll-and-Hyde characters in rise-and-fall stories, Rhodes is alternately engaging and off-putting: clever and charismatic but also soulless as well as heedless of anyone's needs but his own. As he avidly transfigures himself, the dualisms of the successful self-maker are unmasked. Canniness becomes cunning and belief in oneself corrodes into self-deluded egotism. Far from pulling himself up by his own bootstraps, the man on the make is hoisted to the pinnacle of success by a host of people who, in his hubris, he then abandons. The doubleness of these characters and their up-and-down path allows rise-and-fall movies to address the success myth's binary, and contrary, qualities: to play the B-side of the myth's most crowd-pleasing hits. Kazan's film is frequently didactic and heavy-handed. As Rhodes' life falls apart and he degenerates into megalomania, he descends from his penthouse in the sky while the camera belabors his decline by focusing on the elevator buttons taking him down to the bottom. But the film nonetheless puts its finger on the anxieties that lurk behind the optimism of the success myth: the corruptibility and fungible morality of those on the rise (Rhodes' manager cheerily points out that 'Nothing's illegal if they don't catch you'), the loss of authenticity as characters package and sell themselves in the name of success, and the absence of a true meritocracy, since those who are hard-working, deserving, and ethical often go unrecognized.

Figure 2.2 Lonesome Rhodes (Andy Griffith) alone in his penthouse, framed by the iconic New York skyline. *A Face in the Crowd* (1957). Directed by Elia Kazan

Citizen Kane (1941), the most lauded of rise-and-fall tales, provides another object lesson in how these movies articulate the friction between our ambitions and our wariness of where they might lead.[39] Although the young Charles Foster Kane's wealth is inherited rather than earned, he has the requisite humble origins and the eager ambition of youthful success myth heroes. But as he ages and acquires riches and influence, he also acquires the moral taint that often attends success in American movies. Kane's problem is, in some sense, the opposite of George Bailey's in *It's a Wonderful Life*. Whereas George is unable to move away from his origins and his community, Kane moves materially and experientially too far from where he began. The multiple, subjective presentations of Kane's trajectory show his youthful idealism curdling into a hunger for power, position, and possessions. Betraying his old friends and disowning his past, he ends up deracinated and alone, surrounded only by the material spoils of his success. The film's rather facile Freudianism, in which the dying Kane pines for his childhood sled, Rosebud, and the lost innocence that it represents, suggests that mobility – social, geographical, and professional – leads to sorrow as much as to satisfaction.

Here, as in other rise-and-fall sagas, the culture's lust for the riches and rewards that accompany capitalist success collides with its deep populist strain, which looks askance at wealth and position as anti-democratic and corrupting. Ambition and aspiration to the high reaches of success are smiled upon but attainment of the summit is often suspect. We enthrone the successful and aspire to their perch, and we also delight when they are toppled from it. So the spectator is situated to be first tantalized by the protagonist's rise and acquisition of wealth then morally validated by his fall, as well as repelled by his excess of commodities. The ending of *Citizen Kane,* in which his assembled treasures are catalogued by both the camera and the reporters attempting to piece together Kane's life, epitomizes this fickle spectatorial position. Part of the intended pleasure of cinematic visits to the lives and milieus of the rich and famous comes from ogling their belongings and engaging in a sort of vicarious conspicuous consumption of the trappings of wealth. Material goods are the markers of social mobility in America – their ongoing acquisition serving as tangible proof that their owner is continuously moving up rather than stagnating. Kane's obsessive collection and fetishization of objects function to trumpet his success more than to provide him with pleasure.[40] As the camera performs its inventory of his accumulated belongings in the basement of his mansion, craning up to give progressively more panoramic views of a lifetime's worth of possessions, we are, at once, riveted and appalled by this enumeration of his material acquisitions. In the film's final shot, the pined-for sled – the object that was monetarily worth the least but, the film implies, sentimentally and symbolically worth the most to him – is reduced to tinder.[41]

Citizen Kane is the success story as tragedy. Kane's compulsive ambition and acquisition – his inability to stop moving, striving, and buying – is posited as his tragic flaw. Here, as in many of the rise-and-fall renditions of the success myth, the hunger for success becomes an end in itself: a nervous tic that the character cannot keep in check and that ultimately consumes him. The contrapuntal tensions that are latent in all success myth stories are laid bare in this and similar rise-and-fall narratives. The young Kane's commitment to community and collective wellbeing is counterposed with his later hubris, self-regard, and greed. His foray into politics, like his career as a newspaper tycoon, becomes an exercise in vanity. As Kane's early entrepreneurial energy mutates into cupidity, those poles of individual capitalist enterprise are presented as the flip side of one another: the former all too easily contaminated by the latter. Like *It's a Wonderful Life* and *A Face in the Crowd*, *Citizen Kane* does not allay the worrisome insinuation that devotion to private enterprise and individual success is incompatible with commitment to the public good. And unlike more devout versions of the success myth, which downplay or synthesize its competing ideologies, movies such as these expose rather than suppress the undeniable incongruities of success myth ideology.

The lingering appeal of the rise-and-fall pattern, in which the drive for success eventually overtakes reason and morality, speaks to our ongoing need to negotiate the myth's conflicting desires and fears. These rise-and-fall character studies that underscore the paradoxical values espoused by the success myth come in a variety of forms. In 'The Gangster as a Tragic Hero,' one of the earliest and most influential analyses of gangster movies, Robert Warshow attributes that genre's staying power to its enunciation of American culture's splayed stance toward ambition and success. Running counter to America's self-image as cheerful and can-do, gangster films tap a deep vein of despair about what success requires of its seekers – and what it yields once they achieve it. The gangster, says Warshow, 'is what we want to be and what we are afraid we may become.'[42] Ambitious, goal-oriented and strategic, he is the success myth hero viewed through a distorting mirror. Like all rise-and-fall protagonists, the gangster experiences 'steady upward progress followed by a very precipitate fall.'[43] Warshow continues:

The gangster's whole life is an effort to assert himself as an individual, to draw himself out of the crowd, and he always dies *because* he is an individual; the final bullet thrusts him back, makes him, after all, a failure.... At bottom, the gangster is doomed because he is under the obligation to succeed, not because the means he employs are unlawful. In the modern consciousness, *all* means are unlawful, every attempt to succeed is an act of aggression, leaving one alone and guilty and defenseless among enemies: one is *punished* for success. This is our intolerable dilemma: that failure is a kind of death and success is evil and dangerous, is – ultimately – impossible.[44]

Because our national credo insists that ambition and renown are requirements of the good life, notoriety is preferable to anonymity in gangster movies. But in distinguishing himself, the gangster simultaneously isolates himself, moving away from everyone and everything that might once have anchored him to a more acceptable and conventional pathway to success. Skewered by his own grandiose ambitions, he ends up alone and defeated: a victim of his eagerness to succeed at any cost and his willingness to stop at nothing.

What Warshow first recognized, and what later scholars of genre have amplified, is the ways in which the cinematic gangster functions as the avatar of American culture's antithetical inclinations regarding success. The artificial synthesis of those inclinations that is found in traditional Horatio Alger-type success stories is blown apart by gangster movies, which present American ambition gone awry and the success myth story *in extremis*. In such early, definitional examples of the genre as *Scarface* (1932), *Manhattan Melodrama* (1934), *The Public Enemy* (1931), and *Little Caesar* (1931), the central gangster character exhibits the attributes of the ideal American go-getter: determination, smarts, charisma, leadership, salesmanship, entrepreneurial zeal. The actors who play those characters with magnetic charm – Paul Muni, Clark Gable, James Cagney, and Edward G. Robinson, respectively – assure that we will be drawn to and root for the gangsters as they strategize and shoot their way to the top. Even after their ambition turns into obsession and their means turn excessive, these characters are hard to resist. Gable's Blackie, a miscreant from childhood onward, is still jaunty and defiant on his way to the electric chair, charming his fellow inmates, his jailers, and audience members alike with his confident swagger even in the face of death. The gusto and verbal wit of these characters and their fellow gangster brethren across the decades of Hollywood history guarantee that our dramatic sympathies will incline toward them. Their foils – lawmen and other upstanding community members – are generally self-righteous and dull; in spite of their official probity, they offer scant competition for our sympathies and our interest. We initially sit comfortably with this narrative split between those that we root for and those that we acknowledge as morally upright because we recognize the gangster as a familiar and appealing American type: the ambitious outsider who is willing to do what it takes to move upward and onward from where he began. In Thomas Schatz' estimation, he is 'the perverse alter ego of the ambitious, profit-minded American male.'[45]

In spite of the central character's familiar contours and irresistible allure, gangster movies are, as Warshow asserted, inversions of the success myth that ultimately subvert, rather than support, the myth's assumptions and ideologies. The genre constitutes a direct challenge to the success myth's defining convictions: the possibility of mobility and personal reinvention, the promise of success for honest, hard-working young men, and the insistence that success is simply a matter of individual talent and will. Gangster movies expose the sophistry of the success myth's unfounded optimism. In a sort of bait-and-switch maneuver, the genre sets up the spectator to recognize and root for its men on the make, only to then turn on itself and uncover the myth's naiveté and confusion.

Among the mythic contentions that the gangster genre exposes as wishful thinking is that birth station is irrelevant to the attainment of success. In gangster movies, the central character is most often ethnic and working class; whether Italian, Irish, Jewish, or African-American, he is a liminal figure, defined by his difference.[46] In the early instances of the genre, the gangster's particular ethnicity is not especially important, beyond its use as comic relief in the fashion of the era's dialect comedies and ethnic caricatures. The character's ethnicity is simply code for his outsider status and for the challenge of moving up the ladder of success. Ethnic prejudices get masked or displaced, appearing instead as generalized obstacles to success. Nonetheless, gangster movies constitute one of our primary modes for mapping the nexus where the success myth collides with immigrant and class-based marginality. The gangster genre confronts the difficulty of assimilation and class ascension more directly and despairingly than do many of Hollywood's immigrant sagas. Although those films focus on the difficulty of the passage to the new world or the challenges of adapting to American culture or the necessity for delayed fulfillment of the American dream, they usually conclude with the hopeful expectation that the immigrant has the determination and work ethic to succeed eventually. His children, if

not he, will reap the bounty of the American promise.[47] The immigrant
project of Americanization and acculturation may be arduous, but there
is generally little compunction about what is lost in the process.[48] The
anxieties that such films suppress about what it takes for an outsider
to cross the threshold of American success are redirected to the person
of the gangster.[49] He has the hunger for success of the earnest, honest
immigrants, but he lacks the patience and self-sacrifice to wait for the
next generation to achieve his goals. He wants it now and he is willing
to get it by any means necessary.[50]

The classic gangster characters' cynicism about legitimate means
to self-improvement leads them to conclude that the gulf between
their lower class, immigrant origins and the inner circle of success is
bridgeable only through desperate, illegal, and violent measures. The
hankering for swift and great success is like a fever, and they scoff at
anyone who is not similarly infected. Characters who try to pull themselves up by their bootstraps within the limits of the law are derided
as unmanly and stuck. Cagney's character in *The Public Enemy* mocks
his wholesome brother as a 'sissy' who is 'too busy going to school....
He's learning how to be poor.'[51] In *Dead End* (1939), Dave (Joel McCrea),
an unemployed architect is, significantly, still living in the slum where
he grew up. His education and his moral character have gotten him
nowhere, unlike the neighborhood gangster Baby Face Martin, whose
credo is 'Never go back – always go forward.' On the evidence of such
characters, it is virtue, not crime, that doesn't pay. Immobility is the success myth's original sin, and characters who cannot move up and on get
left in the dust of those who are in a hurry.

Several close analyses of the gangster genre locate the character's
compulsive ambition in his identity as an outsider. In *Dying to Belong:
Gangster Movies in Hollywood and Hong Kong*, her study of the genre across
decades and cultures, Martha P. Nochimson points to the gangster's ethnicity, whatever it may be, as central to his determination to move
upward by constructing an acceptable, assimilated, American persona:
to make a self different than the one he inherited. Jonathan Munby's
study of the genre, *Public Enemies, Public Heroes: Screening the Gangster
from Little Caesar to Touch of Evil* posits a similar source of the gangster's
ambition and actions: 'the hyphenated American's frustrated desire for
cultural and economic inclusion... [and] alienation from both roots in
the old world and the projected future in the new.'[52] Success requires a
calculated commodification of the self; the successful mien is a mask,
self-consciously donned to conform to culturally sanctioned codes of
behavior and self-presentation. The gangster – on the outside looking

in and on the threshold between his immigrant past and his American future – is an overeager paragon (and, in Munby's assessment, a parody) of self-making.

In his hurry to cash in on the promises of the Promised Land, the gangster is only too willing to buy into the fantasy of personal trans-formation: to abandon his past and to craft a suitably forward-thinking, irrepressibly all-American self that conforms to the imperatives of the success myth. His flashy clothes, souped-up cars, rat-a-tat weapons, street patois, and arm candy in the form of his moll are consciously crafted projections of his fantasy of successful American manhood. Nochimson sees the gangster figure as a protomodernist performer of his adopted identity. In his need to compensate for and move beyond his origins, he stitches together a persona and plays his role with hammy panache, in an overwrought masquerade of the self-made man on the move.

The gangster is, of course, immobilized in the end. There are so many visually indelible gangster movie finales that hammer home the genre's skeptical perspective on the American success myth's promise of mobil-ity and self-making.[53] Cody Jarrett's immolation on the tower at the end of *White Heat* is one of the few that at least lets the gangster revel in his temporary perch at the top of the world. More often, he dies alone, writhing in the dark streets like the gangsters in *Little Caesar* or *Dead End*. The most self-consciously ironic demise belongs to Tony Camonte in *Scarface*. After begging the cops for mercy ('I got nobody. I'm all alone. Don't shoot') and in return, being gunned down in the street, he lands beneath the flickering electric sign that has been his inspiration and credo: 'The World is Yours.' In discussing the 'obligation to succeed,' Warshow insists that the gangster's fate is sealed not because he bucks the law but because he believes too fervently that the world is his and that he needs to lay claim to it. The folly of mythic expectations is what does him in; as in many of the more subversive success myth movies, the American capacity for hope is both stimulus and delusion, spur and curse. Making an American self requires embracing the myth, but in buying into the American success myth as national imperative, he buys a bill of goods: a promise that fails to deliver because no matter how much he may succeed and acquire, he is conditioned to want more. The national obligation to succeed – to take advantage of the possibility of mobility – puts the gangster in a double bind. He is damned if he does succeed because success requires ruthlessness and results in isolation (since the truism that accompanies, and contradicts, the exhortation to stand out from the crowd tells us that it is lonely at the top, and a similarly pertinent truism tells us that the higher they climb the harder they fall). But he is damned if he doesn't, since failure and anonymity are, as Warshow notes, a sort of death: the demise of the mythical new self to which we are required to aspire.

Flourishing in the midst of the Great Depression, the genre does double duty: invoking the success myth and the self-made man at its center while interrogating the myth's assumptions and the self-made man's presumed infallibility. It is hardly surprising that audiences would want to fall back on familiar stories of upward mobility to comfort and distract them in a time of economic and social crisis. But the element of doubt about the 'obligation to succeed' that creeps into the gangster movies is also not surprising, given the jarring disconnect between the myth and the lives of those consuming it. Lévi-Strauss' claim about myth functioning to mediate or at least articulate ideological contradictions is borne out in the gangster genre, which repeatedly displays the tug of war between our irreconcilable cultural convictions about success, not to mention between American success rhetoric and individual experience.

If the rise-and-fall narratives in early gangster movies implicitly call attention to the schisms at the heart of the American success myth, as the genre matures the gangster's rise and fall is often accompanied by an explicit acknowledgment of the myth's stubborn contradictions. These later, more self-aware instances of the genre put a fine point on its inherent ambiguities concerning the pitfalls of the compulsion to distinguish ourselves and to keep on moving upward. The classic gangster movies' implied equation of the gangster figure with the American entrepreneur suggests that the self-starter can succeed only through aggression and single-minded self-interest, and that all riches are ill-gotten gains. Insinuating that organized crime is a nightmare image of the corporate apparatus, they further imply that there is a fuzzy line between legal and illegal routes to success and an inverse relation between material success and morality. While these ideas are sometimes merely implied in early gangster stories, the similes that equate the crime boss with the businessman and the mob with the corporation become evident in such later movies as *The Godfather* saga (1972, 1974, 1990). Here, over the course of three films, the gangster's rise and fall is simultaneous rather than sequential, and it is distributed among characters. The rise belongs to family patriarch Vito Corleone (Marlon Brando and Robert De Niro) who goes from impoverished immigrant to powerful crime boss (although, as his son Michael would have it, 'My father is no different from any other powerful man'). *The Godfather: Part II* details in flashbacks his steady progress, confirming the possibility of success in America for those with ambition, although also confirming the limited routes to success for poor immigrants and the necessity for ruthlessness on the way up. The fall belongs to his sons, particularly Michael (Al Pacino), who, as the scion of a successful man, a war hero, a graduate of an Ivy League school, and an ostensibly assimilated Italian-American, begins at the pinnacle of worldly success so, according to mythic conventions, has nowhere to go but down.[54] Just as the bygone gangster's fall often began when he separated or turned his back on his gang or his family, the Corleones' fall occurs once Vito's fealty to his clan and his people is succeeded by Michael's detachment and go-it-alone ethic.

There is a marked nostalgia in *The Godfather* films, not just, as several writers have pointed out, for the patriarchal family, for traditional values, and for a simpler, more personalized capitalist system.[55] There is also an elegiac yearning for the romanticized early gangster and his bold ascent against the background of a picturesque early twentieth-century urban America. The spirit of self-making that infused the early gangster prototypes is tainted here by the acknowledgment of what it takes to prosper and survive in the era of late capitalism. In juxtaposing Vito's material rise with Michael's spiritual fall, *The Godfather: Part II* suggests a watering down of the generations – both on the personal level and, more significantly, in the idea of the mythic gangster as the self-made man writ large. His ferocity notwithstanding, Vito subscribes to a strict code of honor that privileges loyalty to his family, the Family, and his ethnic roots. His wish that Michael, rather than following in his footsteps, might lead a life different and better than his endears him to the audience as it echoes the patriarchs of countless immigrant sagas, who do what they have to do so their children can thrive in America. The old Don's loyalty, steadfastness, and solicitousness are replaced, once Michael ascends to the throne, by remoteness, *sang-froid,* and a drive to succeed that is merely vestigial. The gangster is no longer an intrepid go-getter whose immorality is offset by his energy and charm; now, he is simply a jaded, amoral, murderous CEO, presiding over his empire out of habit and spite more than ambition.[56]

In traditional rise-and-fall stories, the audience's dramatic sympathies remain firmly fixed with the protagonist as he climbs, but begin to decathect when he starts his descent. Here, since the upward and downward movements are split between Vito and Michael, the audience's rising and falling receptivity to the characters is likewise split. As the incarnation of the old-school, mythic gangster, Vito retains our sympathies until his end. Atypically for movie gangsters, both he and Michael die in old age of natural causes. But Michael's physical demise, when he ignominiously falls from a chair in *The Godfather: Part III*, is redundant. His spiritual fall has happened far earlier, conveyed in repeated images of desolation and degradation. Although the three-part saga ends with his literal death, the closing moments of the first two films hammer home the fall from grace of the mythic gangster. Each presents Michael as isolated and impenetrable: in the first film, separated from both his wife, Kay (Diane Keaton) and the audience by camera distance, internal frames, and, finally, a door that closes in Kay's and our face, then alone and aloof in the second film, having ordered and impassively watched the murder of his brother. That closing door is Coppola's elegy for the gangster as a tragic hero; in Michael, heroism has atrophied and all that remains is a vestigial simulacrum of the larger-than-life mythic gangster and the American entrepreneurial spirit that he embodied.

Class-passing and voluntary downward mobility

The ambivalence about success and class mobility that permeates rise-and-fall stories appears in another type of success narrative that recurs throughout the history of American cinema. In such movies as *If You Could Only Cook* (1935), *My Man Godfrey* (1936), *Holiday* (1938), *Sullivan's Travels* (1941), *Five Easy Pieces* (1970), and *Lost in America* (1985), the main characters willingly and willfully turn their backs on success to sample life on a lower rung. Having ascended or been born atop the mountain of professional achievement, they decide that the air up there is not as rarefied as it is cracked up to be. They resist the idea that vocation is identity – that what you do is who you are – as they choose to move downward rather than upward in class and profession. Chapter 5 examines in detail films that glorify unemployment, thereby critiquing America's work-besotted notion of success. Their protagonists' refusal to be socially and vocationally mobile constitutes one of the most overt challenges to the myth's equation of economic success and contentment. Films such as the six mentioned above, which invert the classic path of success stories to chart the voluntary downward mobility of their protagonists, likewise enunciate the mixed signals and equivocal attitudes that suffuse Hollywood movies about class mobility.

Among the bedrock beliefs of the success myth is that everyone in America aspires to a consensual, homogeneous definition of success represented by the professional middle class. Barbara Ehrenreich writes that 'The professional, and largely white, middle class is taken as a social norm – a bland and neutral mainstream – from which every other group or class is ultimately a kind of deviation.'[57] The tagline used to publicize *Five Easy Pieces* when it was released says it all: 'He rode the fast lane on the road to nowhere.' Anywhere other than the high reaches of the topography of class and career is not even worthy of a place on the map. If a person is not moving up the class ladder in a professional-level job, he is going nowhere fast. Hollywood movies in which down-ward mobility is a conscious choice represent a dissident (or, at least exploratory) challenge to the dogma that everyone should aspire to a conventionally bourgeois definition of success and an upsurge in class status. As these films consider what happens when their characters spurn the upward track, the mixed messages and warring ideologies that lurk in the fissures of the success myth are once again exposed.

In *Class-Passing: Social Mobility in Film and Popular Culture*, Gwendolyn Audrey Foster uses the term 'class-passing' to denote the performative nature of class and the act of fashioning an assimilable self that is able to cross class categories. The set of class-appropriate behaviors, profes-sions, and acquisitions that telegraph one's status are widely legible cultural codes. They are inculcated and repeatedly reinforced by the movies – and, for that matter, by many other rhetorical and institu-tional aspects of our daily lives – to make us savvy and instantaneous interpreters of class cues.[58] The American success myth is predicated on the idea that identity is fluid and that we can sculpt an ideal, success-ready persona if we are adequately tactical and adept artisans of our own selves. The concomitant assumption is that the social order is supple enough to accommodate those who deserve to move upward. Rather than being victims of circumstances beyond their control, people are free agents who are at liberty to achieve what they can. In this vision of meritocracy, class difference is seen not as a rigid structure of inequality of opportunity and privilege but, instead, as the direct result of distinc-tions in individual drive and talent. In success myth stories such as *The Pursuit of Happyness* or the rise-and-fall tales, characters class-pass to a higher echelon by synthesizing an assortment of class markers (among them new clothing, speech patterns, dwellings, cars, mates) that are a sort of cultural shorthand designed to indicate their would-be new class stratum and professional success. But in a number of movies that betray significantly less certainty that money, work, and class mobility are the means to achieve the good life, characters opt to move down-ward in class, often in a quest for seemingly more authentic, less tangible fulfillments.

The narrative momentum of such movies still revolves around indi-vidualist yearnings for self-realization. But in place of the culturally certified imprimatur of economic success, characters seek self-fulfillment and spiritual satisfaction. These dual poles of individual gratification have a long lineage in American thought. The utilitarian, economic individualism that was inspired by Ben Franklin exists alongside the expressive, ethical individualism articulated by, among others, Emerson and his contemporaries.[59] Hollywood movies seem to valorize the latter tradition, in which individual self-knowledge and self-expression are paramount values, although generally not without some hedging about what is gained and what is lost in the journey away from a life of class privilege.

In each of the six films mentioned above, the male lead at least temporarily repudiates his professional and class identity by renouncing what he variously considers class snobbery, materialism, hypocrisy, or heedlessness. The eponymous Godfrey, a Harvard-educated scion of the upper class, chooses a life of vagrancy over the shallow and childish pleasures of the idle rich.[60] In *If You Could Only Cook*, self-made man James Buchanan (Herbert Marshall), a wealthy CEO of a car company, renounces his position and his pedigreed fiancée to sample life and love as a butler. (As the film's original print ad puts it, 'She gave up her park bench for him! He gave up millions for her!') The Hollywood director in *Sullivan's Travels* who sets off to research a film about poverty by becoming a hobo, the disaffected advertising executive in *Lost in America* who cashes in his nest egg and, with his wife, goes off to 'touch Indians' and pursue similarly romanticized rituals of self-actualization, and the former classical musician of *Five Easy Pieces* who class-passes as an oil rig worker to escape the stultifying life of his upper-class family all hit the road in literal and symbolic journeys away from their lives of privilege and toward what they hope will be more satisfying existences. Each of the films exhibits an ironic awareness that these characters are playing tourist in lower class landscapes while escaping on an experimental basis as they try on their new identities like costumes. When the characters in *Lost in America* lose their nest egg and are forced to take menial, service sector jobs, they ask each other 'What are you?' as if inquiring about a Halloween getup.

These movies also acknowledge the charade of class-passing – even if the movement is downwards – and the difficulty of letting go of class entitlement. The character in *Five Easy Pieces* at times treats both his working-class girlfriend and his co-worker with utter scorn (to the latter he says, 'I can't believe you're comparing your life to mine'), but he is equally contemptuous of the upper-class characters. When the Hollywood director in *Sullivan's Travels* gets thrown into prison, he declares, 'They don't sentence picture directors to a place like this.' He is eventually sprung because of his fame and position. And when the yuppie couple in *Lost in America* loses their life savings and gets a taste of what it is like to live without a safety net, they quickly shift into reverse with their plan to live simply and hightail it back to their former life of privilege. Even Godfrey, who fashions himself as a clear affront to the values of the upper class from which he came, goes from being a 'forgotten man' to a butler to a nightclub entrepreneur in the course of the movie. That each of these characters is, seemingly, just visiting the downward slope and can change direction at will is another demonstration of the confusion that Hollywood movies exhibit about class and success. As American cinema alternates between a staunch (if shallow) populism that romanticizes the simple life of the common man and a fervent love affair with the lives and belongings of the rich and famous, the muddled class consciousness of American cultural practice is on full display.

Other downward mobility films are less conflicted. Just as simple Horatio Alger-type stories handily end at the moment when their young protagonist claims the mantle of success (thereby skirting the issue taken up by the rise-and-fall tales of what happens for the next several decades of his life), some downward mobility plots end at the character's moment of resolve, thereby allowing him to avoid confronting the downside of his downhill motion. *Holiday*'s Johnny Case (Cary Grant), a self-proclaimed 'plain man of the people,' proudly recites his self-made *bona fides* for his prospective father-in-law: son of a grocery store owner; employed since he was ten years old; worked his way through Harvard; toiled at a laundry, a steel mill, an automobile factory, and in a garbage truck; took his first vacation at age thirty. Now, having achieved a good measure of professional success and looking at a bright future, he announces that he wants a holiday 'to find out why I'm working – the answer can't be just to pay bills, to pile up more money.' His dilemma, and the film's plot conflict, comes from being engaged to the wrong woman and engaged in the wrong professional pursuit. The plot of the film revolves around Johnny's need to pick a side in the battle between his success and his soul. Like many American movies, *Holiday* implies that he cannot have both because a man's probity and humanity are in inverse proportion to his professional status and financial success; if he gains the whole world, he invariably loses his soul.

The difficult decision about whether to continue moving up in class and profession or whether to move downward toward a life that privileges play over work and spiritual over material rewards is represented by pairs of opposing characters. Johnny is engaged to Julia Seton (Doris Nolan), a snobby, uptight exemplar of the moneyed elite. But he finds his soul-mate in Julia's offbeat sister Susan (Katharine Hepburn), a free-spirited class traitor and the self-styled black sheep of the family, who spends her days hiding in her childhood playroom bemoaning her death-in-life. Dramatic irony makes the denouement clear from the start, and there is never any doubt about who is Johnny's true kindred spirit. Bereft of a father of his own, he is also torn between the values of two father figures: his friend, Professor Potter (Edward Everett Horton) and his fiancée's father Mr. Seton (Henry Kolker). Potter is a fun-loving man of the mind and spirit. Although he is devoid of social standing and social graces, his lack of *savoir faire* is couched in positive terms since it establishes him as an unpretentious sort. Conversely, Seton is all airs and affectations, like many of the movie's Depression-era tycoons. As a stalwart member of an old money clan, he looks down his nose at the parvenu Johnny. Among Seton's many sins, his reluctance to countenance the young man's self-willed class ascent is his greatest slight to the myth of the self-made man. When Johnny explains that he intends to quit business in order to find himself, Seton announces that he considers the scheme to be un-American. His disapproval of both Johnny's plan and of his son Ned (Lew Ayres), whose passions are making music and getting drunk and whose happiness has been sacrificed on the altar of the family business, makes it clear that the elder Seton – and, by extension, his money-worshipping, class-obsessed cohort – has no truck with expressive individualism. The film concludes with Johnny breaking his engagement to Julia, chucking his job, and, with Susan, joining Professor Potter and his wife on a grand adventure. Because, like most classic comedies, *Holiday* comes to an end at the moment of the consummation of desire, Johnny's embrace of downward mobility remains without consequences. He, and the movie, is able to avoid the ambivalence and confusion suffered by other downwardly mobile characters in stories where a journey to the lower depths forms the plotline.

Although downward mobility tales deviate from classic success stories in their focus on movement that is, according to the myth, in the wrong direction, these movies have much in common with standard issue success tales. Both examine fantasies of transformative rebirth in which identity is fluid and the protagonists possess the necessary autonomy and agency to chart their own course. In all of these movies, self-realization is the greatest good and one's fate is an outgrowth of one's attitude and actions rather than a result of any social or institutional forces. So many of our cultural narratives and ideologies insist that American selves are perennially transitional selves: always on their way to becoming what it is they want to be and never irrevocably what they are. Although movies about success tend to be extremely class-aware, the more simplistic ones highlight class distinctions only to demonstrate the possibility of overcoming them since, as they show, people can exercise active control over their individual destinies by their own choices and actions. Whether the character's movement is up or down the ladder of success, that movement is self-willed and the line of demarcation between classes is permeable and penetrable at will for those who know how to adapt. If the past is a burden, it need not have any bearing on the promise of the future, since the characters in these movies are able to shed their skins and outfit themselves in new, self-crafted identities of their own design. But in both the upwardly and downwardly mobile scenarios, the dualities and doubts that prowl at the edges of this belief in individual agency rear their heads, exposing, yet again, the confusions and crises of self-definition at the heart of the success myth.

Marrying up

The success myth is a decidedly gendered ideal. Stories of self-made men amount to fantasies of masculine self-sufficiency in which the protagonist rebirths himself with, at best, minimal help from the women in his life – or with no help at all in the case of a film such as *The Pursuit of Happyness*, where the woman in his life helps by leaving the picture. If the female character cannot be a habitually supportive helpmeet, she needs to get out of the way of the male character's ascension. Her own thwarted desires are irrelevant to the classic rags-to-riches story of the movie. Whereas men in conventional success myth stories are the putative masters of their fate and captains of their soul, the same, unfortunately, cannot be said for female success seekers in American movies. Traditional success stories from the nineteenth century onward usually relegate women to subsidiary roles: loving spouses, loyal secretaries, nurturing mothers. Women's success is wholly relational and dependent on the fate of the men to whom they hitch their wagons. Chapter 4 explores independent career women in Hollywood films who attempt to pull themselves up by their own distaff bootstraps the same way that men do: through professional skill, drive, and strategy. Although these movie women sometimes do achieve professional and social mobility, it rarely brings them gratification and it invariably comes at the price of their romantic life and interpersonal relationships. For most female film characters with ambitions toward a higher plane, the only sanctioned method for moving up is marrying up: snagging a rich man whose own wealth and prestige allow the heroine to vault to a superior social standing and a more materially rewarding life.

Although the classic success myth is gender specific, the muddled values that shadow that myth are gender neutral. Movies with female protagonists who aspire to greater things are beset by many of the same internal contradictions and inconsistencies about what is desirable and what it takes to move up and move on. However, this clash of ideologies gets rehashed in a different arena, relocating from the professional to the personal sphere as the character moves up by trading not on her occupational skills but on her only asset that has any worth in a patriarchal world: her sexual allure. Our cultural narratives consistently insist that if success at work is the measure of a man, success in marriage is the measure of a woman; if a man's moment of crowning glory happens when he reaches the corner office, a woman's occurs when she reaches the altar. Indeed, by the evidence of Hollywood movies, the only culturally legitimate vocation for women is marriage. A woman may have a job if she uses it to bide time until Mr. Right liberates her from the need to work or, in more contemporary films, if she understands that it needs to come second to her domestic role. In the marrying-up movies, female protagonists bring to their search for a successful husband the same calculation and determination that men bring to their career climb. They deflect their ambitions away from their jobs and toward wedlock: their true vocation. The reward for matrimonially successful women – their 'salary' for a job well done – is their enhanced social status and the material plenitude that goes with it.[61]

Enterprising women who set their caps for successful men and treat husband-hunting as a job appear across Hollywood genres and eras. Usually lowborn, they are Cinderellas who refuse to wait passively to be swept off their ash-covered feet; instead, they are active and goal-oriented hunters whose prey are prosperous prospective husbands. Those movies – often comic – that end at the altar or assume a happily-ever-after union and steer clear of the aftermath of the nuptials are, like classic success stories, able to skirt the issues that may plague the mixed-class marriage down the line (e.g., *It* (1927), *Alice Adams* (1935), *The Lady Eve* (1941), *Gentlemen Prefer Blondes* (1953)). Those – often melodramas – that trace the arc of the marriage and the wedded class-passing heroine are more explicit about the ideological ruptures that dog American movies (*An American Tragedy* (1931) and its remake *A Place in the Sun* (1951), *Possessed* (1931), *Stella Dallas* (1937), *Caught* (1949), *Ruby Gentry*

(1954), *Days of Heaven* (1987)). Whatever the genre, in commodifying themselves to become products with maximum market value, both the comic gold diggers and the tragic social climbers reveal a host of conflicting attitudes about class mobility, gender, and success.

An inventory of these incompatible messages reveals the familiar cultural doublethink. Lower class women should be ambitious but should not overreach. They should, like all Americans, strive to better themselves and move up the class ladder but, if they do, they will not fit in. They should marry for love but no one can live on love alone. They should use what advantages they can to get ahead (in most cases, their shrewdness and their sexuality), but if they do, they will suffer disapproval – not just from other women but, often, from the very men who lust after them.

The head-spinning ideational vertigo that emerges from such films is the equivalent of the similarly mixed messages found in male-centric success stories. Perhaps the gold digger's closest male analogue is the gangster. Both the gold digger and the gangster are hampered by their lower class outsider status, both are brazen and ambitious, but both have only disreputable, desperate means of improving their lot, so they try to better their lives in the only way possible for the likes of them. Like the gangster, the woman who chases success by marrying up is born into a double bind since her class and gender (like his class and ethnicity) limit her options for improving her social status. She is damned if she does go after what she wants, since she is often punished for her striving and her scheming by not being accepted into her aspirational class. And she is damned to a life of low-level jobs and cold-water flats if she does not try to escape upwards.

Not incidentally, both prototypes regularly inhabited the movie screens and the popular consciousness of Americans during the Depression years, when social conditions might well have inspired mass skepticism about the promise of self-making by conventional means. The early gangster cycle's correlative was the cycle of 'fallen women' movies of the early, pre-censorship 1930s, in which the protagonists sleep (rather than shoot) their way to the top – or at least try to. To paraphrase a Lorenz Hart lyric: horizontally speaking, these women are at their very best so, using their most prized asset, they contrive to move vertically by performing horizontally. *Possessed* (1931), *Baby Face* (1933), *Red-Headed Woman* (1932), and *Sadie McKee* (1934) are among the many fallen women movies in which ambitious and conniving lower class women try to seize success the only way they can. *Baby Face* uses the visual trope of the skyscraper, the modernist icon of vertical ascension, to trace the path of speakeasy barmaid Lily Powers (Barbara Stanwyck) as she cynically and skillfully manipulates her way up the corporate ladder floor by floor to the top level and the top executive's bed. (The film's punning tagline – 'She climbed the ladder of success, wrong by wrong' – makes it clear that *Baby Face* is self-consciously in the bootstrap story mode.) Like all characters engaged in self-making, she is a savvy and eager shape-changer, literally fashioning herself anew to conform to each rise in status and position. In spite of her unholy methods, she keeps her eyes firmly fixed on the holy grail of matrimony, declaring that what she really wants is 'a Mrs. on my tombstone.' In a tacked-on ending that, as several film historians have pointed out, undercuts the movie's prior character development and motivation, she ends up acceding to love rather than to riches and acquiescing to a life in the shadow of a small-town industrial skyline rather than the soaring skyscrapers that were emblematic of her crusade to reach the top.[62] As with many of the protagonists who intend to marry for money, love sneaks up on her and overtakes her ambitions and her lust for riches.

Alongside those characters in marrying-up movies who start off as gold diggers and end up choosing true love over money, there are those, such as the title character in *The Lady Eve,* who set their sights on bagging prosperous husbands and end up getting a twofer: rich men that they truly love. More commonly, the machinations of women intent on marrying up yield neither love nor money but, instead, tragedy and despair (*Stella Dallas, Ruby Gentry*). One way or another, these women are punished for their overreaching by finding out that their rich husbands are stodgy and sexless or work-fixated or even homicidal. Whatever the outcome, none of these narrative patterns avoids the myriad ideological discrepancies that bedevil success myth stories. The frankly titled *How to Marry a Millionaire* (1953) exhibits the usual inconsistent values. Three young career women set themselves up to snare wealthy husbands. Their modeling jobs, their soigné clothing, their penthouse apartment are all strategically designed to yield maximum opportunities for them to net their prey. But a funny thing happens on the way to the altar: they find the rich men that they target to be tedious and undesirable and, to their surprise, they fall in love with regular guys. En route to its predictable conclusion, the movie bestows on its audience the voyeuristic pleasure of admiring the clothes, settings, and belongings of the upper class. Like many other success stories, *How to Marry a Millionaire* tries to have it both ways: endorsing love over money and the simple life over worldly success while simultaneously encouraging the spectator to hanker after the lives of the materially and professionally successful.

What emerges most fully from even the comic marrying-up films is the narrow constraints that bind women who want to advance. The women who succeed in wedding for money rather than love are invariably condemned to bad marriages. Those that opt for love rather than money are consigned to a life of straitened circumstances. All have little recourse but to use their wiles and their carnal wares in their drive for matrimonial success. As such, even before her unlikely personality conversion at the end of *Baby Face*, the main character earns our sympathy, if not our approval. Motherless since her youth, pimped by her father and pawed by his roughhewn patrons, she is cynical and opportunistic for a reason. If she is to be commodified by every man she meets, she may as well command the highest price. As with the gangster, her only alternative to stasis is pursuing her ends through disreputable means. But even those lowborn women who are less grasping have few opportunities for upward mobility.

The lack of genuine agency that plagues women in marrying-up movies is readily apparent in *Caught* (1949), a melodrama that exemplifies the plight of ambitious women on film. Early on, the title reveals its double meaning. The heroine Leonora Eames (Barbara Bel Geddes) is a department store model who fantasizes about owning nice things and longs to make the leap to the upper class. In a none-too-subtle gesture, as she talks about catching a desirable man she kills a pesky fly on her knee by slapping it with a flyswatter. Hell-bent on marrying up, she changes her name, goes to charm school to learn a 'personality recipe,' and sets her sights on what she calls 'a real man': someone rich who she can marry to escape her dead-end job. Through luck and guile, she catches one but it is soon apparent that she is the one who is caught. Smith Ohlrig (Robert Ryan), a ruthless business magnate and control freak, treats her like another corporate acquisition. Although initially charmed by him, she becomes a bird in his gilded cage – trapped not only by his intense need for domination but also by her own love of riches. Having been blinded by her ambitions, she is now forced to endure the underside of the dream of mobility and rebirth. A businessman-cum-psychopath and one of Hollywood's many mad capitalists, Ohlrig is like Charles Foster Kane on steroids: obsessed with his acquisitions and intent on having all things material and human under his dominion. He succinctly sums up the secret of his success: 'I can't stand losing. Only nice people lose.' The movie's unease with professional and material criteria for success finds expression in Ohlrig's disease: an increasingly debilitating illness that metaphorically indicates he has become sick with ambition. Apparently, according to *Caught*, success breeds psychosis.

Figure 2.3 Leonora Eames (Barbara Bel Geddes) learns how to cook up a 'personality recipe' for enticing a rich man. *Caught* (1949). Directed by Max Ophuls

Hollywood's habitual split stance on class and success is on full display in *Caught*. 'Smith Ohlrig Weds Former Carhop' reads the headline of the newspaper announcement heralding the mixed-class wedding. Further down in the article, Leonora's mother is quoted as saying, 'I always knew my daughter would be a success.' The director Max Ophuls' famously expressionist camera ogles the vast, rococo spaces of Ohlrig's suburban house while suffusing them in chiaroscuro lighting that denotes the neurosis and imbalance of the characters that inhabit them. Like *Citizen Kane*'s mansion, the architectural grandeur becomes increasingly oppressive and the huge expanses become the visual correlative of the characters' intense loneliness and isolation. As the seductiveness of material plenty strains against Leonora's unhappiness and as her fantasies of class-passing come up against the actuality of her status as an object in Ohlrig's collection, husband and wife turn on one another. Edgy and neurotic, she screams at him: 'Look at me ... look at what you have bought.' His counter-accusation: 'You want too much. You wanted to marry rich and you did. You thought if you had money you'd have everything.... You've had more than a year of being rich – you like it.' And she does.

Eventually, however, Leonora's misery outweighs her lust for riches, so she leaves her husband and goes to work in New York as a secretary to an altruistic pediatrician and man-of-the-people named Larry Quinada (James Mason). Whereas she saw her marriage to Ohlrig as an escape from her career, she now sees her new job as an escape from her marriage. During her job interview, the office nurse tells her, 'I hope you're looking for work and not a husband.' When she meets her employer and he asks what she was doing out on Long Island she replies, 'I was sort of a paid companion to someone who was very rich': an ironic acknowledgment to herself that she was bought by her husband and caught in her own venal net. The schematic plot device of having Leonora choose between the selfless, kind healer and the selfish, loathsome capitalist seems to point the movie toward an inevitable epiphany about what really matters and what true success entails: happiness and altruism rather than money. But *Caught* does not succumb so easily to this escape hatch from the dilemma of defining success. Although she does fall in love with the doctor, Leonora goes back home for a night and gets impregnated by her husband. When she discovers her state, she returns to him explaining, 'I came back for my baby.' With the insight of the devil, seeing through to her gold-digging soul, Ohlrig's rejoinder hits home: 'For money. You want your child to be rich.'

Although *Caught* inches toward being a morality tale about the dangers of loving Mammon and marrying for money, it cannot help but admit that renouncing Leonora's initial conception of success is not so easy. The movie eventually sidesteps the standoff between true love, on one hand, and lust for money and position, on the other, by conveniently having Ohlrig die (seemingly of a surfeit of success in his veins) and Leonora miscarry, thereby clearing the path to a marriage untainted by material desire. All's well that ends well, but the pat denouement cannot erase the ideological dissonance that pervades the movie.[63] A good deal has been written about melodrama as a covertly subversive narrative form for revealing cultural hypocrisies, particularly regarding what historian Richard Sennett called 'the hidden injuries of class.'[64] The endings of *Caught* and other marrying-up movies may endorse the simple life, reject worldly success, and applaud their heroines' eventual revelation about what is truly worth valuing, but they cannot suppress an acknowledgment of the lack of culturally authorized options besides marriage for women on an upward path.

Myth and history

The various narrative patterns displayed by the movies discussed in this chapter – the upward progress of classic success myth heroes, the flat-lined ambition of protagonists whose dreams are deferred or denied, the yo-yoing fortunes of the characters in rise-and-fall sagas, the voluntary downward trajectory of those that opt for class descent – have reverberated since the earliest film versions of the myth. In surveying some of the many films that present the promise of mobility as elemental to the American idea of success, the foregoing investigation has ranged widely across the decades of film history, focusing on an array of movies from many eras and genres that serve to represent ongoing currents of thought as well as recurring narrative conventions. This freewheeling traversal of time periods is not meant to suggest that the success myth is static or utterly impervious to historical change. However much they may hew to long established mythic scenarios and axioms, each of these movies grows out of its particular cultural moment. The Depression-era gangster movies that belie the promise of success for all, *A Face in the Crowd*'s critique of corporate culture and groupthink during the supposedly consensus-ridden 1950s, *The Godfather*'s post-1960s rumination on the longing for traditional values and patriarchal families in a time of social upheaval, along with all of the other movies selected for discussion, emanate from and speak to their own zeitgeist as much as they speak to perennial American aspirations and anxieties.

The success myth, like all myths, adapts and realigns itself to a degree in order to address itself to the tenor of the times, thereby remaining relevant and topical. But in some ways, it is also, like all myths, stubbornly timeless, carrying on with its essential convictions – not to mention the irreconcilable contradictions embedded in those convictions – in spite of fluctuating sociohistorical situations that may refute the fundamental claims of the myth. The basic success myth has a remarkably tenacious hold on the American imagination, even when circumstances fly in the face of its bedrock assumptions. Myth is, of course, historically contingent and ideologically fraught, but it is so tightly woven into the social fabric that those aspects of myth are not always readily discernible. The history of success narratives in America repeatedly suggests that when the symbolic realm of myth collides with the actuality of social and economic conditions, it is often the former that emerges as incontestable, holding sway over our sense of things even when circumstances belie the myth's suppositions. Those suppositions are not eternal verities, but the powerful allure of mythic narratives does make them seem that way.

If a twenty-first century success story such as *The Pursuit of Happyness* can propound the myth, unencumbered by irony or doubt, the pressing question seems to be not how the myth changes with the times but why it changes so little. In his landmark work *Mythologies*, literary theorist Roland Barthes identified 'the very principle of myth: it transforms history into nature.'[65] In flaunting its normative power, myth flouts historical change. Indeed, part of the function of myth is to flatten out history: to endorse its own core premises as expansive and eternal verities. Even the films that challenge those verities tend to echo each other's demurrals across the years. Both the complacent mythic tales that deny our social anxieties about success and the shadow stories that reveal self-doubt and irresolution co-exist throughout film history, sometimes in the same movie. Variform and versatile, the success myth in its many iterations displays less genuine evolution than surface adaptation to changing times and mores. Success narratives acclimate themselves to their age, but their reinvention goes only so far; the difference between new and old tellings of the tale is in shading, not in kind. Contemporary success story protagonists may aspire to a nominally different professional environment than that of their precursors, and their stories may be tricked out in up-to-date garb, but their aspirations, their tactics, and their obstacles are remarkably familiar.

In fulfilling its purpose of articulating deep-rooted, widespread, and everlasting cultural desires and doubts, myth is self-perpetuating and, often, willfully atemporal. To an extent, myths become monolithic by dehistoricizing themselves: by reassuring us that certain beliefs are so culturally definitional, so powerfully etched in our collective self-perception, so essentially and eternally true that they are impervious to the flux of history. In historian William McNeil's estimation,

> [Truth] resides in myth – generalizing myths that direct attention to what is common amid diversity by neglecting trivial differences of detail. Such myths make subsequent experience intelligible.... The simple fact is that communities live by myths, of necessity. For only by acting as if the world made sense can society persist and individuals survive.[66]

Our ardent belief in the success myth contributes to the very idea of our national identity. Striving for success and believing in individual social mobility is, the myth insists, at the core of what it means to be an American, whatever the era or historical condition.

Myth is part of the ongoing conversation that a culture has with itself about itself, and the primary conversational topic of the success myth is work. The vaunted American work ethic is what sustains our belief in the possibility of social mobility and in individual agency in the face of institutional indifference. The remaining chapters of this study focus on work, amplifying and extending this chapter's exploration of the contradictory ideologies that unsettle the success myth's foundation. Whereas the present chapter has pieced together a mosaic of films from different eras in order to build an argument about their aggregate coherence and representative significance, the ensuing chapters pursue a different organizing principle. Each proceeds roughly chronologically to explore the corporate workplace movie, the crossroads of gender, work, and success, and the glorification of unemployment respectively. They share with this chapter the intention to establish a through-line among diverse movies: both those that broach and those that sidestep the cultural tensions that perennially plague the American success myth, not to mention American lives. The sequential design of the ensuing chapters is meant to suggest not evolution but fixity and consistency in the success myth's narrative strategies and ideational confusions. Given the vast assortment of cinematic success narratives that chart their characters' professional mobility, there are inevitable, if regrettable, omissions and gaps. That so many movies variously – and sometimes simultaneously – endorse and challenge the myth's dogma suggests that the American success myth is perpetually pertinent, inhabiting our collective imagination as it attempts to shed light on our social values, behaviors, and identities.

3
Work and Its Discontents:
The Corporate Workplace Film

But in democracies the love of physical gratification, the notion
of bettering one's condition, the excitement of competition,
the charm of anticipated success, are so many spurs to urge men
onwards in the active professions they have embraced, without
allowing them to deviate for an instant from the track.

– Alexis de Tocqueville, *Democracy in America*

If social mobility is the cornerstone of the edifice of success, work is the
basic building block. At its simplest, the American idea of success con-
flates the attainment of success with vocational achievement. Lacking
an aristocracy, American culture exalts the notion of a meritocracy, entry
into which is gained by hard work and professional prowess. In our most
beloved popular culture narratives, successful characters aren't born at
the top of the world; they climb to the pinnacle, rung by professional
rung. Work is the primary measure of self-worth, in the contemporary
American mind, and the material goods that are the signifiers of success are the just rewards for one's labor and the visible evidence of one's
diligence and superiority.[1]

The prototype of the self-made man who remakes himself through
hard work dates back to the social and religious doctrines of the Puritans;
early twentieth-century writers such as Max Weber and R. H. Tawney
extended that notion by positing a linkage between capitalism and
Protestantism, and a view of work as ethically and spiritually based.[2]
Contemporary versions of the success myth have long since lost the
Puritans' view of work as a calling and success as proof of God's favor.
Although the hero who makes it to the top through his superior work
ethic is part of a durable myth that is firmly lodged in the American psyche, in contemporary success sagas, work is rarely depicted as ennobling

65

or important in its own right. Only rarely do latter-day cultural narratives present work as interesting or meaningful beyond its material recompense. More often, work is depicted as toil: monotonous, stressful, and spiritually unrewarding. 'The reward rests not in the task but in the pay,' as John Kenneth Galbraith once neatly summarized the prevailing attitude towards work.[3]

In twentieth- and twenty-first-century success stories, the workplace is usually presented as a proving ground for would-be climbers or, in the more dystopian versions of the success myth, a snake pit for ambitious asps. Careerism has generally replaced the notion of a calling, and work is often seen simply as the route to the riches and recognition that are the emblems of success. The Puritans' spiritual worship has been superseded by reverence for material and professional gain; indeed, in the popular imagination, the visual symbol of aspiration is no longer the church spires reaching toward God but the corporate skyscrapers straining toward Mammon.

As part of the larger construction of social reality, movie versions of the success myth betray profoundly conflicted – and sometimes contradictory – attitudes toward work as a measure of self-worth, reflecting deep-seated cultural misgivings about the centrality of work as the cornerstone of identity. From the screwball comedies of the Depression era to the corporate dramas of the 1950s, from the slacker films of the 1990s to the visions of working life in contemporary movies, there is an ongoing cultural rumination about what is gained and what is lost in the single-sighted devotion to professional advancement. These films are consistently ambivalent about the primacy of professional achievement as an indicator of success. On one hand, hard work is at the core of the American can-do ethic, and success at one's job is equated with adulthood, masculinity, and essential American ideas about social mobility and individual initiative. Alternatively – and sometimes simultaneously – the movies paint the work environment as dehumanizing, spiritually deadening, and, often, corrupt. Characters in success stories frequently find themselves in a double bind: success is gained through one's work, but work doesn't seem to yield contentment. The ambiguity and anxiety at the core of these movies are part of an ongoing American discourse about the vexed interrelationship between work and self-worth, as well as between material and spiritual fulfillment.

Success narratives that are set in the workplace are, like many American success stories, ideationally muddled, as competing cultural myths collide with one another. Rather than professional success leading to happiness, success and happiness are often counterposed, as the main character is forced to choose between material and spiritual (not to mention moral) gratification. Success is presented as a cultural imperative but so are individual contentment and moral probity; alas, in many of the workplace stories, they seem to be mutually exclusive. Likewise, commitment to family is at odds with careerist ambitions, as characters across several decades wrestle with what contemporary parlance dubs 'having it all.'

Corporate capitalism and success

Although they are the products of varying sociohistorical conditions, American popular narratives set in the world of work are consistently fraught with contradictions that reveal profound – if tacit – cultural qualms about the price of professional success. The corporate environment is characterized as particularly inimical to individual contentment. By the latter half of the twentieth century, anxieties about corporate capitalism found their avatar in the organization man, who began to haunt the American psyche and populate the workplace films of the 1950s. Both comedies and dramas that revolve around the workplace tend to focus on the evils of the corporation and the concomitant plight of the individual who comes to understand that he needs to remove himself from the corporate world in order not to be consumed by it. It is striking how durable this storyline is; it recurs in so many films of the last 50-plus years that it is possible to generalize about a standard issue corporate workplace narrative. Across differing economic and social circumstances, in both comedies and dramas, certain visual and narrative conventions consistently define the workplace movie.

The storyline involves a protagonist who initially buys into the corporate *modus operandi* as the path to the top. The young man is willing to work hard and is good at what he does.[4] In his drive to distinguish himself, he often takes, as his exemplar, an older co-worker who has already arrived at the pinnacle of corporate success. Eventually, the success myth hero comes face to face with some sort of ethical lapse, betrayal, or cynicism on the part of those in power. This leads to a moral reckoning and awakening that allows him eventually to turn his back on the corporation and reassert individual identity and control.

These films often end with the character unemployed – sometimes voluntarily, sometimes not. Saved from what the film presents as the clutches of corporate capitalism, he is poorer and sadder but wiser to the ways of the world. It is not that these characters can't win the game; rather, they choose to default because the game is rigged and corrupt.

As comedian Lily Tomlin so aptly put it, 'The problem with the rat race is that even if you win, you are still a rat.' The resolutions of many of these workplace films endorse a sort of maverick individualist stance as the antidote to corporate pressures, bureaucratic facelessness, and institutionalized immorality. Like many American movies and myths, these films are, in essence, about the individual versus the organization – about the tension between self-determination and social conformity or control. The plot invariably revolves around the conflict that arises when an ambitious young man is forced to choose either individual freedom and self-expression or conformity to the collective values of the business world. Along with his fellow genre film individualists, the cowboy and the former cop-turned private eye, the success myth hero finds himself a lone rebel pitted against the mass, represented here by the middle and upper management of the corporation.[5] Those who have made it in the corporation are defined by their conformity, their obedience to corporate mores, and, often, their immorality. Their foil is the success myth hero whose trajectory through the plot leads to his assertion of self-reliance, individuality, and moral probity as the authentic American virtues.

Although these films present bureaucracy as a threat to individuality and meritocracy, most stop short of damning the systemic apparatus of corporate capitalism. In many cases, the blame is put on bad bosses, not on an intrinsically corrupt or ill-conceived system. The problems in the system get localized and focused on an unscrupulous and maleficent individual and his henchmen. If the minions of bad managers can be exorcised from the seat of power, then the young striver can stay. As is typical in many Hollywood movies, the focus is on individual rather than institutional villainy, on personal plights rather than social ills. The structural dynamics that may lead to inequality or immorality are displaced, in the films' cosmology, onto the figure of the evil boss.

In the films in which corporate culture and ideology are themselves targeted as antithetical to individual achievement and contentment, the hero may eventually solve his individual problems with the corporation (usually by leaving it) but, ultimately, the managerial structure remains intact. Indeed, the corporate framework is presented as monolithic and, in spite of their newfound stance towards that framework, the heroes of these films only occasionally attempt to raze it or to rebuild it from within. Rather, the entrepreneurial hero usually goes off to create his own success in isolation from the bad system. The trajectory of the narrative takes the success myth hero from wanting into to wanting out of the existing structure. Dropping out is an act of self-assertion but only occasionally does the protagonist bring about significant change in the corporate apparatus that has oppressed him. The narrative resolutions often fail to ameliorate the problems identified in the foregoing two hours, so even if the protagonist's personal plight is seemingly resolved at film's end, the larger questions and implications are left *in medias res*.[6]

In most corporate workplace films, the specific career that the success myth hero pursues is beside the point. Such corporate milieus as advertising, insurance, or finance are simply class signifiers: a sort of cultural code for the white-collar professional world. The function of the business is less pertinent to the point of the film than is its generalized corporate aura. Since the vast majority of American households define themselves as middle class, it is not surprising that this white collar, careerist version of the success myth dominates the popular imagination, propounding a singular vision of the good life. Barbara Ehrenreich has described the middle class as 'a class which is everywhere represented as representing everyone.'[7]

Demographically, the protagonist of corporate workplace films is generally young, white, male, and frequently of working-class origin.[8] His youth is synonymous with possibility: with the wide-eyed conviction that the business world is his to conquer and its spoils are there for the taking. In most Hollywood movies, success, like romance, is accomplished in youth or not at all. The protagonists in success narratives are in the process of arriving at the top. Those who have already arrived are presented as having paid the exacting price of success: they are settled, cynical, or smug. In the simplistic valuation of many of the workplace stories, aspiration and ambition are good but achievement is suspect. Since the success myth hero is not yet wholly complicit with the corporate apparatus, his progress through the narrative involves a rebellion against the old order which is, at best, tired and, more often, tainted. Of course, the films usually end before the hero either has to join the old order or work to replace it with a new and improved one, thereby leaving intact his moral righteousness and youthful spirit, and begging the question of how he can age in his job and join the mainstream without paddling in sullied waters.

From the Horatio Alger stories of the nineteenth century to contemporary movies, the success myth hero is generally a child of the lower classes. The undercurrent of conflicted class-consciousness that runs throughout American culture embraces a hero whose ultimate achievement is hard won, rather than resulting from unfair advantage. The ideology of class mobility insists that all hard workers have a shot at the big time and that success is a matter of personal will. If the vision of

American life as meritocratic is to prevail, the hero of success stories has to deserve his success and earn it through hard work and high morals. If his origins are not lower class, then it is likely that the main character in success myth narratives will hail from a small town. Symbolically, the city is the ultimate proving ground: simultaneously the locus of opportunity and the urban jungle where only the fittest and most adaptive survive. Whether the hero issues from the lower classes or from a small town, it amounts to the same thing and serves the same narrative purpose. He comes from Nowheresville, and aspires to go somewhere and to be someone. In either case, his origins give credence to the most cherished of American mythic beliefs: that accidents of birth do not hamper us in our lives.

Skyscraper souls

These recurring narrative conventions of corporate workplace films have visual correlatives that likewise reappear in movies spanning several eras. The iconography of the corporation was established in American movies – and lodged in the American mind – early on in the twentieth century. Certain cinematic motifs are repeated so often that they become visual tropes: recognizable metaphors for the films' attitudes toward the corporate environment. As early as King Vidor's *The Crowd* (1928), a particular cinematic presentation of the corporate workplace begins to take shape. The film's evocative visuals and its mise-en-scène of corporate life suggest an overbearing architectural and urban determinism that precludes individuality.[9] *The Crowd* tells the story of John Sims (James Murray), an ordinary young man determined to make his mark in the world. He arrives in New York City from a small town, full of youthful vigor and swagger, and convinced that he is exceptional. As the movie's title indicates, however, the story of John's life in the city involves a gradual paring away of his illusions and his presumptions of individual distinctiveness. The film's final long, group shot, where John and his family are virtually swallowed up by a mass of people, puts the lie to the success myth's most dearly held promise of the possibility of differentiating oneself from the crowd. By positing John as an everyman, the film pinpoints the paradox implicit in the promise of American individualism: every member of the crowd considers himself superior and unique. If the myth that hard work will make us rise to the top were universally realizable, then, far from being lonely at the top, it would be overcrowded. But, by definition, cultural myths – and the hopes that they engender – endure in spite of their implausibility.

Most of *The Crowd* takes place in the domestic sphere, but an extraordinary five-minute sequence near the beginning of the film establishes, through its bravura visuals, an attitude toward the corporate milieu found not only in this film but in many workplace films for decades to come. Vidor's movie, made at the tail end of the silent era, relies on an array of cinematic techniques to make its point.[10] John arrives in the city by boat and, as he declares to a fellow passenger his determination to set himself apart from the crowd, the director gives us long shots of the New York skyline, looking like a tiny erector set version of a great metropolis. In the mythic imagination, New York is The City: the locus of success and the enduring symbol of the promise of the American dream. In these shots of the cityscape, John's silhouette occupies a substantial portion of the frame and, from a distance, the city looks conquerable. But once John is ashore, the film's visual design tells another story.

Immediately after the boat scene, we see a montage of crowded street scenes, strung together with slow dissolves. Mobbed sidewalks give way to a series of overhead shots of elevated trains, cars, boats, and buildings. The accretion of shots, each characterized by a mise-en-scène crammed with multiple signifiers of city life, has the effect of mocking John's assumption of uniqueness. Already Vidor is undercutting John's sense of himself as special by showing us hundreds of people, each presumably harboring similar ambitions and dreams. Here and throughout the film, Vidor presents us with what might be dubbed the 'principle of multiples.' In many of the shots set in public or social spaces, people and objects are multiplied, and the film's title is repeatedly invoked by its cinematic plurality. Privacy and individuality are negated by the enumeration and accumulation of seemingly interchangeable visual elements within the film frame.[11]

A low-angle long shot of the façade of proto-twin towers follows the crowd shots of the city. The camera twists and then begins to tilt up the skyscrapers, accentuating their imposing height. This shot exaggerates the looming presence of the buildings; by keeping the camera on the ground while leaning back and looking up, the tilt makes the high-rise edifice look improbably tall and intimidating. The frame can't contain the entire building and the sky is completely eclipsed by its mass.[12] The camera then begins to crane up the building and we get a view of hundreds of windows. By now, the shot looks almost abstract: a symmetrical agglomeration of rectilinear lines and shapes. After tracking toward one of the windows, the shot dissolves and continues to track slowly into the interior of the building. Once inside, we get a high-angle long shot of a huge room filled with masses of identical desks. Although it is never clear what business the corporation is engaged in, it is all too clear that what it mass produces is legions of indistinguishable workers.[13] Vidor uses forced perspective here and the resulting diagonal composition makes the desks in the rear ground appear to be infinitely receding. The camera finally locates John, at desk number 137, looking notably unengaged in his work. He glances toward the clock which, a close-up reveals, is about to strike 5 p.m. Shots such as this one, in which characters gaze expectantly at an office clock as they wait for the magic moment when they can be sprung from their servitude, are a convention verging on a cliché in scores of workplace films. Taken together, they offer ample evidence of how movie characters across the decades feel about the daily grind.[14] Here, the young man of confidence and initiative has already turned into a goof-off and a clock-watcher who dreams of the big time but spends his days longing for quitting time. Once the clock strikes, Vidor cuts to another overhead shot of the masses of workers eagerly fleeing the office; it seems that John is not the only wage slave who can't wait to leave his work life behind for the day.

The next series of shots take place in a washroom where, once again, Vidor employs the principle of multiples. A long bank of sinks is made to look endless by the open-frame composition of the shot and by

Figure 3.1   A superimposition encapsulates John Sims' (James Murray) attitude toward the daily grind. *The Crowd* (1928). Directed by King Vidor

the bathroom mirrors that, with their infinite regress, exponentially multiply the number of washbasins. Each of the workers ritualistically performs his ablutions. As John joins the rest in washing up, his co-workers pass him and, in intertitles, offer nearly identical small talk utterances to him. John responds with, 'You birds have been working here so long that you all talk alike.' This is perhaps the first of many instances in workplace movies where the employees sling around the contemporary slang as a way of fitting in. Here, as in corresponding movies, a sort of incantatory corporate lingo punctuates the characters' capitulation to the conformist values of their workplace.

Having washed up in lockstep, the workers then race to a large bank of elevators. Once inside an elevator that is wall-to-wall people, John faces the opposite direction from the crowd and is admonished by the elevator operator to face the front. John's sense of uniqueness to the contrary, non-conformity will not be tolerated in the corporate sphere. Vidor puts a fine point on the uniformity and lack of individuation of big-city life in the coda to the office sequence. After making their way through another sidewalk mob, John and his friend Bert wait outside yet another office building for two young women who are also getting out of work. Of course, they are not the only ones waiting. Hordes of men await their dates and, as each woman emerges from the building, the couples pair off in what looks unmistakably like a highly choreographed, ritualized mating dance.

The remainder of the film charts John's disappointment and degradation, as both his work and his home life fall apart. John is far from blameless for his fate; early on, he is depicted as more of a dreamer and a big talker than a hard worker and, even at the end of the movie, he exhibits a remarkable lack of self-awareness. In contrast, his friend Bert manages to hoist himself up to middle management and, significantly, get rewarded with his own office. His private space and sizable desk are tangible indicators that he has been able to remove himself from the mass of interchangeable workers. Bert's success in separating himself from the crowd contrasts with John's inability to distinguish himself. Significantly, shortly after the film reveals Bert's newfound work status and surroundings, John has a breakdown. Beaten down by life and unable to continue to work, he leaps up from his desk and, in an act of rebellion against the environmental determinism of his workspace, he shoves his desk out of line, thereby violating the office's order.

But the film is not so simplistic as to claim that, because some people succeed, failure is wholly one's own fault, and Vidor doesn't make John solely responsible for his plight. Like many success narratives, *The*

Crowd is torn in two directions and Vidor resists easily assigning culpability for John's sorry fate. At first glance, it appears that the film gives a nod to the myth of mobility: if hard work yields success, then the shiftless John is to blame for his lack thereof. His inability to succeed can be attributed to his character defects and his failure of will. But Vidor complicates this reading of the film by ensuring that the audience's dramatic sympathies remain firmly with the character throughout his ups and downs. In contrast, Bert as well as John's putatively successful brothers-in-law are, essentially, ciphers to us, and the film suggests that they have sacrificed their individuality to achieve a small measure of success.

The Crowd's complex visual iconography implies that individual agency is hardly a match for the indignities of modern urban life. This is arguably Vidor's most expressionist film, as workplace degradation and thwarted ambition find their visual analogues in the oppressively uniform architecture of the corporation.[15] In many shots, the urban environment dwarfs the characters, symbolically minimizing their own presence in and control over their world. Vidor's larger point seems to be that, ultimately, the urbanization and corporatization of modern life are to blame for John's alienation, anonymity, and blighted hopes.

The prosperous 1920s were full of paeans to American business enterprise and to the concomitant pace and productivity of big-city life. As historian Loren Baritz has pointed out, 'The celebration of business as the foundation of America's culture, ethic and purpose became a virtual reflex in the 1920s.'[16] Devotion to business success became equated with patriotism when Herbert Hoover famously declared that 'The business of America is business.' And the American success myth even had a brief retrogressive fling with religion in Bruce Barton's widely read book, *The Man Nobody Knows*, in which he claimed that Jesus was, in essence, a businessman.[17] But the anxieties about urbanization and corporate standardization that are embedded in the narrative of *The Crowd* and the film's concern that big business may be antithetical to the entrepreneurial frontier spirit betray an undercurrent to the business-celebrating zeitgeist.[18] The film, appearing in the midst of the prosperous, roaring 1920s, in some ways prefigures the despondency of the Depression. Even in a period of commercial growth and widespread affluence, this story of vocational failure followed by unemployment and facelessness in the big city hit a nerve with American audiences.[19]

Curiously, popular culture narratives infused with angst about corporate capitalism and the spiritual price of success seem to appear with greater frequency in times of prosperity. It is while the national economy is riding the crest of a wave that the fear of drowning in a sea of anonymity and failure is apparently most acute.[20] The vision of the corporation that was limned in *The Crowd* appeared intermittently throughout the 1930s and 1940s.[21] Particularly notable are a trio of films starring Warren William as the all-purpose corporate villain of the early 1930s: a rapacious and exploitive boss who fiercely guards his professional prerogative, using guile to make his way to the top and then stay there. Appearing in the early years of the Depression, *Skyscraper Souls* (1932), *The Match King* (1932), and *Employee's Entrance* (1933) helped to etch in the popular consciousness a recurring success myth type: the soulless exploiter who wallows in material gain at the expense of the sorry souls who work for him. In the first of these titles, William's amoral character will stop at nothing to acquire the hundred-story skyscraper that is the emblem of achievement in capitalist iconography. The predatory corporate scoundrel, a recurring figure in success myth tales, held particular resonance during the Depression years as the embodiment of greed and the target of populist ire.

But it wasn't until the boom years of the 1950s and early 1960s that the corporate workplace film, with its cynical take on corporate life, became full-blown. The incipient motifs of *The Crowd* – corporate-induced loss of individuality, prescribed speech and behavior, fear of failure – are at the thematic center of several workplace films made in the period of abundance following World War II.[22] A spate of movies set in the corporate world reappeared during the 1980s and again in the flourishing affluence of the late 1990s. Ironically, a thriving economy appears to exacerbate the collective angst about the precariousness of success on both the individual and the larger social and economic level.

The organization man of the 1950s and 1960s

By mid-century, the structural apparatus of the corporation largely defined business enterprise throughout many segments of the American economy, as large corporations represented a growing proportion of national businesses.[23] Likewise, the corporate sphere colonized an increasingly larger piece of the American imagination as it became the symbolic locus of cultural anxieties about the loss of individuality, conformity, and the toll on self and family exacted by the rat race. Several popular novels and Hollywood films of the period focus their narrative conflict around corporate mores and their effect on American lives. The decade of the 1950s also saw the publication of a number of highly influential and widely read works of sociology whose reach extended well beyond the confines of the academy. David Reisman's *The Lonely Crowd*

(1950), C. Wright Mills' *White Collar* (1951), and William H. Whyte, Jr.'s *The Organization Man* (1956) collectively gave vent to mid-century America's concerns about the corporate ethos; their titles, in turn, gave rise to catchphrases that entered the vernacular and remain lodged there to this day.[24]

In assessing the effect of contemporary institutions on individual life, all three works struck a somewhat elegiac tone; together they comprised a lament for earlier, presumably more humane forms of social and vocational organization. Each, in its way, championed individualism and equated the corporation with the oppressive mass. Reisman's central dichotomy in *The Lonely Crowd* was between what he named other-directed character types, who strive to conform to externally derived expectations, and inner-directed types, whose internal compass is inculcated early on and serves to keep them on course, whatever direction the prevailing winds are blowing. He maintained that the then contemporary forms of business enterprise rewarded other-directed 'glad handing' and an ability to respond to peer norms rather than to an inner-directed sense of purpose.

For his part, Whyte described his organization man as someone who had taken 'the vows of organization life'[25] by acquiescing to what the author labeled the social ethic, which he contrasted to the Protestant ethic and described as an assault on individuality from the pressure to belong to various groups.[26] Like Reisman, he saw this capitulation to 'group-mindedness' as a degeneration from the model of success that celebrated individual initiative and maverick behavior.[27]

Mills' book, a sustained look at white-collar employment, was the most scathing and incisive of the three. He contrasted twentieth-century business managers with both the small entrepreneurs and the captains of industry, who together staked out the poles of American capitalism in the nineteenth century; in his comparison, the 'salaried bureaucrats,' as he called them, came up wanting in both autonomy and achievement, not to mention contentment. He, too, claimed that in the corporation, 'the forms of power that are wielded, all up and down the line, shift from explicit authority to manipulation,'[28] and he went on to assert that one's status in the corporate hierarchy derived less from skill than from the team-player mentality that Reisman and Whyte also decried.[29] Mills maintained that the older entrepreneurial model of success had been superseded by a corporate-style capitalism in which 'the occupational climb replaces heroic tactics in the open competitive market.'[30] Loyal, plodding organization men supplanted inspired entrepreneurs as the symbol of striving. In a characteristically cynical and pithy passage,

Mills summed up the view of success from the vantage point of the 1950s: ' "Success" in America has been a widespread fact, an engaging image, a driving motive, and a way of life. In the middle of the twentieth century, it has become less widespread as fact, more confused as image, often dubious as motive, and soured as a way of life.'[31]

The same period saw the release of a number of corporate workplace films that seemed like fictional exegeses of these sociological tracts. Hollywood chimed in on the national discourse about the blandishments and hypocrisies of corporate life with *Executive Suite* (1954), *It's Always Fair Weather* (1955), *The Man in the Gray Flannel Suit* (1956), *Patterns* (1956), and *The Apartment* (1960), among others. That last film is the most pointed and caustic in its take on the prevailing workings of big business. Director Billy Wilder's poison pen letter to corporate America, *The Apartment* is teeming with disgruntled white-collar workers, conformist organization men, and achingly lonely crowds. In its mordant presentation of corporate culture, it seems like a full-length serio-comic amplification of the opening segment of *The Crowd*, filtered through its own period's sociology.

Like *The Crowd*, *The Apartment* is set in New York City, capital of the American idea of success. Indeed, the latter film begins with a sequence that is, in effect, a visual quotation from *The Crowd*. Accompanied by a purposeful sounding score, the film opens on the iconic skyline of New York. As the camera cranes up a multi-windowed skyscraper, the voice-over intones actuarial statistics like a mantra. The camera cuts to the inside of the building to view a vast office that, with its seemingly infinite rows of identical desks, its rectilinear design, and its forced perspective, looks uncannily like the one in *The Crowd*. But here the sense of impersonality is even more visually emphatic; the wide CinemaScope frame and the low, fluorescent-lit ceiling together make the space seem, at once, interminably huge and oppressively claustrophobic. After surveying the space, the camera cuts to our protagonist, C.C. 'Bud' Baxter (Jack Lemmon), as he explains in voice-over that he is now on the nineteenth floor of the Ordinary Policy Department, Premium Accounting Division, Section W, Desk Number 861. By the time we reach his desk, he has reeled off the number of employees in the home office (a whopping 31,259), the length of his employment there, and his take-home pay. Wilder succinctly sets the stage for what is to follow by visually and verbally inscribing what he wants us to know about the corporation: it reduces people to numbers and its relentless uniformity makes it all but impossible to distinguish oneself from the crowd.

Figure 3.2 Bud Baxter (Jack Lemmon) responds to the impersonality, uniformity, and sense of entrapment of the corporate workplace. *The Apartment* (1960). Directed by Billy Wilder

As in *The Crowd*, the film then cuts to a shot of the office clock one minute before quitting time. But in *The Apartment*, rather than joining the throngs hustling toward the elevators, Bud remains at his desk. After a series of dissolves during which the office, shown in extreme long shot, gradually empties out, he lingers, looking lost amid the rows of now unstaffed desks. Bud's voice-over dialogue explains why he alone is not in a hurry to leave his workplace: 'You see, I have this problem with my apartment.' The succeeding scene demonstrates his dilemma. In order to enhance his position in the firm and curry favor with the higher-ups, Bud loans out his bachelor pad for extramarital trysts. He allows himself to be taken advantage of (and, on this particular night, locked out of his own apartment), because ingratiating himself with the middle management corporation men seems like the only way he might get a shot at professional advancement and differentiate himself from the other 31,258 employees.

The scenes that take place the next morning further establish Wilder's vision of the corporate way of life. Like *The Crowd*, the film's mise-en-scène employs the principle of multiples. A shot of a huge bank of elevators with hundreds of employees shoving their way in is followed by another view of the office with hordes of workers toiling to the accompaniment of adding machines. A phone bank, diagonally situated across the frame, seems to stretch forever as dozens of nasal-voiced operators chant the company greeting. The middle management types who ride herd on Bud have their own offices: a series of interchangeable rooms on the periphery of the main office, with glass walls (so the throng of subordinate workers is always visible) and windows that look out on more skyscrapers, presumably containing more offices like this one. The CinemaScope frame accentuates the multiples, making the crowdedness – and the concomitant loneliness – that much more vivid.

Wilder characterizes the corporation as a social Darwinist jungle where workers either adapt to the self-serving spirit of the place or suffer the professional extinction of anonymity and stasis. Bud's own scheme for survival seems to succeed when he gets a call telling him to report to Mr. Sheldrake (Fred MacMurray), the head of personnel. On hearing the news, the man in the desk next to him protests, 'But I've been here twice as long as you have.' In the corporate free-for-all, expediency replaces meritocracy, so Bud triumphantly ascends to Sheldrake's office on the twenty-seventh floor to claim his prize. And it is his for the taking, but there is a price: a certain key to a certain apartment. It seems that the supposedly high-minded family man Sheldrake is also stepping out and needs a place to bring his mistress.

The film's dialogue also highlights the adapt-or-die conformist credo of corporate life. Mr. Kirkeby (David Lewis), one of the gang of five who partake of Bud's reluctant largesse, demonstrates the current 'corporatese' by adding '-wise' to the end of words. ('Premium-wise and billing-wise, we're 18 percent ahead of last year October-wise.') When Bud thinks he's about to be bumped upstairs, he parrots Kirkeby in explaining to his bemused next-desk neighbor why he is the chosen one: 'You're carrying previous cargo manpower-wise. I'm in the top ten efficiency-wise and this may be the day promotion-wise.' It *is* the day and Bud gets his own glass-walled office, complete with his name on the door and his own view of the huddled masses of workers in the outer office. He celebrates his promotion by buying a new hat, the 'junior executive model.' Uniform speech and uniform dress mark Bud's trajectory from the lower orders to the ranks of middle management. When it comes to climbing the corporate ladder, other-directedness is the order of the day, and vassal-like fealty trumps both personal morality and professional equity. Although Bud frequently seems uncomfortable performing his prescribed role as corporation man and participating in the you-scratch-my-back-I'll-scratch-yours ethos, the picture that Wilder paints of the business hierarchy leaves him little choice. As Whyte points out in *The Organization Man*, 'It is not for the individual to question the system.'[32]

After Bud's ill-gotten promotion, plot complications ensue. The corporate denizens reveal themselves to be utterly unsavory, as the culture of exploitation explodes with betrayal and bad faith. The most consistently exploited employees are the women of the corporation, who are seen by most of their (married) male colleagues as a ready bunch, ripe for the picking. Women characters in corporate workplace films of the 1950s tend to fall into a few conventional categories: the spinster executive secretary who puts professional duty over personal fulfillment; the loyal wife who stands by her man through his career ups and downs; the young office-worker-cum-mistress who might bridle at her status as a disposable, replaceable item but puts up with it anyway because aligning herself with a successful man seems to be her only available route to success. These characters are generally secondary to the main drama, in which the men's professional ascension takes center stage and the personal dimension is pushed to the wings. Their stories are auxiliary to that of the protagonist, and rarely do they transcend their status as stock characters. In *The Apartment*, the female characters run pretty much true to form. Sheldrake's current mistress, a cheery-seeming elevator operator named Fran Kubelik (Shirley MacLaine), is also the target of Bud's amorous urges. When she is told by Sheldrake's current secretary and former mistress that she is but one in a long line of executive arm candy, Fran tries to kill herself. Her suicide attempt takes place in Bud's apartment, where she has been taken by Sheldrake for a sexual rendezvous; she ends up in Bud's bed, although the circumstances that put her there are not quite as he had hoped.

Bud simultaneously discovers Sheldrake's cavalier attitude toward Miss Kubelik's plight and his own growing love for her, but he nonetheless continues to be seduced by the lure of professional advancement. Sheldrake buys his silence about Fran's suicide attempt with yet another promotion: this one a dramatically vertical rise to the upper reaches of the corporation. His new office, right next to Sheldrake's, is a huge, handsomely appointed affair, furnished with a giant desk, wood-paneled walls, file cabinets, and venetian blinds and accompanied by an expense account. In workplace films, the amount of space a character commands is equivalent to his status and power, and the office mise-en-scène emphatically signifies that Bud has arrived.[33] Convinced that he has artfully played the corporate game, he tells Fran,

> You were wrong about me ... what you said about those who take and those who get took. Mr. Sheldrake wasn't using me, I was using him. See, last month I was at desk 861 on the nineteenth floor. Now I'm on the twenty-seventh floor, paneled office, three windows, so it all worked out fine.

But Bud's self-delusion can't last. Most of the corporate workplace movies are firmly in the *bildungsroman* tradition; hence, by the denouement, the young protagonist has to undergo the requisite moral awakening. His gradual education is often meted out by two contrasting father figures. One, the putatively successful older man, provides a harsh lesson in the ways of the business world. For a time, the young striver tries to emulate this character but the older man eventually ends up serving as a negative indicator. The other, who usually lacks material success but is rich in spiritual assets, functions as an exemplar for the younger man. *The Apartment* offers up these starkly opposing role models for Bud. Sheldrake is the avatar of bourgeois hypocrisy and business sleaziness. In his first meeting with Bud, he self-righteously blathers on about 'an institution founded on public trust' and about 'unbecoming behavior.' Then, moments later, he asks for the key to Bud's apartment. When his wife gets tipped off about his affairs and consequently throws him out of the house, he decides he would like to 'enjoy being a bachelor' rather than committing himself to Fran. He laments to Bud 'You see a girl a couple of times a week – just for laughs – and right away she thinks you're going to divorce your wife. I ask you, is that fair?' To which Bud responds, 'That's very unfair – especially to your wife.' And late in the film, when Bud withholds the coveted key, Sheldrake threatens him in a speech that sums up the precariousness of one's toehold on the corporate ladder:

> I picked you for my team because I thought you were a very bright young man. Do you realize what you're doing? Not to me but to yourself. Normally, it takes years to work your way up to the twentieth-seventh floor but it only takes thirty seconds to be out on the street again.

Sheldrake's opposite number in the campaign for Bud's soul is Bud's next-door neighbor, Dr Dreyfuss. Dreyfuss is an appealing candidate for the role of inner-directed foil to the successful other-directed organization men. He is a shambling, house call-making physician and a folksy family man complete with wife who ladles out chicken soup as a cure for Fran's suicidal tendencies. Assuming that the bacchanalian goings-on behind Bud's door are his own doing, Dreyfuss urges Bud to settle down and become a mensch.[34] Eventually, Bud acknowledges that he has made a devil's bargain by selling his soul for the key to the executive washroom, and he decides to follow Dreyfuss' advice. Like many of his fellow sadder-but-wiser workplace movie brethren, he gets to make a

'To hell with you!' speech, in which he declares his newfound rectitude and independence by turning his back on the corrupt corporation. After refusing to collude once more in Sheldrake's relationship with Fran, he announces, 'I've decided to become a mensch – do you know what that means? A human being.' And when Sheldrake tries one last bribe to keep Bud in line, he rejoins, 'Save it: the old payola won't work anymore.'

This is all well and good: the bad guy has gotten his comeuppance by being denied what he wants and being unmasked as a sleaze, and the misdirected hero has found his way through the ethical thicket of corporate life. But Wilder is too savvy a social critic to settle for the blandishments of a simplistic audience-pleasing ending, and the resolution of *The Apartment* is less resolutely upbeat than it initially appears. At the final fade-out, Bud gets the girl – sort of. The last lines of dialogue include Bud's declaration of love and Fran's response – 'Shut up and deal' – not the most encouraging words with which to launch a new romance. But even if he will no longer be alone, Bud is out of a job and out of a home, since he has decided to leave his ethically polluted apartment to go back to where he came from. He may have gained his mensch-hood but he has lost his shot at the big time; the promise and the perils of New York have defeated him. As in so many of the success myth narratives, personal morality and professional success are presented as mutually exclusive.

Further, as is frequently the case with the endings of Hollywood movies, the main character may have righted himself and overcome his immediate problems but the larger social problems that the film has pointed out remain intact.[35] Although the ending seems to offer up a satisfactory resolution, the lingering questions raised – and never answered – by the foregoing narrative problematize such a resolution. Bud has progressed from having a bad job and no girl to having no job and a girl on the rebound. But at the end of *The Apartment*, the corporate structure is still in place, the corrupt managers are still running the show, and they will, no doubt, easily hunt down another ambitious dupe willing to swap his apartment key for a shot at success. Likewise, Sheldrake will certainly prey on another young woman willing to swap sex for a brush with the company brass. Wilder presents corporate life as a damned-if-you-do/damned-if-you-don't proposition. If one stays within the corporate culture, he is forced to collude with the powers-that-be and compromise his ethics to get ahead. And if one steps outside the corporate arena, he is doomed to dwell in a small-time parallel universe, where virtue has to be its own reward because material success is now out of reach.[36]

Executive Suite (1954), a star-studded morality play about professional ascension and succession, is a more conventional-minded take on the world of business. Unlike *The Apartment*, its ending simplistically allows the protagonist to have his cake and eat it too, but on its way to the unconvincing conclusion, it too corroborates mid-century cynicism toward corporations. The familiar elements of the corporate workplace drama are present here. Once again, the film opens with extreme low-angle long shots of skyscrapers as the stentorian voice-over intones:

> It is always up there close to the clouds on the topmost floors of the sky-reaching towers of big business. And because it is high in the sky you may think that those who work there are somehow above and beyond the tensions and temptations of the lower floors. This is to say that it isn't so.

As the credits roll, we get a conventional view of the bustling city street below. We then see a series of point of view shots from the perspective of an unseen character named Mr. Bullard. He walks down the corridors of a building, rides the elevator down to the ground floor, sends a telegram, exits the building, and drops dead. Thus begins the drama of who will succeed Bullard, an old-style chief executive officer of a successful furniture manufacturing business.

In short order, we are introduced to the executive committee of the company as, unaware of Bullard's death, they gather for a meeting with him in what is reverentially referred to as 'The Tower.' Alderson (Walter Pidgeon) is vice-president and treasurer of Tredway Furniture, a feckless and weary company man who has convictions but little backbone. The backward-looking Jesse Grimm (Dean Jagger), vice-president of manufacturing, resents what he calls 'the boy wonders and slide rule experts,' as he bides his time until retirement. J. Walter Dudley (Paul Douglas), a harried other-directed type, is in charge of sales and is, in the words of his secretary/mistress, 'too busy being popular.' Loren Shaw (Fredric March) is the numbers man, comptroller of the company and the film's representative soulless bureaucrat.

Don Walling (William Holden) is the last to be presented and he is immediately set apart from the others. Unlike his desk-bound colleagues, who are initially seen in their offices, Walling is first seen in the thick of things, working on the floor of the manufacturing plant on a new production design of his own devising. Given his instantly established status as a hands-on, can-do type (and given Holden's status as the preeminent 1950s man's man), it is clear from the outset that we are meant to root for him in the coming struggle for power. The one other aspirant to the throne is George Caswell (Louis Calhern), who is introduced early in the film as he spies Bullard lying dead on the sidewalk. He promptly calls his broker and instructs him to sell short his stock in Bullard's company so he can buy it back at a lower price. The film wastes no time in establishing the foibles of its key players and the cutthroat climate of the corporate world. Given how harried and ulcer-ridden each of the executives seems, it is hardly surprising that Bullard dropped dead of a stroke in his fifties. In *Executive Suite*, stress is simply the occupational disease of the hard-working corporate executive.

The remainder of the film chronicles, with the portentousness of a Shakespearean tragedy, the ins and outs of the internecine struggle to succeed Bullard. In the characters' expositions, director Robert Wise efficiently reveals why most of the potential successors to Bullard are inappropriate. Alderson, the heir apparent, is too weak and burnt-out. He himself admits that 'Avery Bullard didn't want me to be president. He never wanted me to be anything but what I am: a number-two man.' Grimm, the other company elder, has one foot out the door to retirement. Caswell, the only member of the executive committee not on the company's payroll is an outsider, and early on he is presented as scheming and unethical. Dudley, the salesman, is a prime representative of what David Reisman called 'the personality ethic'; he is smooth-talking and personable, but he lacks character. That leaves Shaw, who is hungry for the job, and Walling, who initially doesn't want it. The drama eventually boils down to which of the two will ascend to the CEO perch at the top of The Tower.

In stark, black-and-white terms, the film uses Shaw to demonstrate what is wrong with contemporary corporate-think and Walling to suggest how it might be righted. Shaw is a believer in the primacy of the bottom-line. The quintessential organization man, he announces, 'I have only one interest: the good of this company.' He arrives at every meeting with his vaunted spreadsheets and statistics. Walling sums up Shaw's guiding principle: 'Improve the profits but never the product – that's Shaw's philosophy. To him the whole company is just a curve on a chart.' When Shaw learns of Bullard's death, his primary concern is with the company's stock valuation. Putting business over human concerns, he objects to closing the factory for Bullard's funeral because it will mean a substantial loss in revenue and a 'paid holiday' for the workers. Further, for Shaw, ethics take a back seat to ambition. In campaigning for the requisite four votes that would give him the position, he threatens Dudley with the revelation of his extramarital affair and bribes Caswell with company stock. An oily manipulator, he has got the goods on everyone and will use whatever means necessary to get what he wants.[37]

Shaw's overweening ambition is contrasted with Walling's initial disinclination to pursue the presidency. He is a frustrated entrepreneur caught in the corporate web, and he tells his wife, 'I'm not going to die young at the top of The Tower, worrying about bond issues and stockholders' meetings. That's not why I came here; that's not what I'm working for. I'm a designer, not a politician ... I think.' But he soon realizes that he is the only man for the job. Immediately after reassuring shaken factory hands that the company – and their jobs – will survive Bullard's death, he realizes that 'The whole town is at stake.' This eleventh-hour sense of responsibility for the community's welfare is a familiar theme in American studio films. Film historians have written extensively about the reluctant hero who at first holds back (thereby holding on to his individualist credo), but eventually feels compelled to involve himself for the greater communal good.[38] This character, who faces down the destructive forces and re-establishes order and patriarchy, is a staple of westerns, as well as of what literary critic Leslie Fiedler long ago dubbed 'disguised westerns.'[39] Like a good cowboy, Walling puts his individual interests aside for the good of the community: in this case, his firm.

Once Walling realizes that in order to save the company he must claim the top spot, he goes after it with a vengeance. The climactic set piece of the film is the meeting to elect the new company president. It is held in the conference room of The Tower, which looks like a cross between a dungeon and a medieval cathedral. Shaw enters the meeting assuming that he has the presidency sewn up, since he has bludgeoned Dudley and Caswell into giving him their vote, and he has been given the proxy of Julia Tredway (Barbara Stanwyck), the daughter of the company's founder and the former lover of Bullard. Neurotic and vengeful, she wants to sell her substantial holdings in the company to exact retribution for the neglect that she suffered from both her father and Bullard. She is too world-weary to care about the company's future, so at first refuses to attend the fateful meeting. But after Walling implores her to put the company's interests above her own, she deigns to cast her vote in person.

She thus witnesses, along with the rest of the executive committee, what amounts to the stump speeches of Shaw and Walling. Shaw's oratory is full of such phrases as 'answerable first and last to the stockholders' and 'the primary emphasis must be placed upon return of investment.' But his organization man rhetoric is no match for Walling's impassioned diatribe. He declaims much of his speech while framed by arched, stained glass windows, looking and sounding less like a businessman than like a preacher at the pulpit. Smashing a shoddily made company table, he deprecates the falling standards of Tredway Manufacturing and launches into a tirade about the importance of taking pride in one's product. Walling laments the workers' loss of faith in the company's craftsmanship and he invokes the idea of work as a sense of calling. He then announces that the next president will have to make personal sacrifices and be 'willing to devote himself to the company mind and heart, body and soul.' Holden delivers this peroration in his authoritative baritone, and a series of reaction shots tells us that his listeners are deeply impressed.

He is immediately – and unanimously – elected president. Julia Tredway, who earlier considered following in her father's suicidal footsteps by tossing herself out the window of The Tower, thanks him for saving her life. His wife, who throughout the film has vehemently opposed not only pursuing the presidency, but even remaining at Tredway, tells him, 'If it's what you want, really want, that's all that should matter to either of us.' In this reconciliatory fantasy, we are meant to believe that everything is neatly in its place: our hero gets the promotion, he gets the self-righteous monologue, and he gets his woman to stand by him and support his choice, even though it is antithetical to hers. The film ends with the tolling bells of the corporate campanile assuring us that now that Walling is in the corner office, all is right with the world.

But even such a sappy happy ending doesn't mitigate against the critique of corporate culture that has come before. The film tries to position Walling as a forward-looking man of the future. He lives in a modern, Bauhaus-type home full of trendy, up-to-the-minute furniture and avant-garde art. His youthful vitality and virility contrast strongly with the stooped bodies and effete affect of his colleagues. But his vision for the corporation is strictly retro; he talks of the future but his antidote to bureaucratization and the bottom-line mentality involves harking back to the old-time values and the tradition of quality of the past. Noble though this sounds, there was already in 1954 an air of obsolescence about the patriarchal model of leadership wherein a benevolent father who knows best leads the grateful workers to some corporate empyrean. Like it or not, the audience for *Executive Suite* could not help but admit that the organization men like Shaw and the other-directed salesmen like Douglas seem much more contemporary and believable as corporate success stories than the tradition-bound Walling. Shaw, the profits-obsessed realist, actually reflects the spirit of corporate capitalism better than does Walling, and even a 1950s audience must have sensed it. *Executive Suite* is a cautionary tale that warns us not to let corporations fall into the hands of the Shaws of the world but, on the evidence of the period's writings on corporate life, the warning has come after the fact.

Executive Suite wants us to believe that if only the right man is in charge and the wrong men are routed, the evils of the corporation will be banished. Appealing as this is, it is not very convincing. There is a particularly durable strain of Hollywood wishful thinking that insists that social ills and systemic flaws can be solved by the intervention of exceptional personages. Individualist to the core, American audiences like to believe that a lone cowboy can rescue the town to make way for the coming of civilization and a lone executive can rescue the business to make way for the coming of corporate success. But the films that endorse swaggering individualists as the redeemers of flawed systems have an air of nostalgia and pastness about them. Even Whyte, writing about these films several decades before film theorists discussed the problem of narrative closure, recognized their implausible endings for what they are: an evasion of the issues that have been raised in the previous two hours. Whyte claimed that the essential message of 1950s popular culture versions of the corporate success story was the need to accept the status quo. The hero's seeming revolt against prevailing circumstances is a phony rebellion, negated, at film's end, by his capitulation to the system that he has decried. These endings are, therefore, false victories that reward the hero but fail to follow through on the films' inescapable critique of corporate culture and power.[40]

The reconciliatory ending of *Executive Suite* cannot paper over the sense that Walling is going to become exactly what he has spent the film saying he doesn't want to be. He has pledged to be wholly devoted to the corporation, which will surely exacerbate the work/family tension that runs throughout the film. Even in his current position, he neglects his wife and kid, barely making time for them in the midst of the office intrigue and running out on his son's big Little League game. There is a good deal of discussion among the characters about how Tredway, once a great man, lost his way because he was changed by the pressures of the job. The film implies that, in recent years, Tredway went over to the dark side by subscribing to Shaw's business philosophy. Given the evidence, it is not very convincing that one man can change the corporate culture; rather, the likelihood is that the corporate culture will change him, and Walling's wife implies several times that it has already done so. At the end of *Executive Suite*, as Walling accepts the presidency from his entrenched colleagues, he may think that he has beaten them, but it is clear that he has actually joined them.[41]

A number of other films made between 1950 and 1960 weighed in with similar views of the corporate sphere – and with similarly equivocal endings that tempered their censorious observations of corporate life. *Patterns* (1956) began as a live television show; it was so well received that a second live broadcast was followed by a feature film released one year later. Written by Rod Serling, the film presents the upper reaches of the corporate world as a veritable twilight zone where the office ambience is downright scary and the corporate bigwig is a figure of terror.[42] Once again, the film displays the hallmarks of the genre: a sense of architectural determinism that includes establishing shots of oppressively tall buildings and top-floor executive offices that instantly define the status of their occupants; a young up-and-comer faced with a situation that pits his ambition against his ethical beliefs; the good father/bad father authority figures; a palpable nostalgia for an older, more humane business apparatus; and an ending that hedges its bets. *Patterns* also throws into the executive drama a few telling touches of its own. Here the crane shots up and down the building appear not just at the beginning of the film but are used as visual punctuation at key points throughout, hammering home the awesome power of the executive tower. The company vice-presidents each keep a handy bottle of liquor on their desks, lest they need to dull the pain of corporate life. An endless executive corridor culminates in the office of the boss from hell whose motivating principle goes beyond self-interest to sadism. And in a fight to the death, the adaptive technique is survival of the nastiest. In *Patterns*, as in *Executive Suite*, corporate life is hazardous not just to one's professional wellbeing but to one's physical health and wellbeing as well.

Like *Executive Suite*, the drama here revolves around issues of professional succession. Staples (Van Heflin), an impressive young engineer and businessman, is brought from Ohio to the corporation's home office in New York and is given the red carpet treatment, including a lavish office and a suburban home that is, as he says, 'furnished like a magazine.' Unbeknownst to him and to Briggs (Ed Begley), an executive with several decades of devotion to the business under his belt, Staples has been brought in to replace the older man. The CEO Ramsey (Everett Sloane), a thoroughgoing villain who combines the most shameful qualities of Machiavelli and Mephistopheles, plans to turn Briggs out to pasture by humiliating him so mercilessly that he will take it upon himself to retire. He sets about the task with such a vitriolic sense of purpose that both Briggs, the target, and Staples, the supposed beneficiary of this personnel shuffle, are shocked and horrified. After a particularly brutal tongue-lashing from Ramsey, Briggs collapses in the corridor and, shortly after, dies. In *Patterns*, business pressures are not just demoralizing; they are deadly. Staples consequently decides that swimming with sharks is not his sport of choice, so he announces to his wife his intention to turn his back on professional opportunity and return to Ohio. But first, like every other principled young executive disillusioned by the corporation, he needs to speak truth to power. He storms into Ramsey's office, slams the door, and lets him have it. After announcing his intention to quit because of his hatred for Ramsey, Staples gets hit with a counterpunch. Ramsey, unfazed by the rancor coming at him ('So I'm not a nice human being, what else?'), scoffs at the younger man's righteous indignation: 'You walk out of here with a halo because you spoke your mind. What do you do then? Go to work for some nickel and dime outfit run by nice people?' Apparently this is a convincing argument. Ramsey ends up buying Staples with the promise of a salary increase, stock options, a bigger expense account, and a new title. Staples, in turn, intends to 'do everything in my power to push you out and take your place myself,' and he reserves the right to punch Ramsey in the jaw. We are left with the image of two swaggering combatants ready to go *mano-a-mano* for the soul of the business.

This resolution is right up there in the pantheon of unconvincing movie endings. The audience is evidently meant to cheer Staples' determination to fight the good fight and to prove his manhood in the promised battle royal. But the preceding scenes have presented the corporation as a beast that eats its own, so it utterly strains credulity that nice guys like Staples can tame the beast through skill and good intentions. It is difficult to give credence to individual remedies for systemic ills when the corporate apparatus is presented as frighteningly monolithic. Still, these movies persist in undercutting, at their close, their own appraisal of the world of business; they pull their punches with endings intended to soften the blows that have floored us and to give us hope that it is possible to remain upright in the work arena. The belief in rebirth and self-invention is the cornerstone of diehard American optimism. Endings such as those of *Executive Suite* and *Patterns* suggest that organizations, like individuals, can be reborn out of the sheer determination and good will of an enterprising young man. But the movies are not quite convinced themselves by these dubious resolutions; even the putative happy endings are rife with ambiguity.

A different type of desirable but implausible ending adorns *The Man in the Gray Flannel Suit* (1956). Like the other contemporary workplace films, the movie is roiling with misgivings about the price of success in business. Originally a best-selling novel, *The Man in the Gray Flannel Suit* saw its title become a widely repeated slogan for 1950s dismay about corporate conformity. Unlike *The Apartment, Executive Suite,* and *Patterns,* surprisingly little of the film actually takes place in the office, and the major conflict involves the competing pulls of family and work.

In addition to the title uniform, advertising executive Thomas Rath (Gregory Peck) sports a dysfunctional family and a wife who impugns his masculinity and complains about their house, calling it 'a grave-yard for happiness, fun and ambition.' He also has a hidden wartime past that continues to haunt him. All of the characters in the film are beset by stress and disappointment. A judge who adjudicates a nuisance lawsuit involving Rath keeps his palliative bicarbonate of soda close at hand, and a television executive who interviews Rath for a job suffers from work-induced high blood pressure. Rath himself is torn not only between his home and work lives but also between his sense of what is morally right and his grasp of what is professionally strategic. His wife urges him 'not to turn into a cheap, slippery yes man.' He counters, 'For a man with security it's a cinch to be full of integrity – but a man with a wife and three children....' He decides that 'I never wanted to get into this rat race but now that I'm in it, I think I'd be an idiot not to play it the way everybody else plays it.' But it is clear from the start (not to mention from the casting of the virtue-oozing Peck) that Rath is not the type who will go along to get along. He stands up to his boss, reveals his wartime love affair to his wife, and, in the end, gets patted on the back by both for being true to himself.

There is the requisite big speech in *The Man in the Gray Flannel Suit* but in this film it is spoken not by the young businessman but by the burnt-out CEO who realizes too late what his ambition has wrought. Here the top man is benevolent and paternal – perhaps because his own wife and children have deserted him – and he is himself mindful of the exorbitant spiritual price of his material success. Hence, the tone of his oration is rueful rather than rancorous. He tells Rath:

> Big successful businesses just aren't built by men like you: 9:00 to 5:00 and home and family. You live on them but you never build one. Big successful businesses are built by men like me, who give everything they've got to it, who live it body and soul.... My mistake was in being one of those men.

Rath thus gets his boss' benediction for privileging family over work, and he gets to hang onto his job even though he has criticized the boss' business strategy. (The film throws a hefty inheritance his way as well, just to sweeten the pot and to make his middling status at work more bearable.)

As in many of the corporate workplace films, the protagonist's crisis of conscience and voicing of his convictions are a false rebellion since there is rarely a sense that anything is really at stake. There is nothing to imply that he is actually risking his livelihood, his professional future or his comfortable suburban existence, and these films take pains to assure us that our hero will somehow land on his feet. So the climactic confrontation amounts to little more than a revenge fantasy in which one can say his piece and still keep his job. Inevitably, the main character in these films gets rewarded, rather than fired, for his rebel stance. Nonetheless, the presumptive happy ending cannot erase the tone of what has come before. Although at the film's end, Rath has reclaimed his individuality and integrity, it is hard to believe that, as a soldier in the army of gray flannel suited executives, he will be able to hang onto them.[43]

Even the MGM musical chimed in with a chorus of lamentation for the life of the corporate executive in the 1950s. In *It's Always Fair Weather* (1955), three service buddies convene for a reunion ten years after the war's end. One of them, Doug Hallerton (Dan Dailey) is an executive vice-president for an ad agency. Although he used to be an artistic sort, now he is an overworked, ulcer-ridden organization man. With acerbic self-awareness, he talks about his post-war life as 'ten years of degradation' and notices that his wife looks at him with 'a combination of boredom, disgust and pity.' When his pals suggest they hoist a glass and toast their reunion, he demurs, claiming, 'I'm not too fit, digestion-wise. I've got a little bit of a nervous stomach.' And when they ask him why he gave up painting, he replies, 'Career-wise, it didn't seem practical.' With their characteristic comic economy, screenwriters Betty Comden and Adolph Green establish Hallerton as a character who talks the talk and walks the walk of the corporate drudge.

But, true to the genre, he gets to shed his businessman's fedora and his silly moustache, and tell off the company's Mr. Big. Fittingly, he does so in a song-and-dance routine titled 'Situation-wise' in which, drunk with abandon (not to mention drink), he makes fun of the corporate lingo that he has been spouting, by appending the offending suffix to every word he can think of. (The opening line is 'Situation-wise, saturation-wise, competition-wise, sales position-wise.') Even so cheery a genre as the musical couldn't resist taking a dig at the indignities of corporate existence. Indeed, although the culture of the 1950s is repeatedly cited for its complacency and tranquility, one doesn't need to scratch the surface of the popular culture very deeply to realize that the era was teeming with misgivings about the centrality of work as a measure of success.[44]

Greed is good

The corporate workplace and the types that inhabit it appeared intermittently in movies of the succeeding couple of decades but, for the most part, films of the 1960s and 1970s that featured a critique of the status quo were centered around characters who turned on, tuned in, and dropped out rather than on those who signed on, clocked in, and stayed put.[45] It wasn't until the palmy years of the mid-1980s that another concentrated spate of corporate workplace films collectively mused about the nature of success in business. Within the span of five years, *Trading Places* (1983), *Local Hero* (1983), *Lost in America* (1985), *Nothing in Common* (1986), *The Secret of My Success* (1987), *Baby Boom* (1987), *Broadcast News* (1987), *Wall Street* (1987), and *Working Girl* (1988) all contributed to the cultural discourse about the corporation as an institution central to American life.[46] Collectively, they are true to many of the conventions of the genre, as formulated in the 1950s, but most of these titles add a distinctively 1980s spin to their tales of enterprising young executives confronting the corporate apparatus.

The archetypal film of the era is *Wall Street*; its villain, Gordon Gekko, and his mantra, 'Greed is good,' struck a responsive chord in the gogo 1980s, and came to stand for all that was wrong with the culture of avarice and rapaciousness. This being an Oliver Stone film, there is a simplistic Manichean division between virtue and vice – between the morality of the good guys and the venality of the bad guy – and there is never any doubt about who will win the struggle for the young protagonist's soul. In spite of its up-to-the-minute visual presentation, at its heart, *Wall Street*'s narrative is an old-fashioned, didactic morality tale that, were it not for the computers, portable phones, and digital clocks, would be right at home in the 1950s.

The familiar elements of the corporate workplace drama are all intact in *Wall Street*. But here, the opening skyline shots – complete with flare on the lens and silhouette lighting – present the city as more alluring than daunting, immediately giving a preview of the muddled perspectives of the film. Although *Wall Street* purports to be a barbed critique of corporate values, it is full of internal contradictions, as the film's casting and visual seductiveness end up contradicting its narrative resolution. Shortly after seeing the standard shots of crowds commuting to work and shoving their way onto elevators, we meet Bud Fox (Charlie Sheen), a young, ambitious Wall Street broker. His first encounter of the day is with an older worker whom he addresses as 'Dad,' who tosses out the first of many homilies fielded by Bud in the film: 'Get out while you're young kid. I came here one day when…and sat down and look at me now.' After this comment, the Wall Street grind is immediately established visually while Bud, seated at one of a bank of identical desks, cold calls potential investors. As the camera restlessly tracks around the room, the frenetic pace of the business and the difficulty of distinguishing oneself from the dozens of other brokers are made evident. As in *The Apartment*, the wide screen and low, fluorescent-tubed ceiling visually define the work atmosphere as both confining and frenzied.

The film's exposition reveals Bud to be cut from the same cloth as his fellow filmic junior executives. A child of the working class who is determined to rise above the circumstances of his birth, he is smart and ambitious – and also naive. Bud is constantly reminded of his neophyte status by the older male characters in *Wall Street* who refer to him, at turns, by various diminutives: rookie, huckleberry, sport, *kemo sabe*. Not content to offer the usual dyad of surrogate fathers to choose between, the film is crawling with paternal types who are constantly spouting moralistic homilies at the impressionable Bud. In addition to the aforementioned 'Dad' (who, by film's end, will be mercilessly fired from the firm where he has worked for decades), the sermonizing father figures include Bud's actual father, Carl Fox (Martin Sheen), an airline mechanic and union representative, and another older colleague, Lou Mannheim (Hal Holbrook). Mannheim, the elder statesman of the firm, is full of bromidic advice for Bud: money corrupts, luck in the stock market doesn't last, and one should be true to himself. In his most gnomic pronouncement, he tells Bud, 'Man looks into the abyss and there's nothing staring back at him. At that moment, man finds his character, and that is what keeps him out of the abyss.' Not surprisingly, the firm's young Turks consider Mannheim and his maxims anachronistic; one of Bud's colleagues dubs him a 'loser.'

Bud's father also attempts to save him from the dreaded abyss by imparting such insights as, 'It's yourself you gotta be proud of,' 'Money is one giant pain in the ass,' and 'I'm a guy who never measured a man's success by the size of his wallet.' He is an old-style paterfamilias to both his son and his rank-and-file constituency (who he paternalistically calls 'my men') and he is clearly intended to be the moral center of the film. But his holier-than-thou sententiousness renders him less a character than a mouthpiece for the movie's hortatory moralizing.

The film's antagonist, Gordon Gekko (Michael Douglas), is more than a match for this array of philosophizing father figures. Amoral and proud of it, Gekko is the sort of villain that audiences love to hate. He, too, indulges in his share of pithy advice, but his is of the reprobate variety. 'Greed is good,' he explains, because it 'clarifies and cuts through the essence of the evolutionary spirit.' Himself a working class, City College-educated kid with a chip on his shoulder for the 'Ivy League schmucks,' Gekko is an unrepentant free-market capitalist run amok. He sees business as a war zone; his own inspirational authority figure is Sun Tzu, a sixth-century BC Chinese general whose tactical, take-no-prisoners philosophy girds Gekko for battle. Unlike Bud's father, he does measure success by material markers; spiritual values such as loyalty and friendship are dismissed as obsolete, and love, according to Gekko, is, 'the oldest myth running... a fiction created to keep people from jumping from windows.'

Obviously, when Bud becomes, in effect, Gekko's indentured servant, the audience is supposed to be appalled. Stone paints his characters with the broadest of strokes, and Gekko is the film's Satan writ large, trafficking in souls as if they were tradable commodities. There is no doubt that our dramatic sympathies are designated for the spiritually (if not materially) successful older characters and for the hapless Bud. But there is a problem encountered on the way to *Wall Street*'s denouement: Gekko is far and away the most alluring, engaging character on the screen. The other combatants for Bud's errant soul seem stodgy, self-righteous and tired in comparison. Douglas' dynamic performance and his leading man persona thwart the film's narrative intent. When he is on screen, the drama perks up and the camera, as if in response to the character's dynamism, becomes kinetic, tracking and swooping in an effort to match Gekko's energy.

The official hero/outlaw hero dichotomy that appears in many American movies complicates the audience's positioning vis-à-vis the characters.[47] As in Westerns and gangster movies, the outlaw figure in *Wall Street*, although morally bereft, compels our interest against our better judgment. We know that he is mercenary and money-mad, but he is also much more fun to watch and listen to than the forces of probity. In most corporate workplace films, the representative successful corporate executive is generally played by a character actor or an over-the-hill leading man; most are older and significantly less attractive than

Douglas and few play their characters with as much élan. The characters who steered the corporate ship in the mid-century workplace dramas – played by the likes of Fred MacMurray (*The Apartment*), Everett Sloane (*Patterns*), Walter Pidgeon (*Executive Suite*), Fredric March (*Executive Suite* and *The Man in the Gray Flannel Suit*) – functioned as negative indicators for the young executive (and, by extension, for the audience). They were what he – and we – didn't want to grow up to become. But Gekko, in spite of his malfeasance, is visually magnetic and verbally witty; although the audience may dutifully place our dramatic sympathies with the characters that we should admire, we also can't help but succumb to the pull of the malefactor.[48]

The opposition of success and morality, and the difficulty of satisfying both simultaneously, is a familiar motif in success narratives. The more complex versions of the American success myth give a nod to the protagonist's vexed choices; his ultimate realization – that something is gained but something is lost in choosing one route or the other – is ambivalent and hard won. However, *Wall Street* seems simply confused in its presentation. Clearly, we are supposed to disapprove of Gekko. But in addition to being the most seductive character, he is also surrounded by a veritable department store of desirable commodities. In scene after scene, he wallows in his *nouveau-riche* booty like an exultant pirate, considering it the just reward for his hard-fought, decisively won acts of plunder. His apartment, office, and beach house are shrines to conspicuous consumption. It is hard for the audience not to ogle and covet his modern art collection, his robot butler, and his over-accessorized trophy wife. And it is equally hard to align ourselves with the preachy personifications of the super ego when the id-indulging Gekko looks so good and has such desirable consumer items. Once he hitches up with Gekko, Bud acquires his own designer-accoutered penthouse apartment and, for that matter, he acquires the designer as well. After his moral awakening (helped along by an investigation by the Securities and Exchange Commission and his father's conveniently plotted heart attack), he divests himself of both. Part of the appeal of movie-going involves drooling over how the other half lives, so the audience, although encouraged by director Stone to cheer Bud's newfound ethics, also has a nagging feeling that Bud is a chump to turn his back on his good fortune. *Wall Street*'s dialogue hammers home its moral, but its panoply of visual delights suggests that consumption is more rewarding than morality.[49]

In *Dreaming Identities*, Elizabeth G. Traube's book on films of the 1980s, she calls *Wall Street*'s pontificating a 'patriarchal call for moral restraint,' and she rightly complains that the film's befuddled perspective 'void[s] even the one-sided critique of capitalism of any critical social content. The film celebrates a composite class of industrious producers who share a moral orientation toward work, which in principle is available to all occupations, including speculators such as Gekko.'[50] Indeed, there is one more authority figure in the film to serve as a potential role model: Gekko's archrival Sir Larry Wildman (Terence Stamp), a big-time British investor who, in cahoots with Bud, eventually gives Gekko his comeuppance. He represents the good corporate speculator who wheels and deals while holding on to his moral principles. Although the film couches itself as a debate between benign and malignant forms of capitalism, it is really a simple morality tale that insists the world will be fine if only the demons are exorcised. Once again, there is the presumption that good people can reform a bad system. If we can get rid of the Gordon Gekkos of the world and enthrone the good corporate capitalists, such as Sir Larry, all will be well.

Between its nostalgia for compassionate capitalism and its conviction that it is possible simultaneously to play in the big leagues and play by the rules, *Wall Street* mutes its commentary on the world of big business and gets mired in its own message. Like many other corporate dramas, it focuses on the difficulty of juggling ethics and ambition, individuality and conformity; but it then backs away from identifying the source of that difficulty with the structure and ethos of corporate capitalism. Stone indulges in Hollywood movies' characteristic retreat from the ideas that institutional structures affect individual fates, that systemic ills need systemic remedies, and that heroic, exemplary individuals cannot single-handedly enact the needed reforms. Instead, *Wall Street* pines for a more wholesome form of business practice and a more benevolent sort of businessman, all the while visually and voyeuristically encouraging us to admire what Gekko's success has bought him.

In the end, Bud is redeemed – and headed for jail – but not before his dad gives one final speech: 'You told the truth and gave the money back. In some kind of screwed up way, it's the best thing that could have happened to you. Stop going for the easy buck and produce something with your life. Create instead of living off the buying and selling of others.' Inspiring though this should be, it fails to avert our eyes from Gekko's riches. While the speech is a yawn, Gekko's consumer dream world makes us sit up and take notice; ultimately, the film's commodity fetishism is more alluring than its trite moralizing. Stone's ostensible intentions aside, in *Wall Street* the pleasure principle trumps the work ethic. Ultimately, the corrupt rogue capitalists are more appealing than the repressed organization men or the principled working men. The final shot is a freeze frame of the New York skyline looking more glittering city than urban jungle. In spite of the foregoing narrative, the film concludes its musings on the nature of success with the promise, rather than the perils, of the big city.

The corporate workplace in the era of late capitalism

Most of the other mid-1980s corporate workplace films are comedies, several of which adhere closely to both the narrative conventions of the success myth and the structural attributes of classic comic form. *Trading Places*, *The Secret of My Success*, and *Working Girl* begin with typically jaundiced views of the corporate workplace and their main characters' prospects in it. But since in comedy identity is fluid, accidents of birth can be overcome, and fate is reversible, all ends well. The repressive, hierarchical bureaucracies at the beginning of the films get transformed, by the ascension of the heroes, into meritocratic workplaces where justice and good will prevail. These films are like the comedic flip side of *Wall Street*. They are similarly devoted to the idea that if only the right people are at the helm, the corporation will be right-minded. And, like *Wall Street*, they celebrate the good life and its spoils as, at the end of the films, the protagonists take over the material rewards of the executives that they have supplanted. Their endings wholeheartedly conform to classic comic structure, where both characters and society are reborn into a superior state, and a new, enlightened regime replaces the old wrong-headed one.[51]

Not all of the mid-1980s corporate comedies subscribe to this sort of wishful thinking, however. *Lost in America* and *Local Hero* are far savvier and more uncompromising than the films that stop halfway in their critique of the corporate ethos. Both films are dark comedies that, in their endings, deviate significantly from the classically satisfying finale of comic form. Unlike the more conventional workplace comedies, they don't temper their disenchantment with corporate existence by tacking on pat happy endings. Significantly, neither film takes place primarily in the corporate environment; rather, the workplace scenes serve as bookends to the characters' attempts to escape from the confines of their jobs.

Local Hero is a wistful fable about an on-the-rise young executive who comes to question his profession-driven existence, but the film's whimsical quality doesn't mask a genuine disillusionment with life in the corporate realm in the time of late capitalism.[52] The film begins and ends with its main character in Houston, Texas, home of his employer, the multinational Knox Oil and Gas. The corporate headquarters – all vertical lines and hard surfaces – has a modernist, space-age look. Colleagues talk to one another by phone while looking at each other through the ubiquitous glass walls. Vast rooms, railless staircases, and floor-to-ceiling windows impart an aura of impersonality and other-worldliness. The two main corporation-based characters are MacIntyre (Peter Riegert), a successful young executive who measures his success by the consumer goods it has bought him, and Happer (Burt Lancaster), Knox's eccentric chief executive, who is more interested in astronomy than in business. Both are shown not just in their offices but also in their apartments: lonely bachelor pads that function as visual analogues to their inhabitants' materially abundant but spiritually empty lives. Unlike so many films set in the world of big business, *Local Hero* doesn't present the corporation as inhumane; it is just unfulfilling. And the movie's protagonist is more forlorn than disgruntled, adrift in an insular corporate world and unsure of how to function outside of it.

The central portion of *Local Hero* takes place on the Scottish coast, where Mac has been sent to buy an entire town so that Knox can build an oil refinery on its site. Being a self-proclaimed 'telex man,' he is reluctant to waste his precious work time on travel, so he initially hews to his parochial businessman's outlook, setting his watch alarm to signal the meeting schedule in Houston and quantifying everything from the monetary worth of the townspeople's lives to the awesome landscape, which he describes as 'a whole lot of scenery.' But as he spends several days scoping out the situation, Mac gradually falls under the spell of the town and sheds the trappings of civilization: his suit, his watch, his shoes, and his obsession with money. The shrewd joke of *Local Hero* is that the twee townspeople turn out to be as money-driven and deal-savvy as those in the corporate world, and they are only too happy to sell their pastoral Eden in order to become rich. The newly enlightened Mac has more regret about the impending buyout than they do, and he finds it slim consolation when he is told, 'You should be proud of yourself, making them millionaires... you can't eat scenery.'

In the coda to the film, Happer decides to buy a portion of the town after all, but to erect a space and sea research institute rather than an oil refinery. This is, in some ways, a satisfactory comic ending, since the town is saved – even if it did not want to be – from becoming 'the petrochemical capital of the free world.' Nonetheless, classic comic form involves an essential change in identity and circumstances and, although at the end of *Local Hero* Mac has a newfound understanding of what he wants, he has no hope of achieving it. The film ends with him back in his high-rise apartment, marooned in the middle of Houston while waiting vainly for someone to answer his phone call to the Scottish town from which he is now effectively exiled. With its sense of corporate life as a dead end, *Local Hero* is more despondent than most of the other 1980s workplace comedies. They begin with a repressive corporate apparatus that is then improved by the banishment of the hidebound executives, and they end with the installation of the young, righteous newcomers. But violating the conventions of comic endings, which celebrate rebirths and fresh starts, *Local Hero* ends where it began; its protagonist is sadder and perhaps wiser but still stuck in corporate purdah. The only change is that now he knows what he is missing. *Local Hero* contradicts the delusional endings of most of the other corporate comedies by being emphatic in its conclusion that worldly success and spiritual wellbeing are sometimes mutually exclusive, and genuine change is hard to come by.

Lost in America is even more candid about the high price of corporate conscription. This is a comedy that wears its cynicism proudly and, as such, its ending involves a total sell-out by its main character who comes to realize the impossibility of having it both ways. The movie begins with advertising man David Howard (Albert Brooks) waking up on what he expects to be a red-letter day. He anticipates receiving a much-anticipated promotion, and he is buying an upgraded house and car to go along with his soon-to-be executive status. Alas, the promotion is given to someone else. In a fury, David quits his job, convinces his wife to do the same, sells their house, and sets off on a cross-country adventure, compliments of a substantial nest egg derived from the home sale.

The early scenes in David's place of work give the habitual movie view of the corporate workplace as characterless and inhospitable. As David maneuvers through the labyrinthine hallways that lead to the boss' office, the camera tracks with him, accentuating the endless corridors, the rows of doors, and the bland geniality of his co-workers. Although he makes a convincing case for why he is deserving of the promotion, merit and fairness once again seem to have little to do with job advancement. But there are some early signs that the film will take a slightly different tack in its take on the world of business. The corporate bigwig in *Lost in America* seems less malicious than single-minded, and the corporate aura is not so much pernicious as deadening. That David makes his big, take-this-job-and-shove-it speech at the beginning of the film rather than at the climax is an indication that *Lost in America* will deviate from the structural conventions of most workplace films.

After David quits, he has an epiphany about the path that he has been pursuing, telling his wife that professional ambition is a 'Nowhere road: it's the carrot-on-the-stick and the watch when you're seventy.' Alas, shedding his skin and, as David puts it, 'dropping out' is not so easily accomplished. The film quickly debunks his ridiculous, romanticized notions about life on the road. At the end of the film, having lost their nest egg and realized that they can't support themselves in anything resembling the style to which they are accustomed, David and his wife decide they should hightail it to his firm's New York office and he should, in his words, 'eat shit' by begging for his job back. *Lost in America* doesn't subscribe to the American credo of self-invention and rebirth or to the simplistic, if appealing, assumption that corporate life can be improved by replacing those at the top. Here, the corporate superstructure is impregnable and the only options are to buckle under or get left behind. Nothing is improved, reconciled, or replaced at the end of the film; in fact, David has to take a salary cut and work in a city that he hates. In the blackly comic view of *Lost in America*, the corporate world is immutable and impervious to anyone and anything that might change or challenge it.

The stock market collapse of 1987, which occurred two months before the release of *Wall Street*, coincided with the end of the mid-1980s workplace film cycle. The most significant corporate workplace film of the early 1990s was Joel Coen's deeply caustic and satirical movie *The Hudsucker Proxy* (1994). Set in the 1950s, the heyday of earnest corporate workplace films, the movie is, like many of the Coen brothers' creations, full of self-conscious nods to the conventions of the genre that it lampoons. The mise-en-scène is a caricature of 1950s executive suite movie settings; its monumental spaces and imposing rooms look like corporate headquarters as designed by Albert Speer. An improbably elongated boardroom table is so shiny that it reflects the skyscrapers through the window. Huge banks of filing cabinets, accessible only by ladder, and thousands of mail slots give a sense of the vastness of the enterprise. In the cavernous mailroom, loudspeakers terrorize the employees who, in turn, try to hide from the company's Big Brother-like surveillance. The building's hallways – its corridors of power – stretch into infinity, making those that walk them appear minute. And the 45-floor building is frequently shown in exaggerated perspective, so its height connotes menace rather than opportunity. Indeed, the only opportunity represented by the skyscraper is the opportunity to jump to one's

Figure 3.3   One way to escape the corporate world. *The Hudsucker Proxy* (1994). Directed by Joel Coen

death – which two characters attempt to do. This is a nightmare vision of the corporation in which the expressionist visuals skewer the orthodoxies of both the corporate environment and the corporate workplace movie.[53]

The plot, once again involving business heirship, is set in motion during a board meeting called to celebrate the company's success. In spite of the good news, the eponymous CEO Waring Hudsucker (Charles Durning) gets a running start down the football-field sized boardroom table, crashes through the floor-to-ceiling window, and inexplicably leaps to his death. His second-in-command, the hyperbolically evil, cigar-chomping Sidney Mussburger (Paul Newman), hatches a plot to devalue the company stock so the board can buy Hudsucker's holdings at a fraction of their worth. The scheme involves finding 'some jerk that we can really push around' to run the corporation into the ground. Said jerk is one Norville Barnes (Tim Robbins), a timid mailroom employee who sports a business degree from an obscure midwestern college and some big entrepreneurial ideas. Once he is ensconced in the president's office, Norville invents the hula hoop, becomes amazingly successful, and turns as arrogant and callous as his fellow executives. Having inadvertently thwarted Mussburger's agenda, he of course is fated to get his comeuppance and he, too, eventually leaps from the executive suite window, only to be saved by supernatural intervention. The film ends with a familiar moral as the ghost of Hudsucker tells Barnes, 'In my personal life, I have made grave errors: I have let my success become my identity. I have foolishly played the great man, and I've watched my life become more and more empty as a result.' This platitude notwithstanding, *The Hudsucker Proxy* is a bilious addition to the canon of corporate workplace films and a harbinger of what was to come as the decade progressed.

The irrational exuberance of the late 1990s stock market and dot-com bubble might have been expected to spawn movies that were commensurately exuberant about business opportunity. But that period's corporate workplace entries collectively take a dim view of the business environment and its prospects for success. Apparently, it is easier to bite the hand that pays you when jobs are plentiful and the economy is strong. The films belie official economic indicators by revealing the late 1990s as an age of anxiety about vocational life. *Clockwatchers* (1999), *Office Space* (1999), and *Boiler Room* (2000) present work in the corporate milieu as soul-crushing and repressive. Like *Wall Street* and *The Hudsucker Proxy*, they suggest that immorality or dumb luck are now the only routes to the top. Job insecurity has replaced long-term employment, and avarice has supplanted earnest ambition. Significantly, all three films take place not in the city, the locus of opportunity, but in bland suburban office parks that segregate their workers from the world outside of work. The iconography of success myth narratives gets turned on its ear as the skyscraper, whose empyrean heights represent possibility, is replaced by low-slung buildings with nowhere to go.

It is not just the settings that contradict the conventions of the earlier films. Gone is the implicit paternalism of the 1950s workplace, replaced by a crisis of confidence in authority figures. The fatherly chief executives of *Executive Suite* and *The Man in the Gray Flannel Suit* have been superseded by bosses who are out to eat their own, and the workplace aura has changed from benign neglect to overt hostility. This is the corporation as dysfunctional family, and the dad at the head of the executive suite table is anything but a role model. Furthermore, the corporate world is depicted as fundamentally unfair, since skill is not necessarily rewarded; in fact, it is sometimes punished. Here the right man (or woman in the case of *Clockwatchers*) doesn't get the desirable job. These are failure rather than success narratives in which the protagonists, such as they are, have little hope of pursuing the purposeful career trajectory of their 1950s movie brethren. The best that these films' characters can hope for is the stasis of hanging on to their jobs.

The bedrock assumption of classic success myth stories is that a person's character can be transformed and improved through a formative experience. But from the standpoint of the late 1990s workplace films, this is laughable. In the final frames, the characters are neither wiser nor morally enlightened; they are just more cynical and opportunistic. Whereas the 1950s movies tried to paper over their critique of the corporate environment with simplistically upbeat endings, the relentlessly downbeat endings of the latter-day workplace films confirm, rather than contradict, the mordant outlook of the rest of the movie.

Clockwatchers, set in the pink-collar ghetto of temp workers, revolves around four young women caught in job limbo (one of them dubs their ilk 'corporate orphans' but then amends the label to 'corporate call girls'). The temps, replaceable parts in the corporate machinery, remain anonymous to the firm's permanent employees. As the film's title implies, their ambition is limited to making it through the workday. 'The only real challenge,' proclaims one, 'is trying to look busy when there's nothing to do.' When a permanent spot opens up, it goes to an outsider. The chronically nervous boss dies of a heart attack, and the angriest and most vocal of the temp workers is unjustly axed. Office supplies are doled out so parsimoniously that staples have to be requisitioned one by one. The company sound system pipes in non-stop, noxious Muzak, which is reputed to increase worker efficiency. In short, this is an irredeemably bleak view of the workplace. In place of job security, respect, and a shot at professional success, all that these characters have are escape fantasies.

In the broadly satirical *Office Space*, the workers are brought so low by their jobs that their escape fantasies are accompanied by revenge fantasies. As in *Clockwatchers*, the characters spend their days in a drop-ceilinged room filled with identical cubicles that provide isolation without privacy. They, too, sit around doing nothing while pretending to work. The three young software engineers at the center of the narrative have had all professional ambition drummed out of them. Since they have concluded that, as one says, 'Most people hate their work,' they are appalled at the idea of long-term job security which, in the late 1990s, seems more like a life sentence than a boon. At the mere thought of workplace longevity, one of them wails, 'What if I'm still doing this job 50 years from now?' Their despair seems amply justified by the absurd and unjust practices of their place of employment. When a couple of consultants are hired to downsize the company, they fire the two capable young men who have been dutifully showing up for work and promote the one who has been playing hooky. Hence, the trio's only ambitions are to shirk their work and to wreak revenge on their odious boss and the corporate behemoth he represents. They accomplish both ends, the latter by devising a software program that can skim off fractions of every payroll dollar and deposit them in an account that they set up. They even retaliate against the eternally paperless fax machine by beating it to death with a baseball bat. As outlandish as the tone of the movie is, the ludicrous details of office routines are all uncomfortably familiar.[54]

The ending of *Office Space* further degrades the conventions of classic success stories. Although, when the office building burns, the three disaffected workers evade blame for their scam, there is no sense of satisfaction, progress, or closure at the film's end. The most contented characters at the close of the story are an older worker who has been hit by a car and can live off disability insurance and a downtrodden former employee who has set fire to the building and absconded with the threesome's ill-gotten gains to a tropical paradise: so much for meritocracy. Two of the young men at the center of the story move on to a job not unlike the one that they leave; the third chooses downward mobility and a construction job.

Although, in many ways, *Boiler Room* (2000) is a boilerplate corporate workplace movie, the cynicism about the corporate workplace environment that is tempered in earlier movies is unmitigated here. The workplace movies of the 1950s may have been disillusioned about the corporate aura, but they generally offered up at least one character who was eventually redeemed by his recognition of a moral imperative. In *Boiler Room*, there is no redemption, no moral father figures to show the way, and no sense of purpose for the characters beyond making money. The film casts its jaundiced eye not just on the state of business but also on the state of young men's ambitions. According to *Boiler Room*, newly minted corporate employees are no longer willing to work their way up the ladder. Nor are they eager to make their mark; they just want fast money. As the film's opening voice-over states, 'I just wanted to make a quick and easy buck. Nobody wants to work for it anymore.... There's no honor in flipping burgers at Mickey D's; honor's in the dollar.'

As the film opens, the protagonist, Seth Davis (Giovanni Ribisi), is already, by some lights, something of a success story, thanks to the thriving – if illegal – gambling operation that he runs out of his apartment.

In an effort to please his father, a stern judge who takes a dim view of everything his son does, he tries to go legit. He gets hired by the firm of J.T. Marlin, a so-called 'chop shop' that peddles risky stocks over the phone to naïve investors eager to have a piece of the late-1990s stock market boom. The familiar ingredients of the corporate workplace film are set in place, but the frenzied arena of Seth's new employer couches them in a distorted, dystopian corporate world.

Although the aptly titled *Boiler Room* does offer the requisite visual synecdoche of the New York skyline, the film takes place far from the spires of Wall Street. In spite of its high-toned sounding name, J.T. Marlin is housed in a squat building on provincial Long Island. Its personnel are likewise a far cry from the buttoned-down denizens of the corridors of corporate power. The brokers at J.T. Marlin seem like the mutant offspring of *Wall Street*'s Gordon Gekko. To a person, they are overeager, amoral, and obsessed with money. Here, business is presented as a hormone-fueled game, and the firm resembles nothing so much as a depraved fraternity, complete with hazing rituals. Gone are the long-time employees, role models, and father figures who turned their backs on the bitch-goddess of success in earlier workplace dramas. Only young men populate the firm, and a 27-year-old elder describes himself as 'a fucking senior citizen.' The top brass, sadistic mentors to the new hires, sound like profane, tough-love drill sergeants, telling their terrified recruits that 'You are required to work your fucking ass off at this firm. We want winners, not pikers. People come to work at this firm for one reason: to get rich.' Ambition, in *Boiler Room*, seems more a festering disease than a guiding principle.

The plot convolutions involve a scheme to hoodwink investors, an increasingly ruthless and competitive interaction among the young men in the firm, and a troubled father–son relationship. As Seth gets further sucked into the firm's illicit *modus operandi*, the movie broadly, and somewhat confusedly, ascribes blame for his capitulation to the culture of cupidity. There is the repeated implication that Seth is rudderless and immoral because his father hasn't shown him love. Without adequate authority figures at work or at home, ambitious young men are left to fend for themselves. The movie further suggests that the ethnic insults and macho posturing running throughout *Boiler Room* are symptomatic of the callousness and competitiveness of corporate life.

But the most accusatory finger pointing in *Boiler Room* is self-consciously aimed at the popular culture. The cultural white noise of movies and music speaks more forcefully to Seth than does his disapproving daddy. When the workers at J.T. Marlin get together, they watch none other than *Wall Street* on the VCR, reciting from memory along with Gekko's 'Greed is good' speech like acolytes engaged in a karaoke liturgical rite. One character invokes as scripture *Glengarry Glen Ross* (1992), another film about salesmanship as contact sport. And both the soundtrack and the screenplay feature gangsta rap as a running motif. At one point, Seth claims that selling stocks is 'the white boy way of slinging crack rock.' His walk on the wild side is seductive and exciting, and part of the allure of his ill-gotten gains is that they are, indeed, ill-gotten. Seth's father's life as a moralistic judge and his family's status as upstanding bourgeois citizens seem, to him, dull in comparison. Although, at the end of the film, he feels intense guilt for having lured his father into a bogus stock scheme, there is a hint of Oedipal revenge in Seth's actions.

Boiler Room's evocation of the white boy, white-collar cohort yearning to break out is a late 1990s variation on the movies' ongoing discourse about the discontents of corporate work life. In the final frames, there is no grandiose tongue-lashing to the forces of repression and no great ethical awakening on the part of the young protagonist. When asked if he has learned anything, Seth replies, 'I learned how to fuck people out of their money.' His, and the movie's, last line is 'I gotta find a job.' Simple pragmatism, instead of redemptive moralism, is the order of the day.

The entrepreneur as would-be redeemer

Movie critiques of the corporation, in which the organization man's only choices are to sell out or to get out, amount to a distress signal for maverick American individualism. The cautious careerism of the organization man is an affront to the frontier swagger of earlier success myth heroes: a kind of watering down of the generations. In response to the structural constraints of corporate capitalism, the figure of the swashbuckling, visionary entrepreneur would be a likely candidate for redeemer of rugged individualism and self-will. Ten years after Ben Affleck played a smug, young corporate insider in *Boiler Room*, he played a middle-aged corporation man who gets the smugness knocked out of him when he, along with other organization men, is unceremoniously fired in *The Company Men* (2010). In the film's resolution, the antidote to being beaten down by the corporate world is to become an entrepreneur and start a kinder, gentler company. But like romance films that conveniently fade out at the moment of consummation of desire, *The Company Men* ends with the hopeful founding of the new company, thereby sidestepping any further exploration of the challenges and compromises involved in every business enterprise.

Those movies that do focus on what comes after the entrepreneur's founding of a new enterprise tend to be less sanguine about the possibility of evading the influence of corporate America through initiative and independence. Many of the biopics of inventor/entrepreneurs set in earlier times (e.g., *The Story of Alexander Graham Bell* (1939), *Edison the Man* (1940)) are hagiographies in which the protagonist's 'aha' moment of inspiration is eventually followed by recognition and reward. But more recent movies featuring entrepreneurs generally present the business world the same way as the movies set in the office do: as a monolithic and intractable force inimical to success and contentment. The stigma that attaches itself to the organization man for being sucked into the corporate maw plagues the latter-day entrepreneur in movies as well.[55] In biographical films such as *Tucker: The Man and His Dreams* (1988) and *Flash of Genius* (2008), the visionary entrepreneurs are babes in the woods, and those woods are dense with corporate greed.[56] Brilliant and sincere, these characters are seen as throwbacks to earlier, less tainted models of capitalist enterprise. But their trust in technological progress and allegiance to old-fashioned values is their downfall, since their corporate nemeses hold allegiance only to their own profits. Such portraits of the entrepreneurial visionary as victim of corporate malfeasance are extensions of the workplace films, sharing their anxiety about the possibility and price of individual success.

Even biopics of entrepreneurs who seem to have realized the promises of the success myth and evaded the snags of the corporate ethos are tinged with qualifications and doubts. *The Social Network* (2010), David Fincher's portrait of the entrepreneur as a young man, paints a picture of Mark Zuckerberg that both celebrates and punishes his ambition. In typical success story fashion, we share in the giddy ascendance of an outsider who works his way in and up by brilliantly outmaneuvering those with more advantages and vanquishing all who would stand in his way. He solves his problems with the corporate establishment by bypassing it to create his own business model and set of rules. The early part of the film revels in youthful exuberance and enterprise as Zuckerberg rebels against the old order. He can do as he pleases because, as his business cards proudly proclaim, 'I'm the CEO, Bitch.'

But the final scene punishes him for his hubris. Having outsmarted and outtalked a roomful of insiders, he is left alone with his laptop and his lacks. In the movie's final moments, the camera slowly tracks forward into a tight close-up of his tight-lipped expression. This shot is repeatedly crosscut with another forward track to his Facebook page, which he continually refreshes in hopes that a women who rejected him back when he was a nobody will now respond to his 'add as a friend' request. The rapid-fire dialogue that, until this point, created a wall of sound in the film is replaced first by echoing, receding footsteps that accentuate his solitude, next by his compulsive tapping of the keyboard button as he refreshes his screen, and, finally, by the Beatles singing 'How does it feel to be one of the beautiful people?' from 'Baby, You're a Rich Man.' The 'lonely at the top' ending is a durable cliché in American success stories. As in many of the rise-and-fall biopics, we delightedly share the protagonist's subjectivity on his way up. But as the schisms in his success reveal themselves, we are primed not to envy or admire him, but to pity him. *The Social Network* joins a host of other films that, while proposing entrepreneurial self-determination as an alternative to the deference of the organization man, end up characterizing their entrepreneurs as misunderstood visionaries or miserable visionaries – or both.

All of these films that follow protagonists navigating through the business world paradoxically nurture the success myth while also revealing its implicit contradictions. Although the corporate workplace movie in its various forms has been subtly responsive to social, economic, and historical circumstances, its conventions remain intact, even if adapted or redeployed in accordance with the tenor of the times. From their inception to the present, white-collar workplace movies have remained durable conduits through which to filter both individual ambitions and collective misgivings about work and careerism in corporate America.

4
Success Reassessed: Ambitious Women/Midlife Men

A woman can do anything, be anything – as long as she doesn't fall in love.

– Screenplay of *Possessed* (1931)

If you take away the suit, you will have trouble finding the man.

– Steven Cohan, *Masked Men*

The preceding chapter's examination of corporate workplace narratives exposes the underlying cultural unease with American axioms regarding work and success. Cultural myths traffic in widely shared, but largely unexamined, ideological assumptions about individual desires and social behaviors. From its beginnings, the success myth has conflated vocational ascendancy with success. But many of the movies previously discussed complicate, and sometimes even contest, the success myth's promise of professional achievement as a guarantor of the good life. Across the decades, embedded in the formal and thematic codes of many Hollywood iterations of the success myth, is an undercurrent that dredges up the competing cultural ideologies at the heart of the success discourse. In challenging the equation of making a good living with living a good life, those films contribute to an ongoing polemic which exposes the contradictions and negotiations at the core of the American idea of success.

That polemic, and the ambiguities that inform it, becomes even more pronounced when success myth ideologies coincide with other widely shared cultural beliefs involving gender, romance, and the family. This chapter complements the prior chapter's consideration of the role of work in the formation of individual and social identities by focusing on the intersection of gender, work, and success in Hollywood films.

Together with the earlier explorations, it focuses on the reciprocity between dominant representational systems and social dynamics by illuminating the ongoing role of cultural myths in alternately conveying and containing collective aspirations and anxieties.

Professionally ambitious women

Classic versions of the success myth find women on the periphery of the action while the protagonists strive for success. Generally tangential to the narrative, the female characters in traditional success sagas are most often loyal helpmeets – devoted wives, dutiful secretaries, or adoring mothers – whose competence and nurturance enable the male characters to pursue their goals. As marginalized cheerleaders on the sidelines of the big game, they gaze admiringly while the key players claim their trophies. In such conventional success narratives, personal ambition is an unseemly trait in a woman and careerism is nigh pathological. The only appropriate expression of ambition for female characters involves channeling their energies into marrying well and hitching their stars to men with potential (and, as seen in Chapter 2, even this bid for success by association is often couched as conniving). Accoutrements of male success, the female characters' success is defined relationally while their own subjectivity is suppressed or denied. Nonetheless, there are successful working women in movie versions of the success myth since the beginnings of cinema.[1] The conventions and concerns that attend their many screen appearances point to a persistent dialectic in which gender ideologies collide with the success myth and the cultural primacy of work.

The representation of working women in films from the sound era to recent decades has been abundantly analyzed. The paradigm shift that was ushered in by the second-wave feminism of the late 1960s and early 1970s was accompanied by a commensurably significant shift in how film scholars (and, to some extent, moviegoers) thought about Hollywood's contribution to the ongoing public conversation about gender capabilities and opportunities. The beginnings of feminist film theory were roughly concurrent with second-wave feminism. Film theorists' nascent efforts to unmask the history and practice of gender delineation in film accompanied the larger discourse about women in the workplace and about the social construction of gender norms. The early, sociologically oriented film criticism, which focused on critiquing gender roles and representations, recognized how the dominant popular narratives found in the movies referred and responded to social currents and upheavals. Since then, in considering the intersection of historical, social, and representational discourses, feminist film criticism has highlighted how American movies have made sense of the shifting gender landscape and the place of work in women's lives.

Film critic Molly Haskell's groundbreaking 1974 book *From Reverence to Rape* is a comparative look at the representation of women in films from the 1920s to the mid-1970s. In Hollywood movies, success for women generally goes hand-in-hand with marrying and mothering well. But Haskell spends a good portion of her book surveying the portrayal of working women in film. Her survey of pre-war films involving so-called 'career gals' finds recurring professions considered acceptable for white, middle-class women: among them girl reporter, secretary, teacher, librarian, shop girl, showgirl, model, fashion editor, actress.[2] Embedded in these narratives are consistent attitudes toward women who work. In film after film, work is what a woman does while biding her time until Mr. Right makes his appearance and her real life can commence. 'A woman's work is almost always seen as provisional, and almost never as a lifelong commitment, or as part of her definition as a woman.'[3] Thus, a woman's job is often reduced to a ploy to meet men and a phase that the female character will grow out of once romantic aspirations are fulfilled. Although movie heroines often do have professional lives, they are required to dissociate their fundamental sense of self from their life as a worker.

Those women that, against the odds, make their way into putatively masculine professions do so 'to the detriment of [their] femininity and desirability' and they 'arrive[] at their level of competence only by suppressing their female natures.'[4] Haskell nonetheless considers many of these working women characters complex and effectively drawn. But even the accomplished career women played by such assertive actresses as Rosalind Russell (*Take a Letter, Darling* (1942), *His Girl Friday* (1940)) and Katharine Hepburn (*Woman of the Year* (1941), *Adam's Rib* (1949)) share the fate of the women on the lower rungs of the career ladder: 'Their mythic destiny, like that of all women, was to find love and cast off the "veneer" of independence.'[5] On their way to acquiescing to that destiny, these women are often made to suffer humiliation and scorn. They are mocked for being too masculine (i.e., overly devoted to their job and career advancement) and, concomitantly, for being not sufficiently feminine (i.e., incapable of nurturing, insufficiently erotic, and maladroit on the domestic front). Often these characters undergo a ritual humiliation in which they are chastened for their ambition and reinscribed in the feminine sphere defined by domesticity and romance.

In the decades that Haskell examined, a host of films with working women in supporting, rather than lead, roles further contribute to the received wisdom on the perils of professionalism for women. The likes of Eve Arden and Thelma Ritter repeatedly play wisecracking sidekicks who are smart and capable and, not incidentally, also single and sexless. As *femmes d'un certain âge* in many of the films, they are presented as post-sex and post-hope: lifetime spinsters who work because they missed out on the alternative. For such characters, work is compensatory and their jobs are, in effect, booby prizes that signal their failure in the domestic realm: the only place where women can be fulfilled. According to these classical era movies, then, the options for working women are limited: repressed spinster, harried, unfulfilled professional, or monstrous monomaniac. All of these types of working women suffer because of their professional status; many of the films move toward a resolution in which the social order is reinstated – and female suffering ends – only once the main female character recognizes the repercussions of her devotion to work and is restored to her putatively proper place.

Popular culture's response to the 1940s wartime incursion of women into the workforce was, in the immediate post-war years, to emphatically relegate female characters to the domestic arena or, if women characters did have a profession, to emphasize their anxieties and lacks.[6] From Haskell's mid-1970s vantage point, career women in film never recovered from that post-war insistence on putting them in their place. Her retrospective view across the decades sees the pre-war depictions of working women as far more complex and appealing than those appearing on screen when she was writing. Her book's general conclusion about the representation of working women is that the pre-war characters, although constantly auditioning for professional legitimacy, were more independent and inspiring than their 1970s cohort.

> We can...deplore the fact that in every movie where a woman excelled as a professional she had to be brought to heel at the end, but only as long as we acknowledge the corollary: that at least women *worked* in the films of the thirties and forties, and, moreover, that early film heroines were not only proportionately more active than the women who saw them, but more active than the heroines of today's films.[7]

Haskell's book, along with other image studies including Marjorie Rosen's *Popcorn Venus: Women, Movies and the American Dream* and Joan Mellen's *Women and Their Sexuality in the New Film* (both from 1973), opened the door for an examination of women at work in the movies.[8] But scholarly writers quickly pushed past them through that door on their way to a more systematic, sophisticated hermeneutics that considered how representation gets reified by cultural forms and aesthetic conventions. For those writers, the problem is not simply that images of professional women are not positive or encouraging. There is the larger problem of Hollywood films' (and, by extension, their viewers') unproblematic acceptance of realist claims of access to representational truths and the concomitant denial of the cultural production of meanings and norms.[9] Hence, the subject positions offered to audiences, the nature of the filmic gaze, and the ways that the mechanics of film production construct meaning (all the while, under the guise of realism, masking their narrational strategies) come under scrutiny.

A number of film scholars have performed close analyses of many of the same works that Haskell discussed. But by prying open fissures in the text, they have proposed alternative, subversive exegeses of seemingly unified narratives. In this way, feminist film theory has worked toward a more rigorous approach that anatomizes how the cinematic strategies and realist aesthetics of Hollywood movies situate the viewing subject and reinforce or, in some cases, challenge the norms of representation. In her landmark article, 'Women's Cinema as Counter-Cinema,' Claire Johnston declared, 'In rejecting a sociological analysis of woman in the cinema we reject any view in terms of realism, for this would involve an acceptance of the apparent natural denotation of the sign and would involve a denial of the reality of the myth in operation.'[10] Hence, feminist film analysis shifted its emphasis from simply ferreting out representational trends to determining how the means of production collude in the production of meaning.

This insistence on exploring how the cinematic apparatus naturalizes its modes of presentation and its gender representations has comprised one of the major thrusts of film studies for the past several decades. The eternally unresolved question involves the extent to which dominant cultural narratives, in normalizing certain notions about gender and social roles, function as the handmaidens of patriarchal self-interest. A parallel debate wonders whether film spectators are essentially passive recipients of coded ideologies or, more hopefully, whether those ideologies are so inherently contradictory and impure that they contain the potential for negotiated readings by dynamic, engaged audiences.[11]

This dialectic is on vivid display in E. Ann Kaplan's and Linda Williams' justly celebrated pair of articles on the maternal melodrama *Stella Dallas* (1937). Working-class Stella begins the movie as a secretary in a mill-town factory. It is clear, from the outset, that she views her work strategically as an opportunity to better her social status and escape her dreary home life. And she does, indeed, 'marry up' by snagging the boss, after which she promptly leaves her job to embark on her real calling as wife and mother. Before long, the marriage dissolves and Stella resorts to the only career available to her: mothering with a vengeance. Because she cannot – or will not – conform to expected modes of behavior, and because she privileges her child's contentment over her own, Stella eventually cedes her daughter thereby, in effect, effacing herself. Kaplan's and Williams' variance involves whether Stella's victimization is emblematic of patriarchal notions about appropriate roles for women or whether the film affords its spectators multiple, contradictory identifications and subject positions that challenge gender determinism, and thereby give rein to female subjectivity.[12]

A similar debate has informed discussions of post-war maternal melodramas, including *Mildred Pierce* (1945), in which the entrepreneurial character's business success is counterposed with her disastrous personal life, and the second version of *Imitation of Life* (1959), in which the failed mothering of the protagonist is directly attributed to her successful acting career.[13] Here, too, there is the interpretive proposition that the films' representational strategies and narrative resolutions cannot suppress or resist their inherent tensions and contradictions regarding women as workers and mothers. The scholarly investigation of such canonical classic era films seesaws between whether they function to contain the threat of independent women or whether their competing discourses allow enough textual ambiguity and interpretive wiggle room for spectators to find some measure of validation for women who strain at the boundaries of gender norms. As provocative as these analyses are, they do not put to rest the nagging question of whether it is mere wishful thinking that a film's signification is significantly altered at the level of reception by audiences that are actively and competently engaged in reading against the grain.

Exactly how that grain is aligned gets taken up by later studies of representation that follow Haskell's lead while incorporating the polemics of feminist film theory. For example, Diane Carson turns her attention to the screwball comedy genre and, through the lens of theories of narrative closure and spectator reception, reconsiders some of the same films that Haskell focused on. She claims that the films conclude indeterminately and are therefore able to challenge dominant ideologies. 'Although we may read the films as presenting animated women only to denigrate their defiance, the vitality of their joyful rebellion resists facile dismissal.... Despite all attempts to repress them, these defiant women clearly exceed their subordinate positions.' She goes on to suggest that the female protagonists' verbal assertiveness stymies any attempts to corral their energies. Pointing to the false sense of closure provided by the movies' abrupt restoration of social order, she suggests that these tacked on endings' attempts to contradict what has come before cannot and do not erase the liberatory behavior of the spirited heroines of screwball comedies. By acting up and speaking out, these unruly women 'encourage a reconceptualization of social and political relations.'[14]

Jeanine Basinger also reengages the early work on the image of women in film by amplifying both representational studies and audience reception theories in *A Woman's View: How Hollywood Spoke to Women 1930–1960*, her exhaustive survey of the genre of the woman's film. Basinger's interpretive readings of films about working women complicate the somewhat simplistic conclusions of earlier studies of representation. Like Haskell, she points out the repressive, conservative strain in these movies, most of which remind women that their true career is romantic and maternal love. The movies set up a double bind for audiences, 'providing viewers with escape, freedom, release, and then telling them that they shouldn't want such things; they won't work; they're all wrong.'[15] Nonetheless, through her identification of the films' mixed messages of subversion and acquiescence, she insists they 'accomplish the double goal of covert liberation and overt repression.'[16]

Her focus on the contradictions found in these movies (and, by extension, in the female audience members' response to them) is particularly lucid in her chapter titled 'The Woman in the Man's World.' She examines several movies in which accomplished women achieve positions of rank and power in the professional sphere: doctor (*Mary Stevens, M.D.* (1933)), architect (*Woman Chases Man* (1937)), businesswoman (*To Each His Own* (1946); *Mildred Pierce* (1945); *They All Kissed the Bride* (1942)), star reporter (*Woman of the Year* (1940); *His Girl Friday* (1942)), federal judge (*Tell It to the Judge* (1949)), and even company president in the bluntly titled *Female* (1933). In each case, the professional woman comports herself with confidence and competence. Nonetheless (or, perhaps, as a result), she gets put in her place by film's end. As Basinger points out:

> These films clearly tell women in the audience that being men won't work. They show women that certain occupations are best done by men.... Countless films show women working successfully in all sorts of jobs and achieving wonderful things, and these movies

don't seek to say that women can't do these things, only that if they do, they'll be tripped up by love.[17]

Basinger, like Carson, wrests a glimmer of representational subversion from the spirited heroines' abrogation of the habitual gender hierarchy. She also celebrates that female audiences of the time indulged in at least a fleeting thrill of identification with professionally capable women. But the conclusions of these films – many of which show their heroines giving up their position in order to hang on to their men – are so emphatic in their reinstatement of gender absolutes that it is hard to countenance any prospect of spectatorial liberation.

This capitulation to gender ideologies is perhaps nowhere more explicit than in *All About Eve* when successful actress Margo Channing, having barely beaten back a challenge to her career and her romance from a young rival, ditches her professional life to devote herself to her man. Her renunciation of her professional identity in favor of her new full-time job as wife follows from her earlier pronouncement:

> Funny business, a woman's career – the things you drop on your way up the ladder so you can move faster. You forget you'll need them again when you get back to being a woman. It's the one career all females have in common, whether we like it or not: being a woman. Sooner or later, we've got to work at it, no matter how many other careers we've had or wanted. And in the last analysis, nothing's any good unless you can look up just before dinner or turn around in bed, and there he is. Without that, you're not a woman.

Womanhood, conventionally defined by devotion to marriage and family, trumps careerism, and the two are presumed to be mutually exclusive. Careers are fine as temporary or secondary endeavors but romance is women's reason for being. Basinger herself laments that in such films, 'audiences are asked to participate in a pseudoliberated attitude' and concludes that the working women films from the 1930s, 1940s, and 1950s ultimately functioned to reassure female viewers that their own lives were, after all, preferable to those that risked conventional femininity for professional success.[18]

Second-wave feminism and working women on screen

The paradigm shift of the ensuing decades, in which women entered the higher echelons of the workforce in unprecedented numbers, also saw working women on screen work their way up the career ladder.[19] As a symbolic system with wide reach, movies are particularly well suited to represent and speak to changing social conditions. So whereas vocationally successful women characters were anomalies in pre-WWII films, by the 1980s more and more female film protagonists were seen in executive level positions. But a diachronic comparison of professional women on film suggests that the success myth and many of its attendant ideologies regarding female characters are remarkably durable and resolutely impervious to alteration. Popular culture selectively culls and transforms experience, and the reciprocity between cultural narratives and particular sociohistorical moments is itself contested terrain. As cultural theorist Stuart Hall has pointed out, 'The culture industries do have the power constantly to rework and reshape what they represent; and, by repetition and selection, to impose and implant such definitions of ourselves as fit more easily the descriptions of the dominant or preferred cultures.'[20] What this means for success narratives is that although the dramatic changes in employment patterns were processed in popular culture by having accomplished professional women repeatedly represented in movies from the 1980s onward, usually those characters continued to be punished rather than rewarded for their abilities and ambitions. If anything, the possibility for narrative rupture seems diminished, as the closure of most of these films leaves remarkably little latitude for negotiated readings. In presenting success as a kind of failure, the films' resolutions, which generally force the female characters to capitulate to traditional expectations about gender and work, serve to contain the threat of changing gender dynamics in the workplace.

The outpouring of working women films in the 1980s – and their resonance with the lived experience of working women – has been amply discussed in both scholarly and mainstream publications. In *Dreaming Identities*, her study of class and gender in 1980s movies, Elizabeth Traube notes, 'If Hollywood movies of the 1980s tend overall to reconstruct patriarchal symbols of men and women, the very fragmentation of images and the experimental aura of some of the new composites provides a potential resource, albeit a limited and highly compromised one, for reinventing gender identities.'[21] But the limits and compromises seem to outweigh the reinventive possibilities in these films. If scholarly feminist analyses aimed to locate interpretive fissures in the cinematic edifice, the popular press was less sanguine about representational progress. Journalist Susan Faludi's 1991 bestseller *Backlash* looked back on the on-screen 1980s career woman with despair, claiming,

> In so many of these movies, it is as if Hollywood has taken the feminist films and run the reels backward. The women now flee the office

and hammer at the homestead door. Their new quest is to return to traditional marriage, not challenge its construction; they want to escape the workplace, not remake it.[22]

Faludi sees in the films evidence of the decade's gender regression after a decade of dizzying change.

Indeed, the popular culture response to the incursion of women into the workplace and the elite professions was, by the evidence of Hollywood movies, a sort of ideological retrenchment; most of the films of that era that deal with highly placed professional women end up endorsing gender essentialism and reinscribing women's place in the home. Contrary to claims about the earlier films' internal self-doubts which allowed for multiple subject positions, many of the films of the 1980s and onward seem so strictly encoded that their response to the zeitgeist is to reaffirm clearly defined and distinct gender norms and social codes. Part of the function – and simple pleasure – of classic mythic narratives is to confront perplexing questions only to suggest that the answers are clear. In the case of Hollywood movies, those answers are usually couched in individual solutions to social problems. So in these movies, the issues that confront working women are solved not by substantial and significant systemic change but by acts of individual will. In film after film, working women make their separate peace with the gender wars, often by conceding defeat and retreating back to what is supposedly their proper place in the domestic sphere.

In mid-twentieth century America, managerial level working women were rare, so the early movie incarnations of professional successful women were presented as intriguing curiosities: exotic specimens whose dynamic working lives, albeit emblematic of what they lacked in the personal sphere, were nonetheless titillating for female audiences who had little opportunity to replicate their professional success. From the 1970s onward, when women were becoming more prevalent in the higher ranks of the professional world, their fictional counterparts were increasingly conspicuous but also, alas, consistently caricatured. Several films ostensibly responded to the cultural moment by centering around highly successful working women. But the narrative ruptures that allowed earlier audiences to at least temporarily wallow in the heroines' high-powered existence were notably scarce. Professionally successful, these new exemplars of female ascension up the career ladder were also frequently sexually unfulfilled (or, conversely, sexually voracious and threatening), maternally bereft, romantically thwarted, and altogether forlorn. For instance, the successful television executive in *Network* (1976) is so single-sightedly devoted to her job that her lover, in his parting shot, calls her a 'heartless young woman left alone in her arctic desolation,' and insists that '[our] love is the only thing between you and the shrieking nothingness you live the rest of the day.' If the earlier films contained ambivalent visions of life at the top of the working world, most of these later narratives replaced that ambivalence with an emphatic insistence that, for women, career accomplishment could not coexist with personal contentment. The options for ambitious career women seemed to range from murderous (e.g., *Fatal Attraction* (1987), *Basic Instinct* (1992), *The Last Seduction* (1994), *To Die For* (1995)) to miserable (most other movies of the era showcasing career women).

Interestingly, the few films of the period that deal with blue-collar (*Norma Rae* (1979)) or pink-collar (*Nine to Five* (1980)) workers allow their protagonists a measure of triumph over patriarchal and corporate repression. In both films, the heroines wreak revenge on sexist bosses and unjust working conditions, while maintaining sisterly solidarity and generally congenial home lives. But their professional counterparts in other movies do not fare so well. The white-collar, professionally successful characters face off against similar sorts of systemic gender bias, but their battle is a lonely one and their adversaries are frequently other women who function as deterrent examples of the perils of ambition. These films offer audiences more rigidly encoded subject positions and far less latitude for multiple identifications.

For example, in *Working Girl* (1988), a particularly cynical piece of antifeminist backlash, the successful corporate executive, Katharine (Sigourney Weaver), is a ruthless and manipulative harridan who tries to thwart the entrepreneurial ambitions of her young secretary, Tess (Melanie Griffith).[23] The latter, who sums up her professional credo with the line 'I have a head for business and a bod for sin' eventually exposes and replaces her boss in a denouement that we are clearly meant to cheer as a triumph of probity over dishonesty, regular folks over pretentious snobs, and youth over age. As Tess repackages herself as an acceptable substitute for her abrasive boss, the film reinscribes the young, sexually accommodating woman at the center of the narrative by exorcising the tough, self-determining one. The movie is seemingly untroubled that, while Tess does devise a workable business plan, she gains admission to the corridors of power mostly by manipulating and exploiting her status as an object to be looked at.[24] Her professional ascension necessarily comes at the expense of the other woman, who is demonized for being overly ambitious and, therefore, a threat to the essentially masculine workplace. Although Tess' corporate work environment is rigidly hierarchical, gender segregated, and inhospitable to change, the film's ending suggests that what is needed is not structural reform but, rather, a ritualized expulsion of the element that is hostile to the status quo: to wit, the aggressive professional woman.

Almost 40 years earlier, in *All About Eve*, the ambitious young parvenu who tried to vamp her way to the top was exposed as fraudulent, and the seasoned professional at least got to retain her dignity and her man, if not her identity as a career woman. But in *Working Girl*, the middle-aged, successful female character is demonized and ostracized, and the audience is positioned to approve of her comeuppance as the righteous restoration of a just social order. Like the corporate workplace dramas analyzed in Chapter 3, many of the working women films revolve around this opposition between youth and age: between the optimistic ambition of young career women and the jaded opportunism of their older colleagues. By pursuing a sort of 'divide and conquer' strategy, these films pit woman against woman, encouraging them to aim their ambition at interpersonal rather than systemic obstructions. Given Hollywood's habitual tendency to redirect social problems to the personal realm, a catfight presumably makes for more engaging cinema than a work action. Consequently, audiences are encouraged to cheer as young, ambitious protagonists such as Tess best their bosses by reactively fashioning more attractive, compliant working woman personae.

Other midlife, midcareer movie women of the era are likewise consigned by their ambition to solitude, lack, and regret. They work their way up only to opt out following an epiphany about the price of their success. In *Baby Boom* (1987), the incompatibility of motherhood and professional success once again comes to the fore when the main character, J.C. (Diane Keaton), inherits a baby and, as a result, gets ousted from her life as a corporate executive. She, herself, is adamant that they cannot coexist: 'I can't have a baby because I have a 12:30 lunch meeting.' The movie ends with her happily ensconced in the country with the new baby, a new and improved man, and a new career as a baby food entrepreneur. Hewing to comic form, the ending is presented as – in Northrup Frye's famous formulation – desirable if not plausible.[25] J.C. eventually redefines success on her own terms (and, not incidentally, discovers her heretofore latent maternal instincts), but the movie makes it clear that the sorts of success available to her as a woman are far more limited than those available to men.

Broadcast News (1987) showcases yet another successful but disconsolate professional woman who wins at work but loses everyplace else.

Figure 4.1 J.C. Wiatt (Diane Keaton) tries to figure out how to hold a baby and a business meeting simultaneously. *Baby Boom* (1987). Directed by Charles Shyer

Jane Craig (Holly Hunter) is a high-powered television news producer who the film follows from her days as a precocious and overambitious pre-adolescent to her midlife status as a professionally accomplished but romantically deprived woman. (As her assistant tells her: 'Except for socially, you're my role model.') Throughout, the film makes a point of pointing out her officious efficiency, suggesting that the very qualities that make her successful in the workplace also make her unappealingly obnoxious in her personal dealings. In the film's most telling character detail, Jane schedules five minutes each day to sit and cry; when the time is up, she calls an abrupt halt to her indulgence in self-pity and reverts to her purposeful professional self. The wistful ending of the film leaves no doubt that her devotion to her career is directly responsible for her status as an unhappily single woman. In this and like-minded films, female professionalism is equated with masochism and suffering. The repeated implication is that it is the heroines' ambition, rather than the structural attributes of the work and social spheres, that is responsible for their misery.

These films and others of the era that featured successful profes-sional women occasioned further debate in film theory circles about the cinematic balance – or lack thereof – between textual rigidity and spec-tatorial liberty, and about the ways that social changes get absorbed and interpreted by popular culture artifacts. In *Working Girls: Gender and Sex-uality in Popular Cinema*, Yvonne Tasker ferrets out varying interpretive possibilities from films of the 1980s and 1990s. Citing Richard Dyer's claim that popular culture products are fundamentally ambivalent and complex, having 'both oppositional and hegemonic potential,'[26] she turns her attention to what she dubs the 'new *film noir*' as a site for the ongoing cultural dialectic surrounding women who work, addressing 'contemporary culture in its own appropriate paranoid fashion.'[27] The dark, destroying seductress is an ancient archetype, but her incarnation in the latter decades of the twentieth century took a contemporary turn by conflating her with the successful working woman.[28] Tasker finds in these new *noirs* a postmodern knowingness that winks at the persona of the *femme fatale* and its evocation of powerful women as sexually enticing and dangerous but also vital and capable. In this ambiguous persona, Tasker sees an effort to work through attitudes toward independent women. Citing 'the relocation of the threat posed by the deadly woman...to the context of work,' Tasker analyzes how these films 'articulate an opposition between two versions of femininity, one associated with domesticity, one with a dangerous rejection of such conventional roles.'[29] In such films as *Fatal Attraction* (1987), *Presumed Innocent* (1990), *The Last Seduction* (1994), *Judicial Consent* (1994), and *Disclosure* (1994), professional capability and immorality (or, in some cases, amorality) go hand in hand. As in *Working Girl*, the workplace is a sexualized space where women wield their newfound power with a combination of good old sexual allure and newfound managerial prowess. Although the films clearly vilify the aggressive working women as threats to their beleaguered male colleagues, Tasker sees the narrativization of professionally successful women as fraught with double meaning. The film's demonization of these characters is accompanied by spectatorial fascination with their lives. Audiences are encouraged by the mise-en-scène to leer voyeuristically at all that their success entails. Their verbal wit and bitchiness, their enviable wardrobes and offices, their freewheeling sexual adventurism are cinematic turn-ons; but their ultimate loneliness and their ethical deficits are turn-offs, and we are left with the films' reassurance that the former enticements are not worth the latter lacks. If, as Tasker claims, these films evoke a collision of responses to the entry of women into the upper reaches of the workforce, they seem ultimately more symptomatic of cultural anxiety toward empowered professional/managerial women than of approval.

The more things change...

In the new millennium, when almost half of the American workforce is female and women are well represented in executive and professional positions, self-styled third-wave feminism has tried to reframe the terms of the discourse by focusing on the fundamental ambiguity of gender denotations and the discursive power of representational forms and, hence, of the culture industries. But efforts to expand and contextualize the subject positions available to women and to avoid simplistic binary oppositions (e.g., the working woman vs. the stay-at-home mother) find little reflection in mainstream cinema. After decades of women's professional advancement, the fingerprints left on the infamous glass ceiling have left barely a trace on the film screen. So would-be post-feminist movies – a simultaneously hopeful and benighted term – offer up plenty of women in powerful professional positions, but those women generally confront familiar dichotomies and choices: reject their professional identity for something seemingly more satisfying or remain alone and abandoned in the desert of careerism. Only rarely is there a suggestion that perhaps the structural, systemic qualities of the professional sphere are antithetical to a work/life balance and might themselves benefit from adaptation to changing social circumstances.

Essentialist gender stereotypes die hard, and most of Hollywood's recent female embodiments of professional success hew closely to their cinematic foremothers. So in 2003's tellingly titled Diane Keaton vehicle *Something's Gotta Give* (an exhortation that might well serve as the subtitle of virtually all of the working women films that insist on aspirational compromise), writer Erica Barry inhabits the familiar persona of the professionally successful, personally unfulfilled woman. Kate (Catherine Zeta-Jones), the no-nonsense master chef in *No Reservations* (2007) is cold, controlling, and lonely until she is humanized by her orphaned niece and romanced by her male sous-chef. In Miranda Priestly (Meryl Streep), *The Devil Wears Prada* (2006) gives us yet another cinematic dragon lady at the helm of her business but cast adrift in her personal life once her husband gets fed up with her careerism and ditches her. The film's young striver, Andy Sachs (Anne Hathaway), having discovered in Miranda a negative indicator for how she wants to live her life, decides, at film's end, to take a less power-vested job in a city less associated with big-time success. Miranda's filmic trajectory, in turn, transforms her from overreaching executrix to abject loner, thereby turning the film into a cautionary tale for women who aim too high. In its exposé of corporate hypocrisy, the film positions our dramatic sympathies with the younger woman; the reassessment of the costs of success is meant to signal a victory of authenticity over ambition.

The pair of women in *The Devil Wears Prada* – one at the beginning of her career and one an established success, one eager and the other jaded, one compliant and the other imperious – is a familiar, and remarkably durable, plot device in films about working women. The dialectic represented by the two characters changes little over the years, so going back from *The Devil Wears Prada*, to *Working Girl*, to the 1950s' *All About Eve* and *The Best of Everything* (1959), the older woman is consistently positioned as a warning to her younger counterpart of things to come if she follows her careerist ambitions. In the latter film, a melodramatic potboiler based on a Rona Jaffe novel, powerful publishing executive Miss Farrow (Joan Crawford), who is universally dubbed 'the witch' by the young women in the steno pool, abuses her young colleagues, all the while inflicting self-abuse by begging her married lover to pay more attention to her. After quitting her job because she thinks she has found true love with another man, she finds out 'It's too late for me.' She returns to work, sadder, wiser, and lonelier than ever, thereby inspiring the young heroine to get out while the getting is good. This notion that careerist women are compensatorily consigned to work because they fail at love is distressingly unchanged 50 years later. *The Devil Wear Prada*'s Miranda Priestly, too, ends up ruefully stuck in her work-obsessed persona, while her younger counterpart scales back her ambition to achieve balance, contentment, and romance.

Expanded opportunities to the contrary, in Hollywood movies the choice for working women often still seems to boil down to either renouncing their professional drive or being punished for it. And for audiences, despite feminist film theory's longing for narrative rupture, there is little to grab onto by way of negotiated readings. The films may encourage us to ogle the successful women's material surroundings and belongings and to envy their heady ability to say and do what they

Figure 4.2   The moment of truth as Andy Sachs (Anne Hathaway) rejects her boss Miranda Priestly's (Meryl Streep) version of professional success. *The Devil Wears Prada* (2006). Directed by David Frankel

please, but the narrative offers condemnation or, at best, pity for these characters, so any feeling of spectatorial identification with them leans toward the masochistic. The textual strategies ultimately tend to undercut or contradict the occasional fracture in the films' dominant codes. Nonetheless, the closure of these movies sometimes fails to mask their presentation of the limited options available to women in the film and, for that matter, to those watching the film who must choose among equally constrained subject positions. While working women movies for the past several decades may leave audiences little leeway to celebrate rather than censure professionally successful female characters, they do at least offer a chance for spectators to grapple with the gendered assumptions that underlie the American idea of success. The persistent repetition of these representational and narrative conventions may not be progressive, but it nonetheless bespeaks an ongoing cultural need to process gender and success ideologies. Although individual film iterations may show little change or development, and although cultural narratives generally do not proceed in lockstep with social advances, the films' cumulative, if inchoate, presentation of gendered limitations imprints itself on the popular imagination and at least encourages an awareness of these stories' inherent ideological contradictions.

Second-wave feminism and working men on screen

While the foregoing films have contributed to the framing of cultural attitudes toward successful women, they are not alone in wondering about the equation of professional achievement with contentment and success, and in revealing a long simmering, deep-seated discomfort with the conventional prescriptions of the success myth. As the preceding chapter suggests, the movies are rife with disaffected organization men and with narratives whose development and denouement imply a renunciation of professional success as the cornerstone of adult identity. For much of film history, many iterations of the success myth signaled a collective desire to work through the myth's inherent ideological contradictions or, at least, scrutinize its assumptions. That desire was only amplified by feminist discourses of the past few decades that opened up a larger cultural consideration of gender dogma.

Much has been written about male-centric movies' responses to second-wave feminism and to the influx of women into previously male spheres. Several films from the 1980s onward seem symptomatic of the social disorientation caused by changing gender roles and possibilities. With male prerogative in the extra-filmic world supposedly on the wane,

Hollywood volleyed back with a line-up of movies celebrating masculine authority and power. Susan Jeffords' books of the late 1980s and early 1990s, *The Remasculinization of America: Gender and the Vietnam War* and *Hard Bodies: Hollywood Masculinity in the Reagan Era*, see the macho militarism of the likes of *Rambo: First Blood* (1982) and *Robocop* (1987) as a direct response to the period's supposed feminization of American manhood.[30] From her perspective, the hypermasculine body that actively asserted its power betokened a reassertion of patriarchal order, and the climactic combat-filled action scenes were a ritualistic casting out of feminized or foreign elements that would taint that order. Other film historians and theorists have written extensively about masculinity as a sort of masquerade in which the fetishized male body of recent films functions as armor-cum-costume, and that body's exertions lead to the reconsolidation of hegemonic control.[31] Such films seem symptomatic of American anxiety about what Robert Bly, guru of the 1980s men's movement, called 'soft men' (whose counterparts are, presumably, hard, ambitious women who are responsible for the supposed crisis of masculinity).

Another popular strain of movies of the era, including *Kramer vs. Kramer* (1979), *Mr. Mom* (1983), *Three Men and a Baby* (1987), *Look Who's Talking* (1989), and *Mrs. Doubtfire* (1993), responded to the perceived threat posed by ambitious women by not only idealizing domesticity but by having their male protagonists take on the stereotypically feminine tasks of child-rearing, nurturing, and housekeeping. In each of these films, the main female character is professionally successful and, not incidentally, domestically neglectful. If women insist on taking their place in the male world of work, men in these movies respond in kind by discovering their inner homebody and thereby besting women at their own game while obviating the need for a mother. Although these films' transgressions of traditional gender roles may, at first glance, appear progressive, audience subjectivity is firmly aligned with the male nurturers and against the female strivers. Several critics have noted how the appropriation of women's experience works to conceal and deny female subjectivity. In her book *Feminism Without Women: Culture and Criticism in a Post-Feminist Age*, Tania Modleski has noticed 'how frequently male subjectivity works to appropriate "femininity" while oppressing women ... the extent to which male power is actually consolidated through cycles of crisis and resolution, whereby men ultimately deal with the threat of female power by incorporating it.'[32] In general, these films end up reasserting masculine capabilities on all fronts while denigrating women's ability to 'have it all,' in the phrase beloved by the popular press.

The Mr. Moms and the Rambos seem like contradictory responses to the zeitgeist and, indeed, they reveal a genuine confusion about gender roles and relations.[33] Susan Faludi, who proved to be an equal opportunity zeitgeist-chaser, followed up *Backlash* with a best-selling book about thwarted males. Her 1999 book titled *Stiffed: The Betrayal of the American Man* detailed the dissatisfactions and disappointments of middle-class men in the latter decades of the twentieth century.[34] Hers was one of several books wondering what went amiss, why American manhood seemed so diminished, and how men could reconceive their identities in the new gender cosmos. Faludi's book and other popular literature of the period exhibit a range of stances toward shifting gender dynamics; likewise, several films of the period complicate the notion of gender as a consistent, unified social position.[35] In *Slow Motion: Changing Masculinities,* her book about male identity in the latter decades of the twentieth century, Lynne Segal points out that in response to recent feminist-inspired changes, 'A diversity of "masculinities" jostle to present themselves as the acceptable face of the new male order.'[36]

Work and its malcontents

The films that celebrate hypermasculinity and those that exalt men's dominion in the domestic sphere are not the only ones in the past couple of decades to offer a spectrum of male subject positions. Another of those diverse masculinities jostling for attention in recent years is found in a spate of movies in the early years of the twenty-first century that focus on midlife men coming to terms with the realignment of gendered notions of success. Together with many of the women-centric films discussed above, they reassess the bedrock assumptions of the success myth by musing about professional accomplishment as the be-all-and-end-all of the good life and as the marker of one's standing in the social sphere. Alongside the working women films, they present another version of the cultural discomfort with socially mandated gender expectations and with the idea of measuring status and fulfillment by the level of one's professional achievement.

American Beauty (1999), *Wonder Boys* (2000), *Adaptation* (2002), *About Schmidt* (2002), *Lost in Translation* (2003), *Sideways* (2004), and *Broken Flowers* (2005) comprise such a concentrated take on success and work for males at midlife that their aggregation seems to indicate a delayed response coming-to-terms with the shifting gender and work landscapes of the preceding decades. These are certainly not the first or only films to focus on the travails of midlife working men.[37] But their latter day reassessment of the equation of professional achievement with success is distinguished by a self-conscious awareness of the performative aspects of both gender and work, as well as of the constructed nature of social identity. Their contemporaneous appearance and their remarkable consistencies of characterization, narrative, and subtext mark a particular cultural moment when the cracks in the consensus about what constitutes success radiate out to include middle-aged, middle-class, seemingly successful men.

The protagonists of these seven films are, for the most part, professionally successful and financially comfortable, but they nonetheless find their lives lacking. Although they earn a good living, the good life eludes them; neither their affluence nor their professional status can quell their sinking sense of wellbeing. Their professional identities prove to be shaky scaffolds on which to construct their self-images. These are men unmoored: beset by confusion about who they are and what they want. Their anguished *cris de coeur* of midlife stultification expose the fragility of socially crafted desires and identities. With a finger to the prevailing winds of public discourses about gender, work, and identity, these films suggest that culturally mandated expectations regarding both gender and success are not just in conflict with individual desires; they make it difficult to figure out what those desires might be. Hence, these are comic/ironic quest narratives with elusive grails. *Bildungsromans* for the middle-aged, their narratives revolve around a search for an alternative masculine identity and for a way to usher oneself into the later years of one's life and career.

Work, for these characters, is no longer a defining endeavor; for each, a flagging engagement with work precipitates midlife angst. The writers' blocks that the protagonists of *Wonder Boys, Adaptation* and *Sideways* wrestle with serve as analogues for the larger sensation of futility and dysfunction that all of these characters feel. These characters' particular blockages are characterized less by the inability to generate than the inability to stop generating: to sift through the welter of accumulated ideas and select what is pertinent. All three films poke fun at their characters' prolixity, with *Wonder Boys'* Grady Tripp being stuck at page 2611 of his novel-to-be, *Sideways'* Miles penning a similarly weighty tome, and *Adaptation's* Charlie Kaufman unable to finish his screenplay because he insists on putting everything in his life into it, right up to the moment when he writes. The characters' inability to choose and to then move on flies in the face of American cinema's conventional notion of masculinity, in which a man is defined by his decisive actions and difficult choices. Classic movies' most pithy credo of masculinity – 'A man's gotta do what a man's gotta do' – here morphs into the concession that a man has no idea what he's gotta do or what he wants to do, so he doesn't do much besides whine about his predicament.

The characters in the other films are even less devoted to their work and less defined by their professional identities. *About Schmidt* begins with the retirement of the eponymous character. The movie opens with a familiar bit of film iconography analyzed in Chapter 2: the low-angle shot of looming office towers as representatives of capitalist achievement and masculine ambition. Once the camera cuts to the inside of the building, another familiar set-up, analyzed in Chapter 3's analyses of *The Crowd* and *The Apartment*, introduces Schmidt (Jack Nicholson) sitting at an empty desk in an empty office, staring at the clock, which reads 4:59. Like an impatient child at the end of the school day, he is anxious to be sprung from his corporate servitude. But his response to the final moment of his decades-long career is utter impassivity. The following scenes introduce him as a man drained of emotion and disconnected from life. At his retirement dinner, when a colleague launches into a generic speech about 'the knowledge that you devoted your life to something meaningful ... to being productive' the camera slowly tracks in on Schmidt's poker-faced reaction. The early scenes take pains to present a life devoid of meaning or connection. Although he apparently loathed his job, without it he is without identity and routine. Weeks after his retirement, when he goes to visit his replacement to offer advice, he is rebuffed. Unneeded anywhere, Schmidt realizes that he is obsolete and irrelevant, and he plunges into a midlife malaise.

Figure 4.3 Warren Schmidt's (Jack Nicholson) deadpan response to the end of his working life. *About Schmidt* (2002). Directed by Alexander Payne

American Beauty also charts the end of a career but here the character, in the grip of a more angry response to the disappointments of his seemingly ideal suburban life, purposely gets himself fired. When asked to write a memo detailing why the company should keep him on his job, Lester Burnham (Kevin Spacey) responds with, 'My job consists of masking my contempt for the assholes in charge ... I jerk off while I fantasize about a life that doesn't so closely resemble hell.' When his much younger boss calls to tell him how out of line he is, he claims, 'Nope, I'm just an ordinary guy with nothing to lose.' He later applies for a job in a fast-food restaurant and when the manager points out that he is too old and too overqualified, he announces that he is 'looking for the least possible amount of responsibility.' The film's mordantly satirical view of a middle-class man at midlife posits such men as role-players chafing under the weight of an ill-fitting costume that disguises, distorts, and eventually eradicates their sense of self.

Bill Murray's characters in both *Lost in Translation* and *Broken Flowers* are likewise adrift in midlife alienation. Respectively a successful actor and a successful computer entrepreneur on the downward slopes of their careers, these characters struggle with the lack of identity that comes from renouncing work as the centerpiece of life. Murray's famous deadpan befits these portraits of men unable to shake their suspicion that, in spite of their professional achievement and recognition, something is amiss and something is missing. Jaded and bereft of significance, they can barely rouse themselves for a half-hearted engagement with their lives. In *Lost in Translation*, actor Bob Harris is on a job in Japan, self-contemptuously shilling for a liquor company. His jet lag becomes a metaphor for his pervasive sense of dislocation as he moves through his life like a sleep-deprived somnambulist, watching himself go through the motions with stoical resignation.

Similarly, in *Broken Flowers*, Don Johnston spends most of the film reacting with bemusement to life going on around him. We first view him sitting placidly in the dark, his mask-like face staring at the television screen where his alter ego, Don Juan, embraces life with gusto. Johnston's own embrace of life is indifferent at best. His name ironically invokes not just Don Juan but also, as several other characters point out, television icon Don Johnson, and the film misses few opportunities to accentuate the gulf between the swashbuckling masculinity of movies, television, and other symbolic systems and the effete masculinity of Murray's character. His career has enriched him monetarily but has endowed him with no sense of purpose or direction (in a telling detail, although he made his fortune in computers, he doesn't even own one since, at the beginning of the film, he has no desire for connectivity of any sort). Similar to *Lost in Translation*, the film is rife with stone-faced reaction shots. An extended montage without dialogue in the middle of the film consists entirely of the character's impassive non-reaction to life going on around him. Unlike classic movies' prototypical men of action, both of these characters can only react – and they can barely rouse themselves to do even that. Their world-weariness and apathy are couched as ironic responses to masculine self-assertion and decisiveness. Men of inaction, they cannot see the point of exerting themselves so they opt, instead, for a willful inertia and resort to irony as a defense against anomie.

Together the seven films present two paradoxical versions of masculinity: flaming neurosis, accompanied by compulsive logorrhea (*Sideways, American Beauty, Adaptation, Wonder Boys*) or listless catatonia (*Broken Flowers, Lost in Translation*).[38] Both are a far cry from the idealized masculinities of classical American cinema. In contrast to the films that Jeffords cites, which reassert the patriarchal order by having their protagonists triumph in conflicts with other men or with overreaching women, these films give us characters in conflict with themselves, victimized mostly by their own flagging conviction in conventional routes to contentment. Seduced and abandoned by the success myth, they respond either with an outpouring of verbalized frustration or with abject silence.

Some of these characters react to their diminishing presence in the world of work by retreating to the private, domestic sphere generally associated with women. Traube, among others, has noted that capitalism's split between home and workplace has naturalized gender distinctions, so that the home is equated with feminine nurturance and dependence, while the workplace represents social power and freedom.[39] But many of these characters do their work at home and those that do 'go to work' find their workplace utterly inhospitable. In *About Schmidt, American Beauty, Broken Flowers,* and *Adaptation*, much of the action (such as it is) takes place inside the characters' houses. In each, the scene design of the home is a carefully conceived representation of the character's situation. Middle-American kitsch (*About Schmidt*), bourgeois suburban orderliness (*American Beauty*), high-tech bachelor modernism (*Broken Flowers*), low-tech bachelor mess (*Adaptation*) all function as stylistic metonymy for the incongruity of these characters in their home environment. The mise-en-scène and the multiple single shots of the characters tend to isolate them in the frame, adding to the sense of disharmony with their domestic habitat. Whatever the style, the home is an alien space for these characters: they are literally out of place there since, as men, they belong in the public space of the work world. Domesticity, rather than being a comfort, is a sort of house arrest for these men; they retreat there because, having dislodged themselves from the traditionally masculine realm, they do not know where else to go, but they remain equally disconnected and ill-at-ease in the private and public spheres.

When *Sideways* finally delivers its main character home after a series of misadventures on the road, his bachelor apartment is so dark, claustrophobic, and forlorn that he escapes to a desolate chain restaurant to drink a prized bottle of wine. Even the films that take place far from home are haunted by – and flummoxed by – the domestic. *Lost in Translation* has a running gag in which Bob's wife keeps calling him about her redecorating project, hounding him about carpet samples and the like. On the job and in his off hours, this character is stalked by minutiae: perennial reminders of absurdity and meaninglessness. The sterility and anonymity of the Japanese hotel where he is holed up likewise function as signs of alienation for both character and audience. Like the tourist motel in *Sideways*, the setting accentuates the character's estrangement from his own life and from the domestic ideal that is supposed to accompany success. Discontented with work and out of place in their homes, these characters cannot be at home anywhere.

Several of the characters respond to their sense of incongruity at home and at work by hitting the road: that enduring American symbol of personal reinvention and revelation. Typically associated with youth and adventure, the road movie genre conventionally has its protagonists face a series of challenges en route to greater self-awareness.[40] The pull of the road is a siren call and the expanse of the American highway offers not just physical mobility, but the promise of spiritual transformation and regeneration. But in *About Schmidt*, *Broken Flowers*, and *Sideways*, there is an ironic usurpation of the iconography of the road and the idea of moving on to find oneself. Here, the road leads only to the frontier of old age where self-awareness seems to be an ever-receding mirage. If, in conventional instances of the genre, the road symbolizes the heady freedom of being liberated from commitments and feminizing domesticity, these films present the flip side of American rootlessness in which roaming becomes a kind of lonely self-exile. These are road warriors who cannot find the battlefield and who, instead, career down dead ends, a point made clear by *Broken Flowers'* repeated shots in the rear view mirror as well as by bits of dialogue ('So if I continue down this road, I will find the Riverview Cemetery?' and, at the end while hailing a taxi, 'Circle Drive, please. No rush'). The road trips in both that film and *About Schmidt* are punctuated by multiple cutaway shots of generic highways: a recurring refrain suggesting that the roads may proliferate but they are indistinguishable and they lead nowhere.

Even the cars that bear these characters away from their disappointments conspire to rob them of their dignity and masculine identity. The semiotic significance of consumer goods functions, in film, as a visual shorthand: an efficient expository technique for conveying characters' statuses and situations. Several cultural historians have pointed out the link among consumption, commodities, and identity.[41] The car as an icon of sexuality, affluence, and masculine power was firmly established in the popular mind at least as early as the 1930s gangster cycle. But there are no testosterone-fueled hot rods or motorcycles for these aging wanderers. When they tool around in, respectively, an RV (*About Schmidt*), an old Saab (*Sideways*), a series of rented Ford Tauruses (*Broken Flowers*), and a 1966 Ford Galaxie (*Wonder Boys*), there is no mistaking the insinuation that these are men past their prime and potency. The characters are all too aware of the image that their vehicles telegraph. Johnston's cars have been rented for him by his friend, neighbor, and foil: a lively and contented family man who is as energetic as Johnston is enervated. At one point, Johnston complains to him about having to drive such a nondescript car, unbefitting of his image of himself. Schmidt's oxymoronically titled mobile home was selected by his wife before her death and he is vaguely embarrassed by its associations with domesticity. In *Sideways*, Miles' car ends up being deliberately crashed into a tree so it can serve as an alibi for his philandering friend's injuries. And Tripp's car, which transports drugs, stolen goods, a tuba, a dead dog, and the one extant copy of his manuscript, is likewise brutalized when his editor slams it into a building. The car as an artifact of conspicuous consumption and masculine self-assertion is, in these films, conspicuous only as a symbol of the characters' battered sense of identity.

The buddies that take off together in many conventional road movies are here replaced with loners, shut off in their car from life around them. Only *Sideways* presents two characters on a journey. They are the usual ill-matched couple: Miles (Paul Giamatti) a sad-sack curmudgeon and Jack (Thomas Haden Church), an aging roué determined to indulge in one last fling before his pending marriage. Jack eventually ditches Miles to take up with a woman they have met on their trip so Miles, like the wanderers in the other movies, ends up alone for much of the film, dining and drinking solo while staring into space. These films systematically sever their characters' ties to the usual anchors of adult life: job, marriage, home, family, friends, community. When there are family or friends around (*Adaptation, Sideways, Wonder Boys, American Beauty*), they are more irritants and disappointment than comforts or companions.

A strong leitmotif in several of these midlife odysseys involves a symbolic regression in which the protagonists either literally revisit places or people from their past or emotionally revert by indulging in a second adolescence. The characters in *About Schmidt, Sideways, Wonder Boys*, and *Broken Flowers* pay visits to childhood homes or past loves in an effort to recover their youth and their sense of purpose. But nostalgia proves to be a poor road map for the future, and each gets ejected from his past having garnered little in the way of enlightenment. Schmidt's childhood home is now a tire store. Johnston's old girlfriends are a catalogue of disappointments in *Broken Flowers*. *Sideways'* Miles steals money from his mother and then steals away from her home before she wakes in the morning. And *Wonder Boys'* Tripp, after breaking into his estranged wife's childhood home in a town called Kinship, comes away with anything but kinship. Each of these movies puts a fine point on their characters' inability to connect with both their present and their past, not to mention their inability to imagine a satisfying future.

Those characters that do not physically go back to sites of their past nonetheless feel a relentless pull toward retrospection. The self-contemptuous Charlie, in *Adaptation*, writes his own birth into his screenplay, having already detailed the birth of the earth in his hopes of figuring out, as he puts it, 'What am I doing here?' And *American Beauty's* Lester wallows in arrested development by giving free reign to his dormant id: saying what he pleases to whom he pleases, hitting on his daughter's teenage friend, smoking dope with the high school-aged neighborhood dealer, cruising in his car with the radio blasting, and altogether ditching his responsibilities to indulge his adolescent-like desires. In this movie's gothic satire, adulthood is a grim, joyless affair, so Lester's retreat from its mandatory role-playing is seen as a step toward liberation.

Lester's first instinct once he decides to repudiate bourgeois propriety and indulge his lust for his daughter's friend is to reclaim his youthful body. After examining his sagging torso in profile, with its telltale middle-aged paunch, he decides, 'I wanna look good naked.' He embarks on a weight-lifting regimen and, as he begins to get results, the audience is privy to several shots of Lester flexing narcissistically as he gazes in the mirror. The midlife male body is a central signifier of marginality in these films: its girth and fleshiness a metaphor for the characters' wayward existence and waning masculinity.[42] The cinematic male hard body is habitually presented as an eroticized spectacle to be admired, envied, and feared. But these soft, aging bodies are spectacular only in their comic contradiction of the ideal male form and in their tendency to make a laughable spectacle of themselves. If the masculine ideal is a body poised for action, these are bodies divested of power, attraction, and capability.

Adaptation begins with a voice-over self-hating lament about the character's fat, balding middle-aged form: 'If my ass wasn't fat, I'd be happier. I wouldn't have to wear these shirts with the tails out all the time. Like that's fooling anyone. Fat ass!' The verbalized inadequacy and insecurity about the body sounds familiar but misplaced, coming, as it does, from a man.[43] Charlie Kaufman (Nicolas Cage) is so paralyzed by his own deficiencies that the only way he can cope is to create a fictional doppelganger who is as confident, action-oriented and romantically successful as he is not. Miles, in *Sideways*, is a similarly lacking physical specimen by the standards of movie paragons. Balding, overweight, and round-shouldered, he shambles through the movie with self-loathing, at one point curling up on his bed in the fetal position. His opposite number is his college roommate Jack, an aging lothario as clueless as Miles is self-aware. Both this movie and *Adaptation* present self-awareness as a paralyzing pathology. But Jack's more forceful masculine mode and his pride in his physicality take a beating as well when he has his nose broken by an irate lover and later arrives naked and shivering back at the hotel, having been chased away by the irate husband of yet another woman. The midlife body, whatever its shape, is allowed no dignity in these films; its comic abasement is tinged with a genuine despair about the aging body's distance from the youthful masculine ideal.

This is nowhere more manifest than in *About Schmidt* where the audience's extra-diegetic acquaintance with Jack Nicholson as bad-boy icon makes his incarnation as Schmidt that much more poignant and disturbing. The firebrand of *Easy Rider* (1969) has traded his motorcycle for a recreational vehicle; the aggressive, socially smooth rogue is replaced by a repressed, ill-at-ease loner. The camera takes pains to accentuate Schmidt's lack of physical and social facility, repeatedly isolating him within the mise-en-scène or cutting to close-ups of his fleshy, timeworn face. As he moves further into his existence as a widower and retiree, he becomes increasingly slovenly. Unshaven and uncombed, he slouches around in slippers and an old trench coat. Schmidt's dismay about his own physical decline and vulnerability gets projected onto the women in the film. Before his wife dies abruptly, he catalogues his disgust with her aging body: 'Every night I ask myself the same question. Who is this old woman that lies in my house...why is it that every little thing she does irritates me...I hate the way she sits, and the way she smells.' The camera placement during this tirade – first at chair height with his wife's rear end ominously approaching the camera as she sits, then offering a close-up of her armpit – places the audience within Schmidt's subjectivity. In the film's most widely discussed scene, Schmidt shares a hot tub with his daughter's soon-to-be mother-in-law, played by Kathy Bates. The camera cross cuts between Bates' character, proudly fat and naked, and reaction shots of Schmidt who, not knowing where to look, sits with a tight-lipped, embarrassed smile. When she reaches for his knee, he lunges out of the pool, displaying his own corpulent, over-the-hill body. But the spectator is firmly aligned with him so the camera encourages us to react with amused horror to her body but not to his: to find hers grotesque but his merely past its prime.

Even those characters whose bodies have not gone to seed have their masculine deterioration accentuated through costume. Tripp spends much of *Wonder Boys* in a woman's chenille bathrobe, looking more like a blowzy *hausfrau* than an accomplished writer and professor. In *Lost in Translation*, Bill Murray's character begins the film in a natty suit but, as he becomes increasingly dissociated from his life, he sports shirts so garish that the young woman with whom he has been passing time takes one look at him and notes, 'You really are having a mid-life crisis, aren't you?' In *Masked Men*, his book about masculinity in films of the 1950s, Steven Cohan claims that 'The breadwinner's public face is a masquerade, a performance put on to deflect attention from suppressed ambitions and emotions, his conformist appearance obliquely resonant of lost sexuality and what he has renounced.' He goes on to claim that the corporate uniform of a somber suit is a symbol of men's 'devotion to the principles of duty, of renunciation and of self-control.'[44] Once those men doff their grey flannel suits, they become stripped of identity. Out of corporate uniform and in mufti, these men, too, seem at a loss about how to declare and define themselves. Without their professional garb to confer identity, their sense of self is in free fall.

Added to the indignities of aging, ill-clad bodies are the various physical wounds that these characters suffer. Broken noses (*Sideways*), blackened eyes (*Broken Flowers*), dog bites (*Wonder Boys*), and, improbably, waterbed injuries (*About Schmidt*) are among the stigmata of masculinity in decline. All told, the midlife body's depreciation in these films is emblematic of the instability and tenuousness of masculine power and authority. This awareness of obsolescence and of the end of youth, vigor, and power marks these characters as marginal. Their marginality contradicts the reigning representations of masculinity in film, and points these characters toward a different sort of masculine subjectivity. Kaja Silverman has written extensively about the 'vulnerability of conventional masculinity,'[45] and about how certain films 'complicate the notion of "the feminine." '[46] Her comments about alternative masculine subjectivities are applicable to these characters, who are marginalized not just by their age but also by their flagging convictions about work and about the standard markers of success. Silverman cites a body of films that suggest alternatives to conventional masculine representation and goes on to claim that these marginalized subjectivities 'are those which absent themselves from the line of paternal succession, and which in one way or another occupy the domain of femininity...not as disenfranchisement and subordination, but rather as phallic divestiture, as a way of saying "no" to power.'[47]

That the repudiation of traditional forms of social power might be liberating rather than debilitating is a provocative suggestion, but it is one that these films are not entirely convinced of. Although some of their characters may indulge in a passive (and sometimes involuntary) renunciation of hegemonic masculinity, they tend to be ambivalent about occupying, or even visiting, the domains of femininity. Their responses to women range from intensely hostile (*American Beauty*) to fearful (*Adaptation, Sideways*) to simply baffled (*Lost in Translation, Broken Flowers, About Schmidt, Wonder Boys*). Although they refuse the gendered prescriptions for success and contentment that have previously ruled their lives, they find little comfort or succor in alternative ways of being. In these films, the domestic sphere is as alienating as the work environment, and relationships with women neither compensate – nor, for that matter, cause – the characters' loss of a clear sense of self. Only *American Beauty* directly suggests that male anxiety stems partly from female ascendancy and the collapse of gender norms. The other films aim their plaint at a broader cultural failure to imagine alternative identities for men outside of classic success dogma.

Their appropriation and adaptation of feminist thinking about professional and personal identities qualifies them as what one writer once called 'melodramas of beset manhood.'[48] Film theorist Tania Modleski decries such films as part of a discourse that 'relocate[s] the struggle of feminism against patriarchy to a place entirely *within* patriarchy and within the psyche of the patriarch himself.'[49] Certainly there is an element of that in these films, particularly in *American Beauty*. The uncertainties that were amplified by feminist discourses about how to balance work and family life, or about how to craft a satisfying identity outside of work, here are firmly fixed within male subjectivity. The relative absence, marginality, and lack of subjectivity of women in these films, and the male characters' unhampered ability to choose when and whether to shed their identities as working professionals, set these films apart from those with female protagonists. Further, whereas the films that focus on working women tend to suggest that it is the characters who bring upon themselves their lack of fulfillment through their own failings or choices, the male-focused films suggest that it is the culture and its expectations that somehow fail them.

Of these midlife men movies, only *Wonder Boys* has a conventional happy ending that satisfies spectatorial desire for closure and for romantic union. Tripp ends the film having finally made a commitment to his long-time lover: 'I lost my wife, my book, my job, everything that I thought was important. But I finally knew where I wanted to go. And now I have someone to help me get there.' The protagonist's rebirth supplies the conventional ending of romantic comedy which, however improbable it may be in terms of the character's unexpected transformation, is what audiences have been conditioned to expect and applaud.

As regenerative crises go, that is as good as it gets in these movies. The other films end *in medias res* with the characters' romantic fates and, more significantly, their odysseys of identity unresolved. The final shot of *Sideways*, which shows Miles being admitted to the home of the woman that he desires, at least leaves open the possibility of union and romantic fulfillment. But the other films end with their characters as disconnected and bewildered as they have been throughout. *Adaptation*'s about-face ending can only be taken as the resolution of Kaufman's overdue script, rather than as a record of the actual course of his life. *About Schmidt* concludes with Schmidt alone and weeping, as he reads a letter from the only person with whom he feels he can connect: the African child that he sponsors from afar in a desperate attempt to matter to someone. *American Beauty* ends with its main character shot dead, having been killed for sexual desires that he did not, in fact, have (and having been unable to act on those that he did). Finally, *Lost in Translation* and *Broken Flowers* wind up in stalemate, with their characters at an impasse about who they are, what they want, and how they should live. However they end, all seven films are tinged with an elegiac quality and a final suggestion that the lost souls at their center have, at best, a tenuous hold on their identities and their desires. It is this very refusal of closure that suggests how difficult it is to overcome the contradictions inherent in the success myth in all its versions.

Success up in the air

Comparable reassessments of culturally prescribed definitions of successful manhood continued to appear frequently in films as the decade progressed (e.g., *Thank You for Smoking* (2005), *The Weather Man* (2005), *Little Children* (2006), *Up in the Air* (2009), *Greenberg* (2010), *Everything Must Go* (2010)). Jason Reitman's *Up in the Air* is a particularly intriguing entry into the catalogue of movies about midlife men who come to reconsider their formula for a successful, fulfilling life. Like the decade's earlier films of midlife male malaise, it is a lament for what is lost when one's primary criterion for success is professional. What makes the film especially pertinent to this discussion of gender, work, and success is its two main female characters: working women at different stages of their careers whose own efforts to find satisfaction and balance in their lives set the protagonist's quest in sharp relief. Although the organizing sensibility of the film is male, the female characters' subject positions are crucial to its agenda of rethinking the role that work plays in a successful life and reassessing the meaning of success.

Ryan Bingham (George Clooney) is a professional hatchet man, hired by companies around the country to fire their employees for them. Euphemistically referred to as a 'termination engineer' or 'career transition counselor,' he is a hired gun who swoops in from above to do the dirty deed then gets out of town and moves on to the next frontier of downsizing. The first moments of the film neatly sum up Bingham's life as well as his existential insecurity. Under the opening titles, an elaborate series of matte shots showing cloud-filled skyscapes are intercut with cityscapes seen from the air. The scene that immediately follows the title sequence is a montage of single shots of employees reacting, in turn, to the news that they have been fired. Throughout this sequence, the camera stays focused on the recipients of Bingham's professional *modus operandi*, keeping our attention on their subjectivity rather than his. When one furious person who has just been given the boot says to him, 'Who the fuck are you, man,' the film finally cuts to a reaction shot of Bingham as he comments, in voice-over: 'Excellent question: who the fuck am I?' This, of course, is the fundamental question for all of these movies' men at midlife; once again, the narrative revolves around its protagonist's halting efforts to find a belated answer to that question. Here, too, geographical wanderings serve as analogues for ontological journeys. In the airport scene that directly follows the firing montage, Bingham's voice-over informs us that 'To know me is to fly with me...this is where I live': in airplanes, hovering over more grounded lives. The arc that Bingham travels in the course of the movie forces him to realize that he spends his life not just literally, but also metaphorically, up in the air, uncommitted to anything except doing his job efficiently.

In this version of the midlife quest for self-defined success, the central character starts out full of smug surety that his is a wonderful life. He fancies himself a savvy operator, going about his business with well-practiced buzzwords and well-worn routines. The movie's repeated montages of those routines – packing his suitcase, going through airport security, gazing out of airplane windows – are accompanied by Bingham's self-satisfied palaver about how much he loves this life of perpetual motion. He moonlights as a motivational speaker who motivates people to avoid attachments and stasis. His canned presentation closes with a purportedly big insight: 'Make no mistake: Relationships are the heaviest components of your life .... Moving is living; the slower we move, the faster we die.' His voice-over happily brags that 'Last year, I spent 322 days on the road,' which, alas, means that he had to spend '43 miserable days at home.' His home, such as it is, looks uncannily like a hotel room: anonymous and unlived-in. As in the previously analyzed films, not to mention in scores of male-centric American stories, restless travel is a repudiation of domesticity and the female-inflected private sphere.[50]

His interactions with a series of women are what trip up his swagger and shake him out of his complacency. Natalie Keener (Anna Kendrick), the young hotshot who is hired to modernize and digitize the firing process is, initially, a more hard-nosed version of Bingham. Even he is appalled by her pitiless devotion to professional efficiency, regardless of the collateral damage left in its wake. After a series of wake-up calls (her boyfriend dumps her, one of the people she fired kills herself, she realizes how lonely Bingham's itinerant existence is), she ups and quits. But not before she indulges in a classic 'I've-seen-the-light' speech, in which she points out to Bingham how shallow and meaningless his 'cocoon of self-banishment' is. Her epiphany about work, relationships, and ambition humanizes her and sets the stage for Bingham's own recognition of the imbalance and aridity of his supposedly successful life.

Bingham's most significant relationship is with a woman who appears to be his female soul mate, since she initially gives the impression of being as soulless and rootless as he. Like Bingham, Alex (Vera Farmiga), seems to live on the road, measure her success by her air miles, and delight in freewheeling, hit-and-run sex unencumbered by any expectation of commitment. 'Think of me as yourself, only with a vagina,' she tells him. When Bingham asks her to accompany him to his estranged sister's wedding, she gamely accepts. But revisiting his old hometown haunts and rethinking his work-obsessed, rootless existence makes him decide that he wants something more from Alex. His 'make no mistake' anaphora comes back to haunt him, as he realizes that he has made a big mistake in privileging his career while sacrificing personal bonds.

Although each of the female characters in the movie also struggles to forge a truce between their ambitions and the demands and rewards of home life, relative to Bingham's existence up in the air, they have their feet on the ground. Bingham's sisters, homebodies who, unlike him, have never strayed far from their roots, seem to have made peace with their modest, family focused aspirations and limited worldview. Thanks to a donation of air miles from Bingham, his younger sister ends up finally being able to indulge her heretofore thwarted wanderlust. Natalie finds a new job that, seemingly, will require of her less travel and less torment in the service of business. The film's eleventh hour plot twist suggests that Alex has already figured out how to have both a whirlwind life on the road and a rooted home life, not to mention a life that fulfills both duty and desire.

Strikingly, the time-honored narrative practice of featuring two working women, one young and one middle-aged, is put to unconventional use. Rather than being competitors or having the older woman serve as a warning symbol of the price of success for women, these two characters empathize with one another. Together, they share a rueful awareness of the challenges and compromises that accompany professional women's drive for success as they push against gendered expectations and limitations. These characters are neither pitied nor punished for their ambitions. Well before Bingham finally admits that wandering as a way of life is more a curse than a boon, both women seem to know what they are up against in longing for a satisfying life on both the home and work fronts.

The movie's climax, in which all of Bingham's bonds – romantic, professional, familial – are in tatters, leaves him painfully aware of the unbearable lightness of being chronically up in the air. For a film that, up until this point, has seemed to adhere to classic comic form by moving its main character toward enlightenment, romantic union, social integration and positive change, this is the wrong ending. But as its protagonist progresses from publicly extolling 'the virtues of the unencumbered life' to privately longing for some ties that bind, *Up in the Air* reveals itself to be a drama masquerading as a satiric comedy. Even after Bingham admits that his success is hollow, he cannot change himself or his circumstances. The final shot shows him, once again, at an airport, staring in a stupor at the continuously changing departure board and wondering forlornly where to go next.

Considered together, the movies dealing with professionally ambitious women and professionally disaffected men point to a deep crack in the cultural consensus about what constitutes success and about how gender, work, and success are intertwined. Some individual films may appear to reconcile doubts about the success myth by perpetuating simple polarities and typologies – for instance, the unhappy professional woman versus the contented woman of limited or conventionally gendered ambitions. But even those movies generally contain enough narrative fissures to suggest that the options and solutions are significantly more complicated than their textual strategies might acknowledge. Jeanine Basinger points to 'the great secret of the Hollywood film: its ambivalence, its knowing pretense.'[51] She goes on to write about Hollywood's talent for 'saying one thing and showing another [and for] the raising of social questions within a safe context.' So those social questions get translated into the *lingua franca* of Hollywood film and, in the process, they may appear to be mediated and mitigated. But movies do not just allay collective concerns; they also arouse and address them. Cumulatively, if not individually, these films dealing with work, gender, and success are full of internal doubts about both the success myth's privileging of professional achievement, as well as about the stability of gender norms and ideologies. Over the decades, the pervasive preoccupation of such a large number of Hollywood films with the interplay of gender, work, and success attests to a communal need to confront the contradictions of the success myth. Even if the resolution of those contradictions is elusive, the movies give vent to a cultural yearning to revisit, once again, how we think about what we do and who we are as men and women, as workers, as strivers for success.

5
Hallelujah, I'm a Bum: The Glorification of Unemployment

I loaf and invite my soul

– Walt Whitman, *Song of Myself*

The standard ingredients of the American success myth – the promise of social mobility, the irrelevance of accidents of birth, the cult of individual enterprise, the dividends paid by hard work, the cornucopia of consumer goods that are the reward for toil – are so much a part of our daily fare that to question them seems subversive. Ideology, by definition, is normative, and the norms of the success myth are among the most intrinsic of American ideologies. But the recursive loop between myth and ideology is stretched to its limits by Hollywood movies that manage to foreground the myth's ideological inconsistencies. Such films put the cultural contradictions regarding work, success, and fulfillment in their crosshairs, setting their sights on the ways in which the American idea of success is conflated with vocational achievement, material attainment, and individual will. In counterposing contentment with conventional notions of success, they suggest that one needs to be sacrificed in order to achieve the other. The prior two chapters have shown that this marked ambivalence is consistently evident in stories revolving around professional success as an indicator of self-worth. On the one hand, work is equated with masculinity, adulthood, and deep-seated American ideas about individual initiative and mobility. Alternatively – and sometimes simultaneously – work is seen as demeaning and spiritually deadening, and only an escape from the workaday world allows one to regain his individuality and integrity.

This contradictory vision of work reveals itself not only in movies set in the workplace but also in a range of films – from Depression-era comedies to slacker films of the 1990s to the current crop of movies about grown-up men who resist growing up – that posit unemployment as an appealing antidote to the drudgery of holding a job. As many stories as there are about hard work leading to success, there is an equally durable contrarian strain in which liberation from work, whether voluntary or otherwise, is romanticized as a desirable state that affords social freedom and spiritual fulfillment. Given the primacy of the American work ethic and our national devotion to professional productivity and advancement, these films that exalt the state of idleness comprise a seemingly odd, but persistent, cultural inclination. Their glorification of idleness and its practitioners reveals a deep schism in our collective notions of success, work, and leisure. In aggregate, they comprise an ongoing rumination about what is gained and what is lost by fetishizing work as the route to success and gratification.

There is a long lineage of films that glorify unemployment and revel in idealized fantasies about life without work. Marx's notion of alienation from labor in capitalist societies reaches its full expression in these narratives, in which a succession of hoboes, bums, vagabonds, beatniks, hipsters, and slackers either opt out of work culture or are ejected from it. More often than not, they get rewarded for their escapist escapades by undergoing – and sometimes imparting to others – spiritual redemption. Collectively, this cavalcade of jobless characters serves to illuminate our cultural ambivalence about work as a cornerstone of adult identity, while simultaneously exploring American attitudes about leisure, laziness, and play.[1]

Work, play, and success

To be sure, there are a number of movies from the Depression era onward that offer frank and bleak looks at the condition of joblessness, but they are vastly outnumbered by those that gaze at the unemployed through rose-colored lenses.[2] Unsurprisingly, most of the films that romanticize unemployment hew to conventional comic forms, conventions, and character types. In his classic treatise on comedy, 'The Mythos of Spring,' Northrup Frye explains that the comic spirit is moral; its intent is to challenge behavioral and cultural norms, thereby acting as a corrective to repressive social conventions. Classic comedy's rebelliousness toward the social order marks it as a progressive form, since it imagines a better, more just world where people are driven by desires rather than duties, and passion rather than reason. Since comic narratives move toward deliverance from an unsatisfactory social order, their endings, in Frye's phrase, 'do not impress us as true, but as desirable.'[3] The audience bestows upon these wished-for endings the benediction that 'this should be,' even as we must admit that, this side of the proscenium, it cannot, in fact, be.[4] Most of the comedies dealing with unemployment precisely conform to Frye's schema in imagining a utopian world free from the degradations of work but nonetheless equally, and implausibly, free from the deprivations that come from having no job, no pay, and no professional identity. Far from suffering for their lack of work, the protagonists of these stories thrive in their unemployment, as the idealized endings suggest that idleness is its own reward.

Comedy's subversion of expectations and customs makes it a form well suited for a critique of work. By nature, the comic protagonist is a rebel and an outsider who is positioned, or who often positions himself, against the status quo and in opposition to dominant social institutions. His creative, emancipatory spirit challenges normative values and assumptions, and his contentment with his lack of employment seems to undermine the ideological bases of work and success. In these comic narratives, joy in joblessness is an affront to the defining qualities of mythic 'Americanness': diligence, productivity, professional ambition.

Often in these films, the central character will play at being a worker while he is temporarily (and usually disastrously) employed. But, far from being genuine attempts to join the ranks of the employed, his forays into the work world are presented as a form of masquerade. Like a child trying on costumes and identities, he may don workers' weeds but only as a narrative device to reveal the ways in which his habitual unemployed status is preferable to the working life. Disguise, the ancient strategy of comedy, allows him to mock those who are gainfully employed and to belie the illusion that work is in any way fulfilling.[5] As is frequently the case in comic form, it is the stripping away of social masks and costumes that exposes the essential self and its desires. When the comic protagonist casts off his professional regalia and leaves the world of work to return to the parallel universe of unemployment, it is clear that, spiritually, he has come home.

In the movies that glorify joblessness, the opposite of work is not merely the lack of work; the opposite of work is play. Johan Huizinga's influential study of *homo ludens* (man at play) makes a case for the play instinct as the fundamental element of all cultures. According to Huizinga, the defining principle of play is that it is purposeless – an end in itself.[6] It is this lack of teleology and rational endeavor that marks playfulness as a transgressive threat to the ideologies of the success myth. As Barbara Ehrenreich points out in *Fear of Falling*, her book about the inner life of the middle class, 'pleasure of any kind was subversive to the "production" of useful adults.'[7] Work is purposeful, productive, and strategic – and so are the adults that labor at it. But the ludic instinct has no end beyond its own delight in frolic. Reveling in their release from work, the central characters in the narratives of unemployment are often presented as childlike in the best sense. In eschewing the burdens of adult existence, they remain happily at play, free from the restrictions, delayed gratifications, and repressed desires of the working life. The genre of screwball comedy that came into being during the Depression revolves around its protagonists learning to play and turning their backs on the adult world's stringent standards of behavior.[8] In the comedies of unemployment, the protagonists likewise either learn to play during the course of the movie or infect other characters with their already well-formed ludic tropism.

The comic protagonist's regression to child-like behavior and the resultant transgression of adult codes of conduct has been well explored by theorists of comedy.[9] Geoff King, for one, couches the ludic impulse in Freud's pre-Oedipal stage with its fluid, yet-to-be-formed identity and lack of social restrictions. If, for Americans, there is equivalence between one's work and one's identity (what you do professionally is what you are), then the lack of a job is commensurate with the lack of a stable, unitary identity. The comic character's status as shape shifter allows him to evade the strictures of a singular self and play at what King calls the 'fluid, unstructured, unstable possibilities' of the pre-Oedipal phase.[10]

This plasticity of identity marks the character as liminal and socially ambiguous. Victor Turner's articulation of liminality, originally an anthropological term, is applicable to the comic protagonist: 'Liminality may perhaps be regarded as the Nay to all positive structural assertions, but as in some sense the source of them all, and, more than that, as a realm of pure possibility whence novel configurations of ideas and relations may arise.'[11] In *The Ritual Process: Structure and Anti-Structure*, Turner defines the liminal as 'neither here nor there; they are betwixt and between the positions assigned and arrayed by law, custom, convention, and ceremony.'[12] If, in the American *weltanschauung*, job equals identity, then the jobless person is free of identity or, perhaps, free to play at different identities rather than declaring himself one thing or the other.

Both Freud's concept of the pre-Oedipal and Turner's articulation of liminality imply a passage through these stages to a more definitively formed self. What is notable about many of the unemployed comic characters is that they are eternally 'neither here nor there,' never landing on one ultimate identity, as they happily dwell in 'the realm of pure possibility.' If work equals identity, then their lack of work marks them as eternally formless. In this, their sense of play is genuinely transgressive of adult social conventions and professional exigencies. As antitheses to the gainfully employed, they indulge in their creative playfulness which serves as counterpoint to the drudgery of the legions of the employed.

Literary theorist Mikhail Bakhtin's influential writings on the spirit of carnival are likewise germane to the function of the unemployed protagonists of these films. In *Rabelais and His World*, Bakhtin's study of medieval folk culture, the carnival represents a break from strict social hierarchies and civilities. In the privileged site of the carnival ritual, the world turns topsy-turvy as unruly, indulgent behavior briefly becomes the norm. Everyday decorum is mocked and parodied, and there is an exuberant hybridization of high and low social strata and modes of comportment. This inversion of the societal apparatus 'extend[s] the narrow sense of life' and allows for the 'temporary suspension of all hierarchic distinctions and barriers among men … and of the prohibitions of usual life.'[13] In legitimizing – or, at least, temporarily giving a stage to – the marginalized elements of adult society, carnival represents an ethos of insurgency and resistance to rigid social constraints.

Similarly, in extolling the joys of unemployment, these comic films gleefully undermine the apparatus of work and the ideologies of the success myth. Here, the prescriptive convictions of the myth and of the American work ethic are turned upside down: work is grim, its rewards are specious, and the responsibilities of adulthood are soul-killing. Play, rather than work, is the ethical imperative. Like the antics of the carnivalesque jester, which ridicule the pretensions of the court, the comic protagonist's lack of ambition and aversion to toil calls into question the value of work and the values of those who do it. But the function of carnival is not merely to denounce entrenched hierarchies and principles. As Bakhtin suggests, it also serves to illuminate the creative potential for genuine social upheaval: for a recasting of abiding customs and values.

Idleness was considered an ideological affront to industrial society well before American movies trumpeted the joys of shiftlessness.[14] Ever since Benjamin Franklin articulated a secular version of the puritan work ethic, American culture has been run through with cautionary bromides and exhortations about the relation between hard work and good character, and about the centrality of work to our moral life. In this work-besotted nation, individual enterprise and compulsive ambition are presented as the DNA of our national character: hence, the cultural suspicion of time away from work. At best, leisure pursuits are couched as what one does to recuperate from work; work is at the front and center of American existence and leisure is what fills the negative space not inhabited by work.

Because leisure is thought of as what one does when not working, in the popular imagination leisure and lack of work are sometimes seen as synonymous. But as Joanne B. Ciulla has pointed out in *The Working Life: The Promise and Betrayal of Modern Work*, there is a distinction between idleness as a willful act of rebellion against work and idleness as an enforced state resulting from lack of work. As she rightly says, 'People who have lost their jobs or cannot get jobs are not free *from* work. If anything they are *not free to* work, since they have little choice in the matter.'[15] Nonetheless, in the romanticized Hollywood versions of unemployment, joblessness is usually commensurate with leisure. In many of the comedies that feature unemployment, the major difference between the idle rich and the idle poor is that the former are better able to afford material comforts while the latter are better able to wallow in spiritual verities and pursuits. Both are generally more content with their state than are those working stiffs who are unlucky enough to dwell in between the class extremities represented by these avatars of joblessness.

In these movies, it is not just the idle rich who have the double, and enviable, boon of being free from labor *and* free from want.[16] Although the jobless protagonists may wear rags and occasionally go hungry, in keeping with the comic spirit, they experience few acutely felt threats to existence. The plots tend to revolve around not how the hero will fulfill basic material needs but how he will achieve spiritual transcendence, thereby throwing into relief the spiritual deprivation of those who toil. This endorsement of what historian Anson Rabinbach has called the 'enlightened glorification of contemplative idleness' begs the question of whether these films' portrayals of unemployment comprise a genuine interrogation of work as the measure of success or whether they merely traffic in the illusion of ideological challenge.[17] Their apparently oppositional stance toward the ideology of work as the essence of life is undercut by their glorified gloss on unemployment which rarely acknowledges the downside of joblessness. By muting the real significance of class distinctions, and by ignoring or romanticizing the real privations of unemployment, perhaps the films only seem like refreshing dissents from success myth orthodoxies.

Whether popular culture narratives collude in maintaining, rather than challenging, existing social relations and conditions, and whether they function to keep audiences complacent and self-satisfied, is the crux of an ongoing debate in film studies. Many seemingly provocative movies resolve themselves in an endorsement, rather than a critique, of the status quo. On second look, some of the films featuring unemployed characters seem less intent on critiquing the failings of the working life than on trumpeting the triumphs of maverick individualism. By suggesting that agency is achieved through autonomy rather than through collectivity, many of these movies endorse the idealized, if ideologically problematic, myth of the self-determining individual. Although they may offer pointed comments about the inhumanity of the industrial workplace and the enforced conformity of the working world, this subtext tends to take a back seat to their insistence that pluck and will – the can-do American formula for success – will see them through.

If, as Robert Warshow famously pointed out, the gangster is the American success myth writ large and the end-point embodiment of the credo of success at any price, then the succession of unemployed characters is a funhouse mirror distortion of the legions of other mythic iconoclasts in American movies who achieve success on their own terms and avoid identification with a community.[18] This is untrammeled individualism wearing a hobo's costume. Like the protagonists of films set in the corporate world, which are discussed in Chapter 2, these characters have the luxury of leaving the soul-killing workplace rather than sticking around and trying to turn it around. At bottom, many of these films are more of an endorsement of individualism than a critique of work. In Hollywood, individual solutions and escapist fantasies regularly trump genuine ideological heterodoxy. The suggestion that collective action and systemic overhaul are necessary to redress dissatisfactions with the working life is left for the rare films that deal seriously with labor issues and social change.[19] Most American movies that focus on the working life exhibit Hollywood's habitual hostility toward collective action or political solutions. Although they may not shy away from presenting sociological and economic problems, they raise these conditions only to have them magically resolved by individual self-assertion.

Of course, utopian, comic flights of fancy are not intended as designs for living or as calls to action. Rather, they are vicarious wish fulfillments that generally give us worry-free heroes, consequence-free actions, and ambiguity-free endings. As fantasies of the unemployed life, these films are cumulatively of interest less for how they resolve their would-be challenge to the apparatus of work than for what that challenge suggests about our collective confusion and anxiety about work as the basis of a successful life.

A number of theorists have written about the movies as a site for the mass audience's displaced latent desires.[20] That those desires are frequently unrealizable because they are essentially irreconcilable is a truism that our cultural myths tend to paper over. Robert Ray methodically applies to Hollywood movies Lévi-Strauss' notion of the reconciliatory function of myth: 'myths are transformations of basic dilemmas or contradictions that in reality cannot be solved.'[21] Ray finds that the thematic paradigm of American movies overcomes opposing desires by concealing the necessity to choose between them. In a discussion of *Citizen Kane*, he cites 'the irresolvable conflict between American myths of success (celebrating energy and ambition) and of the simple life (warning that power and wealth corrupt).'[22] Those movies that glorify unemployment bask in the wishful thinking that one can escape from work without missing what work provides: a sense of purpose and structure for one's life, a vocational identity, a professional community, and, on the material side of the equation, a paycheck and all that it can provide.

The apparent contradictions inherent in the success myth and the fissures in its attendant ideology are inscribed in a variety of comic movies spanning several decades. They vary in the extent to which they rattle or bolster the foundations of the myth. Writing about gross-out comedy, Geoff King has suggested that a hallmark of comedy is 'the dialectical exchange between subversion and reconfirmation' of cultural norms.[23] But he goes on to explain that 'Whether it is taken to be subversive, conformist, or an unstable mixture of the two, comedy that presents a transgression of dominant cultural norms can tell us a great deal about the conventions of the society in which it is produced.'[24] In the case of the comedies of unemployment, they can also tell us a great deal about our latent, and often contradictory, attitudes toward work and its lack.

Vagrants and Hoboes and Bums, Oh My!

It is unsurprising that the first cycle of films to posit unemployment as an exalted state arose during the Depression. A number of films from the early 1930s to the onset of the war indulged in this glorification of unemployment as a release from regimentation. From the 1930s onward, success in the movies was, as often as not, defined as freedom *from* work rather than *through* it. American films of this period are rife with a succession of happy-go-lucky hoboes and soulful tramps, whose spontaneity and integrity are contrasted with the spiritual deadness of their foils: miserable drudges and soulless tycoons. Long before the neologism 'workaholic' entered the American lexicon, ambition and dedication to one's job was frequently presented as a sort of pathology.[25] From the revealingly named *Hallelujah, I'm a Bum* (1933) to the appealingly titled *Holiday* (1939), unemployment is, if not always a state of grace, then an acceptable alternative to the rat race.[26] This view of joblessness offered reassurance to audiences of the time that being unemployed was preferable to being unhappily employed, and that lack of work at least gave one a shot at spiritual, if not material, fulfillment. Several historians have suggested that these films comprise a sort of mass placation that posits joblessness as a desirable, rather than a desperate, condition. In examining some of the films from that era, Peter Roffman and Jim Purdy contend that they pander to audiences by encouraging acquiescence to an economy rife with job loss and lack:

A number of paradoxes are played off against one another. To be wealthy is not impossible, since the American dream is still feasible; it is only undesirable because it makes you a snob. To be unemployed is not to be forced into want and suffering, but is a liberating choice made by all endearingly spontaneous eccentrics. While these films appear to be socially critical, dramatizing an apparent rejection of upper-class materialism, they are essentially offering the familiar rationalizations of the Depression status quo – that unemployment makes you a richer human being.[27]

Theirs is one of many suggestions that Depression-era comedies served as a sop to the un- or underemployed masses by demonizing the idle elites and pitying the hapless drones while sentimentalizing the (often involuntarily) idle little people.

Hallelujah, I'm a Bum, released during the depths of the Depression, could be considered the urtext for films that glamorize unemployment. Its credits are a roster of A-list talent: director Lewis Milestone, whose preceding films included the much lauded *All Quiet on the Western Front* (1930), *The Front Page* (1931), and *Rain* (1932); writers Ben Hecht and S.N. Behrman; composer Richard Rodgers and lyricist Lorenz Hart; star Al Jolson as the eponymous bum and silent movie comedian Harry Langdon as the resident contrarian.[28] Although the film performed poorly at the box office, its title phrase and song became part of the vernacular of the times, and Jolson's genial tramp became the *beau ideal* for an enduring stock character. With its dialogue comprised mostly of rhyming couplets and its genre status a strange hybrid of melodrama, social commentary, and musical comedy, *Hallelujah, I'm a Bum* is a film oddity. But as a cultural artifact of the Depression zeitgeist, it is a fascinating document of the American-style uplift-cum-denial that threads through movies about joblessness.

Jolson plays a self-proclaimed bum named Bumper (aka 'The Mayor of Central Park') who sums up his *raisons d'être* as 'panhandling, manhandling, inebriation, and repopulation.' Although he does indeed live a marginal existence in Central Park, he is not entirely an outsider, and he is more indifferent than hostile to social conventions. When, later in the film, he asks his friend, a rabid communist, what he thinks of Angel, the woman that Bumper has fallen in love with, the latter says, 'She dresses like a capitalist,' to which Bumper shoots back, 'Some of my best friends are capitalists!' Indeed, he is friends with the mayor (Frank Morgan) who, like him, prefers leisure to work, and who gives him regular handouts, seemingly because he envies Bumper's carefree life. The film doesn't miss an opportunity to make fun of the pomposity and hypocrisy of public officials, while also aiming cynical barbs at both capitalists and communists. Although Bumper doesn't work (he calls himself 'a gentleman of leisure without money'), the film's opening finds him, like the mayor, on vacation in Florida where, he proudly claims, 'I always spend the season.' On his homecoming to his Central Park haunts, he gathers his fellow bums with a whistle and proudly sings the title anthem (the lyrics of which include 'I love to breathe the air and feel I'm free ... I never have to care what becomes of me ... I don't give a stitch if I never get rich .... When a bank will crash, I don't lose my cash ... I find great enjoyment in unemployment').

Bumper's life of ease is contrasted with the traditions and travails of various strata of the social world of New York. While the mayor dines at the elegant Central Park casino (like his model Jimmy Walker, whose reign as mayor and man about town came to an end as the film was in production), Bumper and his lunch mate sit outside, using a garbage can for a dining table. And while Bumper whiles away the hours, his nemesis Egghead (Harry Langdon) picks up trash in the park and harangues its shiftless denizens with party-line Bolshevism ('Those rich, idle shirkers who live on us workers ... You're parasites all, you're brothers in crime. When the revolution comes you won't sit pretty ... the workers will rule the world someday ... your socks and pants may have holes, but you're plutocrats down to your souls'). With its intermingling of the high and low born and its interchanging of values, Central Park in the film certainly qualifies as one of Bakhtin's carnivalesque sites. There the social world is turned upside down with bums and plutocrats living with – and off of – each other.

Figure 5.1 Bumper (Al Jolson) sings of his disregard for money and employment. *Hallelujah, I'm a Bum* (1933). Directed by Lewis Milestone

When Bumper later finds $1000, he explains his decision not to keep it in yet another emphatic expression of the bums' creed: 'What Do You Want With Money?' ('Money is a curse. It's risky business and worse...you're better off just broke'). This production number is the occasion for the movie's most bizarre moment: an Eisenstein montage of angry bums, replete with colliding shots and extreme close-ups of synecdochic body parts. In spite of the clear invocation of Eisensteinian aesthetics, the political sensibility of *Hallelujah, I'm a Bum* is anti-agitprop, as it encourages the audience not to go out and agitate but, instead, to appreciate their lot in life and to aspire to nothing more than what they have. By making fun of politicos as well as plutocrats, the movie remains true to Hollywood's 'reelpolitik' in which individual freedom is paramount, and political convictions or communal actions are either laughably futile or alarmingly suspect.

Into the middle of this beggar's operetta, Hecht and Behrman drop an overwrought love story involving the mayor, his mistress, Bumper, and an unseen other man. When the mayor accuses his beloved of two-timing him, she throws herself off a bridge in the park, only to be rescued by Bumper – who promptly falls in love with her – and to become conveniently amnesiac. The ensuing love triangle seems notably beside the point; as is often the case in films where the major agenda is to ballyhoo the blithe spirit of the unemployed protagonist, the love interest is merely a prod for the main character's brief and unsatisfying foray into the world of work. Bumper's compatriots make known their disapproval of his intention to join the working world so that he can take care of his lady love. The bums stage a kangaroo court, which the movie's creators use as yet another occasion for work-bashing. Bumper is accused of deserting the cause of happy unemployment; he pleads guilty to this 'repulsive offense' and is acquitted because he is declared insane. After he does take the job – in a bank, no less – he declares to his sidekick Acorn, 'It feels good to have money in your pocket,' to which Acorn, like a true work shirker, replies, 'Yes, but you waste so much time getting it.'[29]

The oddly abrupt ending of the movie seems to defy both comic conventions and the film's portrait of unalloyed insouciance. Once Angel's memory is restored, Bumper regretfully but graciously cedes her to the mayor. His brief paroxysm of ambition behind him, he returns to the park. The final long shot shows a dejected Bumper separated, in the mise-en-scène, from his trusty partners in sloth. This is certainly not 'as it should be' according to the precepts of comic endings, and his sylvan home and enviably carefree life are presented as meager recompense for losing his girl. But the lingering impression of the film comes not from the histrionic plot or its ambiguous resolution, but from the imprint that the Jolson character and his devil-may-care existence made on the American imagination. The compelling image of unemployment as a state of grace spoke to a collective desire to believe such simplistic formulations and to rely on the movies to redress the inconsistencies and irreconcilabilities in our attitudes toward work and leisure that our lives cannot.

The glorification of unemployment and the concomitant ambivalence toward work is crystallized in the films that Charlie Chaplin made during the Depression. Since his entry into film, Chaplin had used the tramp character to cast light on the follies of work, ambition, and conformity. The titles alone of many of his two-reelers betray an ongoing meditation on work: *Making a Living* (1914), *His New Profession* (1914), *His New Job* (1915), *Work* (1915), *Easy Street* (1917), *The Idle Class* (1921), *Pay Day* (1922).[30] Throughout the 1920s, Chaplin honed his representation of work. Typically, in his movies, the tramp is by definition unemployed and by temperament unemployable.[31] On the rare occasions when Charlie does have a job, work is not depicted as productive labor. Rather, work is a necessary evil: a self-perpetuating and point-less exercise. For example, in *The Kid* (1921), the tramp maintains his window-repair business by having his sidekick, an adorable urchin, toss stones through people's windows so that, moments later, the tramp can offer to repair them. Likewise, in *The Gold Rush* (1925), when Charlie needs money he devises a scheme whereby he gets paid to shovel snow from a doorway only to pile it onto the next stoop, thereby keeping his job prospects alive.

Although sound became the norm in the movies by the late 1920s, well into the 1930s Chaplin kept his silent tramp character as the per-fect avatar of Depression-era anxieties about the centrality of work as a measure of one's worth.[32] In his two masterpieces, *City Lights* (1931) and *Modern Times* (1936), Chaplin continued to muse on the ideology of work and the notion of unemployment as a preferable alternative. In both films, unemployment is hardly depicted as an exalted state; hunger and homelessness are the norm for the tramp character and his fellow vagabonds, and the degradations of life on the street loom large alongside the films' comic set pieces. But each of Charlie's reluc-tant forays into the world of work is so disastrous and humiliating that, in comparison, joblessness is posited as the lesser of two evils.

The opening of *City Lights* finds the tramp comfortably and obliv-iously dozing on a statue while a civic ceremony takes place around him. As in most of Chaplin's *oeuvre*, idleness is the tramp's natural state; like an underclass *flâneur*, he aimlessly roams the city with a seeming lack of ambition as he loiters without intent. Charlie eventually takes on employment not to better his own plight but only to help some-one else: in this case a blind girl with whom he is smitten. His first job involves picking up the droppings of the various animals that stroll the city streets. From the outset, it is clear that the tramp is minimally invested in his work and his lack of commitment is greatly exacerbated when an elephant lumbers by. Immediately after Charlie is fired from that job for habitual lateness, a low life asks him if he wants to make some easy money and he agrees to a rigged boxing match in which both participants will evenly split the purse. Since the universe in Chaplin's films is unfailingly hostile, the plan naturally goes awry and, after a hys-terical and highly choreographed boxing match, Charlie ends up being knocked out. In spite of his best intentions, the tramp is clearly not cut out for any sort of paid labor. As Gerald Weales has so vividly put it, 'the juxtaposition of the two work sequences suggests…give up your independence and you may end up either shoveling shit or having it knocked out of you.'[33]

The series of jobs that Charlie lands in *Modern Times* offers no less bleak a vision of work life. The film opens with an ironic intertitle that immediately declares its perspective on work by describing what follows as: 'A story of industry, of individual enterprise, humanity crusading in the pursuit of happiness.' *Modern Times* is an anomaly among Chaplin's features since the tramp character is first introduced to us wearing not his usual glad rags, which are a parodic take on the habiliments of a gentleman of leisure, but in worker's overalls since, uncharacteristically, he is gainfully employed on a factory assembly line. But from the outset it is apparent that industry and individual enterprise are emphatically unhappy pursuits. Following the opening titles, we see a visual simile equating men going off the work with sheep to the slaughter. The factory where Chaplin works has turned its workers into cogs in its Rube Goldberg-like machinery.[34] While the company boss does jigsaw puzzles, interrupting himself only to order the assembly line to speed up, the workers perform their repetitive tasks like automated puppets. Twice in the film, workers are bodily sucked into a huge mechanical apparatus, and the famous feeding machine sequence puts a fine point on the inhumanity of industry's drive for greater productivity and efficiency.

Factory employment, the film tells us, denies its workers the satisfaction of seeing a job through from start to finish, denies them any break from their work,[35] and even denies them workers' solidarity, as the employees inevitably turn on each other when things go awry with the process. The tramp regains his humanity and individuality after being swallowed up and then spit out by the machine; only then does he recover from his assembly line-induced twitch, and as he begins to move balletically rather than mechanically, the tramp's familiar spirited defiance of conformity returns. Of course, this most reasonable response to the drudgery of the assembly line is deemed crazy and Charlie is promptly fired and hauled off to an insane asylum.

The tramp goes through four more jobs in the film – ship builder, night watchman in a department store, machinery repair assistant, and singing waiter – and, until the last, he fails at each. A game but inept employee, he clearly prefers the life of the streets. In what is arguably the film's most radical critique of modern times, the tramp is pictured as being happier in jail, where he is housed, fed, and left alone, than out, where he has to fend for himself. As in *Hallelujah, I'm a Bum* and *City Lights*, the jobless character pursues employment primarily to help his love interest, an orphaned gamin who is his spiritual counterpart. After the two share a fantasy of bourgeois contentment and plenty, Charlie declares, 'I'll do it! We'll get a home even if I have to work for it.' The tramp does have middle-class aspirations, but he ultimately refuses to put himself through what he has to do to achieve them. Although in both films he is clearly identified with the lower class, he reveals himself as a sort of bourgeois-wannabe. He is happy, in *City Lights*, to align himself with the intermittently benevolent millionaire and to enjoy the perquisites of wealth. In *Modern Times*, although he satirizes the joys of a settled, affluent life, he is also wistful about its blandishments. Like Jolson's character, his liminality allows him to sample and imagine alternative identities and lives.

In spite of Chaplin's famously leftist political stance, his films of the 1930s often espouse an essentially individualist, every-man-for-himself credo as the route to survival in a social Darwinist world. Indeed, although his films exhibit a great deal of class consciousness, they reveal little class solidarity. Whereas Jolson's bum had a coterie of vagabonds to provide collectivity and social connection, Charlie makes his way without a community of fellow sufferers. As the quintessential survivor, the tramp is used to sticking up for himself. In one of *City Lights'* funniest moments, Charlie drives the rich man's car but, spying a cigar butt on the sidewalk, leaps at it and instinctively shoves another hobo out of the way to claim his prize. Twice in *Modern Times*, Charlie opportunistically pushes to the front of a crowd in order to get a job. When he does manage to land employment, his fellow workers are consistently hostile and competitive. And although he is twice hauled off to jail after mistakenly being identified as a protest leader, he has little use for or awareness of political or collective action. When a workers' strike puts an early end to one of his jobs, the tramp expresses only dismay at being once again out of work. Throughout his *oeuvre*, Chaplin seems more interested in individual struggle than in social struggle. As in many films that extol the joys of joblessness, to the extent that there is a political stance, it tends to be libertarian: leave the bum alone to make his own way in the world, however antagonistic to his individualist spirit that world may be.

In both *City Lights* and *Modern Times*, there is a damned-if-you-do-damned-if-you-don't sense of work, and the films' famously ambiguous endings remain unresolved about how to balance personal needs and societal demands. Chaplin clearly privileges joblessness over employment as a more humane and spiritually fulfilling state, but his depiction of unemployment is far from rosy, and he repeatedly acknowledges that being without a job has real consequences. Unemployment may signify independence and autonomy, but it also involves hunger and homelessness, and a lack of connection and sense of purpose. *Modern Times'* veritable obsession with hunger and food is a motif that undercuts its romanticization of the hobo's life. Likewise, in *City Lights*, the preoccupation with where the tramp sleeps runs throughout the film, and in both movies, the material conditions of the tramp's existence come to the fore. Although Chaplin's major subtexts involve the nature of love, friendship, and dignity, these musings on spiritual fulfillment are balanced by a clear-eyed concern with material survival that keeps the films from becoming wholly maudlin about the joys of idleness.

Unemployment as a lifestyle choice is, in essence, a patronizing notion that offered audiences of the time a comforting – if evanescent – rationale for their involuntary plight. To equate the decision not to work with the inability to find or keep a job is a cynical ploy in the depths of the Depression, as if a narrative reassurance that it's not so bad after all can contradict the day-to-day privations and indignities of joblessness. But Chaplin's manifest ambivalence about work – about the opportunities and oppressions of modern times and city life – saves his films from indulging in a purely sentimental view of unemployment. That Chaplin equates unemployment with spiritual salvation and the working life with servitude and materialism; that he rejects the existing social order but doesn't posit much in its place; and that his characters, in the end, retreat from society rather than trying to reform it doesn't indicate a failure of consistency or vision. Rather the films' ambiguities are at the crux of our ongoing national discourse about the culture's contested notion of work and social identity.[36]

The joys of joblessness

That discourse carried through to several other types of film in the 1930s. The screwball comedy genre, with its daffy heiresses, gruff tycoons, and unlikely couples, who often achieve union through their shared mastery of playfulness, offered a further demonstration of the movies' starry-eyed stance toward joblessness. Unlike the otherworldly tramps of Jolson and Chaplin, who were seemingly born to be unemployed, many of the middle-class characters in the screwball comedies had to earn their unemployment the hard way: by suffering through the travails of work before achieving deliverance from it. Other films of the period carried on with the spirit of the earlier tramp characters but couched their narrative not on the streets, the tramp's domain, but in domestic settings.

Several of Frank Capra's films from the 1930s and early 1940s celebrate the boon of joblessness; even when his characters are employed, much of his film output insists that one's professional identity should take a back seat to one's identity as part of a community of like-minded souls.[37] His most vivid exploration of the pleasures of the non-working life is *You Can't Take It with You* (1938), a ludic treatise *par excellence* and an ensemble comedy that offers a veritable rogue's gallery of dilettantes, amateurs, and eccentrics. The title of this paean to escapism betrays the movie's philosophy toward the fruits of one's labors. Characters who work are, at best, benighted and are beset with all manner of work-related woes, both physical and spiritual. This movie sports a fat cat businessman who is plagued with stomach troubles and a real estate man bedeviled by a stress-induced eye twitch. Here characters are literally sickened by their toil, as if ambition itself were a sort of nervous tic.

The story involves the romance of Tony, a high-born young man (James Stewart), whose father (Edward Arnold) is a business tycoon and whose mother (Mary Forbes) is a dyed-in-the-wool snob, and his love interest Alice (Jean Arthur), whose large family is comprised of irrepressible bohemians.[38] The Sycamore household is a den of liminality where three generations of adults engage in perpetual play. Apart from Alice's job as a stenographer, the family has no visible means of support, although it is revealed that many years ago Grandpa Vanderhof (Lionel Barrymore) turned his back on a successful business career and developed an expertise in stamp collecting, which seems to yield a meager income. In spite of their lack of money, the family enjoys a large house, plentiful meals, servants, and all the time in the world to pursue their passions. Even infirmity is taken in stride; although Grandpa broke his leg while sliding down a banister on a dare from his granddaughter, with characteristic good cheer he confides that ever since he was a kid he wanted to play on crutches.

Like many comedies of the period, *You Can't Take It with You* is a story of individual redemption in which the professionally fixated characters need to overcome their repression of desire in order to be spiritually reborn.[39] The Sycamore household is a home for wayward workers, several of whom come for a visit and, lured by the siren song of idleness, end up permanently joining the festivities. As more than one character gets seduced by the felicities of the non-working life, the film suggests that everyone has a secret, better self longing to emerge from under the guise of the working professional. Grandpa, who is taken to speechifying about success and failure, is the mouthpiece for Capra's musings, and much of the dialogue amounts to proselytizing for unemployment and for indulgence in one's passions as the route to self-actualization and happiness. Unemployment is presented as a spiritual calling and there is a quasi-religious undercurrent to this gospel

Figure 5.2   Members of the Sycamore household opt for play over work. *You Can't Take It With You* (1938). Directed by Frank Capra

of fun. Much of Grandpa's dialogue suggests that joblessness is next to godliness, and that God smiles on – and takes care of – those that devote themselves to their own pleasure.[40]

Following the precepts of conventional romantic comedy, the film ends with the eleventh hour reconciliation of opposing forces as Tony's parents are brought into the fold after they drop both their resistance to the young lovers' union and their upper-class, uptight ways. As Northrup Frye drily noted, 'Comedy regularly illustrates a victory of arbitrary plot over consistency of character.'[41] To achieve this ideal ending and reveal his authentic self, Tony has to quit his job in order to be worthy of Alice and her family. Whereas in the comedies that center around jobless outcasts, the main character may reluctantly sign on to a job not out of concern for his own material wellbeing but in order to win or support his girl, in *You Can't Take It with You* and several other romantic comedies of the period, the male protagonist has to renounce work in order to make himself deserving of the affections of his more freewheeling mate.

Of course, forswearing work and embracing a life of leisure and pleasure is easy if there is a family fortune behind the decision. So many of the films about unemployment hedge their bets by endorsing their characters' repudiation of work without even hinting at any problems that might attend the lack of a job. The characters that choose self-realization over work get to flirt with freedom while still being wed to the security that their privileged backgrounds provide. By blithely ignoring any real consequences of choosing unemployment, these films deny the imperative to balance the desire for freedom and self-expression with the need to be fed, clothed, and housed. In accordance with the comic spirit, the tensions between personal and professional exigencies, and between license and restraint, are magically resolved. Characters get to be spiritually *and* materially satisfied with no sacrifices in either area, and audiences get to indulge in the pipe dream of having it all.

Further, when the idealized endings mute the divisiveness of class distinctions, they suggest that there is little significant difference between the haves and the have-nots. Even the bum and tramp characters of the early 1930s are often presented as flipside entrepreneurs, making their way in the world through determination, resourcefulness, and connections. In these movies, being down and out is, after all, not so different from being on the upside of success in terms of the personal qualities needed to survive and thrive. In some ways, the idle rich and the idle poor cancel each other out as characters with any real claim on our concern: the former are not so bad after all and the latter are not so bad off after all.

Although the settled bourgeois existence and the careerist course are discredited in film after film, the characters that pursue those paths are often presented as curable of their materialism and their workaholic pathology. What makes comedy delightful is the intrinsic suggestion that both characters and societies are capable of changing for the better: of achieving 'this should be' status. *You Can't Take It with You* is such a captivating fantasy not just because of the eccentric charms of the family of happy dropouts but also because of its insistence that everyone – even the putative successes – has a shadow self that would like to chuck it all and pursue a happy-go-lucky, work-free life. The dissident lower-class idler and the consummate insiders represented by the leisure class are brothers under the skin; it is the lowly workers, tethered to their jobs and incapable of giving license to their authentic selves, who seem hopelessly aberrant in the comic cosmos.[42]

George Cukor's *Holiday* (1938), which was briefly discussed in Chapter 2's consideration of voluntary downward mobility, offers yet another protagonist who flips into reverse during his climb up the ladder of success. Johnny Case (Cary Grant) is a self-made man and proud of it. Although he thinks that having money is 'a pleasant accomplishment,' when he announces his intention to retire young and 'save part of my life for myself,' his fiancée, Julia, scoffs at it saying, 'You don't know how exciting business can be...there's no such thrill in the world as making money,' and her financier father accuses Johnny of being 'a young dreamer' which, in his book, is an insult. Since, in comedies, young dreamers always get to realize their reveries, we recognize that Johnny will end up leaving his job and his planned future with Julia. Although the audience knows the outcome right from the outset, Johnny has to come around to the need to cast off his ambitions and let his inner child emerge.

Indeed, *Holiday* couches its musings about what makes for a contented life in a series of scenes contrasting childishness and adulthood. Like many of the films that celebrate unemployment (and, for that matter, like much of American popular culture), this one presents adulthood as a grim affair while promoting child-like whimsicality and irresponsibility as something to be cultivated.[43] These movies' insistently unemployed characters' refusal to settle into adult responsibility is a cinematic strain of the impulse cited by Leslie A. Fiedler in his seminal work *Love and Death in the American Novel* in which he pinpointed the American nostalgia for childhood innocence and the fantasy of fleeing from the demands of maturity.[44] In the comic universe, *homo ludens* is the ideal; *homo faber* (man the maker or laborer) is the negative indicator of how to live one's life.[45] Whenever they emerge from their hideout, the Seton siblings are infantilized by their paternalistic father who will not stand for any challenge to his authority or his values. Until Johnny comes along as catalyst, these adult children experience the worst of both worlds: like children, they have no power, and like adults, they have no fun.

The plot of *Holiday* presents contrasting, and simultaneous, engagement parties: one in the adult quarters, which one character compares to a ghostly museum, and one in the old playroom where, once Johnny happens in, he, Linda, and Linda's brother Ned perform acrobatics, play with puppets, make music, and generally comport themselves like children at play.

The film also gives us opposing world views: one that values money, status, decorum, and steadfastness and one that privileges imagination, play, self-expression, and escape. Not for nothing does *Holiday* end on New Year's Eve. Reborn with the new year, Johnny recognizes his love for the unconventional Linda and his disdain for the life that Julia and her father represent. He quits his job, ditches Julia, and, with Linda, sails away to a better life – a perpetual holiday. The flight from the settled life is presented as a hard-won victory. Like many other characters who opt for unemployment, Johnny exercises control over his fate by surrendering his job. The notion that one seizes rather than cedes control by being unemployed is a fond illusion that, even during the Depression, was remarkably impervious to real-life experiences to the contrary.

Although most of the job-chuckers in the late 1930s and early 1940s movies were middle or upper class, the lower-class wastrel did make occasional reappearances during this period. *The Magnificent Dope* (1942), for example, combines the liminal loafer figure of the early 1930s with a romantic comedy plot. Fiancés Dwight Dawson (Don Ameche) and Claire Harris (Lynn Bari) run a success school that is, alas, failing. They cook up a contest to find the biggest failure in the United States and make a success of him by schooling him in their techniques, thereby garnering some much needed publicity. Lured by the $500 prize money, Thaddeus 'Tad' Page (Henry Fonda), who describes his occupation, such as it is, as an occasional 'boat renter-outer,' sends in an application declaring, 'My ambition, if I've got any, is just to continue doing what I'm doing and living the way I'm living.' His letter explains that he is entering the contest not out of his own interest in the prize money but only so he can buy a fire engine for his town. He believes that entering contests is the only way he can get cash since getting a paying job would be against his better interests: 'Being a success is a job in itself . . . it wouldn't give me time to do the things I like to do.' Dwight and Claire are dumbfounded by what they dub his 'lazy man's philosophy' and his complacency about doing nothing. Needless to say, he wins the contest. Concluding that he is too contented, they decide that the first thing they need to do is to make him dissatisfied.

This send-up of self-help programs echoes the components of the earlier comedies of unemployment: a laidback bum, a rich industrialist who is reformed by his interaction with said bum, a woman for whom the bum grudgingly takes a job, and a comic resolution that reveals the bum's philosophy to be the right-thinking one. Realizing that 'We didn't pick the biggest failure . . . we picked the happiest guy in the United States,' Claire naturally falls in love with Tad and breaks off with Dawson. The film's final image reveals that the success school has reinvented itself as a business that teaches people how to relax.

Underneath this amiable portrait of an artless young man is a sharp satire that mocks not only the ideologies surrounding work and success but also the American doctrine of reinvention and continuous self-improvement. Dale Carnegie's *How to Win Friends and Influence People*, which is arguably the granddaddy of self-help books, was published in 1937 and became an instant bestseller. Carnegie's promotion of what has come to be known as 'people skills' as the key component of financial success became the business gospel. With its anti-materialism, its skepticism about ambition (Tad philosophically points out, 'I've known a lot of go-getters... been pallbearer to about ten of them') and its disparagement of the sort of unctuous, glad-handing bonhomie that Carnegie endorses, *The Magnificent Dope* is a bit of apostasy to that gospel.

The figure of the contented bum and the comedy of unemployment appeared less frequently during the war and early post-war years only to re-emerge in the late 1950s beat era and the countercultural 1960s. Although the Depression period offered the most concentrated collection of films extolling the joys of the jobless life, throughout the ensuing decades many movies of this ilk maintained their grip on the American imagination by continuing to engage in flights of fancy about the blessings of being out of work. Together, they speak to the persistence of our collective yearning for something better – or something other – than our work lives and selves.

Dropouts and slackers

Although the decades following the war are identified, in the popular mind, with the explosion of youth culture, some of the comedies of unemployment that best capture the era's zeitgeist involve mid-career characters coming to grips with their midlife malaise and their cynicism about professional success. In several of the corporate workplace movies of this period, the reactive flight toward unemployment and away from the repressive corporate ethos comprises the coda of the film. *The Apartment* (1960), for one, offers a comic take on a young executive who, in the film's final moments, realizes he needs to shed his executive skin to expose his authentic self. Several other films with workplace settings similarly highlight the oppressive nature of work in late capitalism by positing dropping out as an act of self-assertion. In these stories, characters willfully choose to leave the game because the price of winning is too high. Professional failure is presented as nobler than life as a wage slave; in Hollywood's simplistic trade-off, material and spiritual success is often an either/or proposition. Particularly telling of the 1960s anti-establishment ethos are films in which the character's unemployed status is the starting point and centerpiece of the plot, providing yet another occasion for the privileging of the work-free existence over the working life.

A Thousand Clowns (1965), adapted from the hit Broadway play by Herb Gardner, proffers yet another iconoclastic jobless protagonist whose non-working status throws into sharp relief the oppressions and repressions of the world of employment. This stage-bound adaptation relies mostly on its self-consciously clever dialogue to convey its take on the soul-numbing acquiescence required to make one's way in the work environment. Its one bit of visual expressivity comes with the title sequence. Murray Burns (Jason Robards), a New York-based children's television writer who quit his job five months ago, tells his nephew that 'In a moment you're going to see a horrible thing – people going to work.' This is followed by a series of shots of crowds marching lockstep to their jobs while the soundtrack blares military music. Overhead long shots alternate with sidewalk level views of legs and feet trudging along, with nary a facial close-up in sight. Together these shots deindividuate and disparage those poor drudges whose quotidian routine involves slogging off to the daily grind.

This sequence, which is repeated at intervals throughout the film, sums up *A Thousand Clowns'* none-too-subtle outlook. Those who work are conformist dupes; those who opt out are free-spirited, clear-sighted visionaries. Although the movie does inject some balance to this view in the characters of Murray's nephew, brother, and lover, all of whom urge him to grow up and get a job, our sympathies are clearly steered toward the unsocialized charmer who evades conventional behavior and adult responsibilities. Once again, the protagonist is an adult-sized child – a middle-aged kid, as another character calls him – who spends his days playing: flying kites, yelling witticisms at empty streets, throwing confetti at ship launchings. When someone urges him to return to reality for a moment, he replies, 'I'll only go as a tourist.' Many of the jokes in the movie revolve around the role reversal of uncle and nephew. The latter reads the want ads, ingratiates himself to those in authority, and worries that Murray is becoming a bum, while the former obstinately insists on continuing to play as the social service net descends on their household.

The film's closure is an inside-out take on conventional comic endings. Rather than turning his back on work to find himself, Murray sells out and suits up, returning to his hated job in order to retain custody of his nephew. Like his unemployed movie brethren before him, he grudgingly goes to work only out of love, not out of ambition or material want. But unlike most of them, he is there to stay, since his custody arrangement is contingent on his job security. It is a defeatist ending for a comedy – a 'this should not be' capitulation to the values that the movie has decried, which suggests that the dropout ethic is not as sustainable as one might wish.

When *A Thousand Clowns* was released, film critic Pauline Kael called it 'romantic crackpotism – harmless American nonconformity.'[46] Those are charges that could be levied at many of the comedies of unemployment. These films flirt with bohemianism and with the lottery-like fantasy of being free from work and also being free from want. Their plug for iconoclasm does not have much heft since these characters are fairly toothless and non-threatening vis-à-vis the social order. Indeed, many of them are quite well assimilated in spite of their eccentricities, with friends in high places and material needs well tended. Further, although we are encouraged to place our dramatic sympathies with the characters who evade work, most of them are so otherworldly that we are not meant to identify with them. They function not as behavioral models but as sentimentalized symbols of our uneasiness when confronted with the dialectic between labor and leisure, toil and pleasure. These films do not so much endorse the jobless existence as they enunciate questions about the place of work in our lives and offer appealing, if unrealizable, fantasies about reconciling our opposing desires.

Virtually all of the dropout characters get by on what might be labeled their cuteness quotient. Chaplin's tramp, Jolson's bum, Grandpa Vanderhof, and even Murray Burns are a common type in American cultural narratives: the lovable oddball who, while endearingly off-beat, is effectively neutered and marginalized by his difference. He cannot be taken too seriously as a challenge to ideological or behavioral norms. In the comedies of unemployment, these characters function as mascots in the game of success. They are there to amuse us with their costumes and their antics while we take occasional breaks from tallying who is winning in the race to the top. Their connotative function is not to offer unemployment as an authentic alternative but, rather, to represent our confusions, frustrations, and desires in regard to work, success, money, conformity, and personal agency.

The period's most winsome pet bum appeared not in the movies but on the television sitcom *The Many Loves of Dobie Gillis* (1959–63). Beatnik Maynard G. Krebs and his plaintive cry 'Work!' is, as David Sterritt points out in *Mad to Be Saved: The Beats, the 50s, and Film*, a lampoon of the nonconformist rebel. His cuteness quotient is high and his threat potential concomitantly low. As Sterritt explains,

> The indolence, aimlessness, and insouciance attributed to Beats by mainstream opinion would be perceived as humorous and appealing (if not laudable or enviable) if embodied by a suitably sweet character... as a specimen of the Beat Generation, he was a caricature whom right-thinking Americans could laugh into inconsequentiality every single week.[47]

Such characters are part of a long tradition in American popular culture of undercutting any challenge to conventional behavior or values by couching it as harmless eccentricity rather than as genuine ideological insurgency.

In some of the latter-day movies that focus on the unemployed, the countercultural character does have teeth, but the narrative nonetheless manages to dull his censorious bite. *Down and Out in Beverly Hills* (1986), directed by Paul Mazursky, offers up a bum with fangs who is eager to sink them into the flesh and soul of his haute-bourgeois hosts. At first glance, the film appears to be another familiar tale of an enlightened dropout. The central character is a homeless and jobless drifter named Jerry Baskin (Nick Nolte), a man of strong appetites, weak morals, and bad hygiene. When he loses his only companion, a mangy cur, he tries to commit suicide in the perfectly tended pool of a Beverly Hills millionaire. Out of a combination of bobo guilt and *nostalgie de la boue*, the businessman and his *nouveau riche* family more or less adopt the bum. He moves in and then proceeds to move in on each of the initially repulsed characters. Predictably, he connects with and brings spiritual and/or sexual satisfaction to every heretofore-neurotic member of the household, including their pampered dog.

But unlike the early 1930s vagrants, Jerry is neither sweet nor harmless. He is much more of a trickster character, less holy fool than all-knowing tempter. The trickster, a common archetype in myths and legends from across the globe, is a schemer and a breaker of taboos. Through guile, he unmasks the arbitrariness and foolishness of social codes and mores. The trickster is profoundly liminal and adaptable, which accounts for his ability to worm his way into varied situations. Carl Jung writes of the trickster as a primitive, animal-like being who has the animal's cunning and survival skills as well as the animal's lack of consciousness.[48] In many versions of the trickster myth, he is also the epitome of animalistic libido. Most of the early movie bums

Figure 5.3   Vagrant Jerry Baskin (Nick Nolte) indulges his animal appetites. *Down and Out in Beverly Hills* (1986). Directed by Paul Mazursky

are desexualized, which contributes to their transcendental quality. Although Jolson's character longs for the girl, he is unsurprised and resigned when she leaves him. Chaplin also pines for togetherness with his female characters but his yearning seems more for companionship than for sexual union. But Jerry is all animalistic id: he beds all three of the females in the household and even gets down on all fours to share the dog's food from his bowl. Much less ingenuous than the earlier tramp characters, he manipulates each situation to his advantage and uses his wiles to satisfy his wants.

The film's plot premise and its contrast between the bum and his benefactors – between bohemian authenticity and bourgeois hypocrisy – is loosely based on Jean Renoir's *Boudu sauvé des eaux* (1932). But as Janice Morgan points out in her astute comparison of the two films, *Down and Out in Beverly Hills* blunts its own satirical edge by backing away from the clear-cut perspective of Renoir's and others' films that equate joblessness with personal freedom and integrity.[49] In most of the movies with jobless protagonists, there is no question about who lays claim to the moral and spiritual high ground or whose choices are the right ones. In Mazursky's movie, there is the familiar longing of the working characters for the carefree life of the unemployed bum. But it is countermanded by the bum's easy acquiescence to the life of material ease and excess represented by Beverly Hills: the Mecca of Mammon. Morgan writes that 'this bum is soon commodified into a much more glamorous – and especially, more expensive – version of leisured freedom...this is the kind of freedom only money can buy.'⁵⁰ Although the movie's exposition efficiently trashes the moneyed class, the camera sensuously caresses their icons of plenty. As in many of Hollywood's would-be social critiques, the panoply of material goods up on the screen holds a greater claim on our attention and admiration than the moralistic verities of the script. Our voyeuristic enchantment with the good life prevails over the script's claim that maybe it is not so good after all. Although the movie traffics in such comic conventions as the mixing of classes and the unmasking of characters, the comic milieu is less Bakhtin's carnival than a tantalizing trade show where high born and low come to ogle the consumer wares together.

The earlier characters' joblessness was intrinsic to their being; they were not so much lazy as philosophically devoted to the conviction that, in order to be their own person, they had to avoid the social and occupational demands of work. But here, Jerry's idleness is revealed to be not a matter of principle but a streetwise strategy to live parasitically off others. Whereas the family considers him a charity case, he acts like an entitled guest. The ending of the film, when he threatens to leave but, with remarkably little urging, decides to stay, epitomizes the thematic paradigm by suggesting that irrevocable and exclusive choices are sidestepped in American movies. In the conclusion's opportunistic quid pro quo, the family gets to continue grafting their fantasies of escape onto Jerry while feeling benevolent and safely bohemian, and Jerry gets to continue indulging his omnivorous appetites. Together, the bum and the businessman are presented as social Darwinist survivors, scratching each other's backs while patting themselves on the back in self-satisfaction. The film glamorizes both unemployment and opulence, as it seems to suggest that, in the booming mid-1980s, spiritual fulfillments and moral imperatives are merely quaint.

Morgan's reading of the ending concludes that this is cynicism masquerading as subversion. Indeed, although the ending gives us a tentative reconciliation of opposing forces, in other ways it does not measure up to the conventions of comic subversion in which a flawed social order is replaced by a superior, right-thinking one. Instead, with its suggestion that the bum got himself a good gig with good benefits, the ending reinstalls and reconfirms the flawed values of the existing social order. In that, the film is more satire than conventional comedy.

Considered in the context of earlier films in this mode, the ending could be taken as an attempt to demystify and deromanticize the tramp figure for a more cynical age. In many of the earlier films, including Chaplin's and Jolson's, if the society is untransformable and the jobless outsider is unable or unwilling to conform, the best that he can do is exile himself in order to maintain his incorruptibility, not to mention his unemployability. But in Mazursky's more clear-eyed, if despairing, view there is no principled dropping out of the competition for success and survival. The escapist fantasy of the earlier films is replaced with a more jaundiced and opportunistic answer to the bum's plight: if you don't want to work, you had better come up with a workable scam. The ending seems to endorse a creed that might be summed up as, 'If you can't beat 'em, exploit 'em.' This is, indeed, cynical but, as a commentary on its times, it is also dead-on.

The work-averse refusenik crops up in other guises in the age of commodity capitalism. Sometimes he is a middle-aged malcontent who opts for underemployment rather than unemployment, as he knowingly bails out of his career in order to search for what he hopes are more authentic satisfactions (*Five Easy Pieces* (1970), *Lost in America* (1985), *American Beauty* (1999)). Alongside these disaffected midlife dropouts are legions of slackers who range from teenagers to young adults (*Stranger Than Paradise* (1984), *Dazed and Confused* (1993), *Clerks* (1994), *Reality Bites* (1994), *Mallrats* (1995), *Kicking and Screaming* (1995), *Slackers* (2002)).[51] Spiritual descendents of the earlier bums and tramps, they may not yet have entered the workforce but they are nonetheless precociously anti-work. If they are, in fact, employed they are likely to be underemployed in service jobs, in spite of being well educated. The anti-work stance in this period loses its class associations and gets embraced by middle-class characters as one more lifestyle option. Although the stakes of joblessness do not seem as acute, the joys do not either. Whereas the earlier embodiments of the anti-work ethic were presented as less neurotic and more contented than those who worked, the slacker characters are a mass of neuroses and insecurities.

Even though the slacker film does not reach full flower until the 1990s, there are scores of proto-slackers in the post-war decades. The beats and angry young men of the 1950s and the hipsters and anti-establishment college kids of the 1960s pointed the way for the slackers' indulgence in in-your-face rebellion against the drive for professional stature and identity.[52] Just as the title character in *The Graduate* (1967) cannot quite decide what he wants, other than sex, from his post-college life, the do-nothing slackers both flout work and, all the while, agonize about their inability to commit to a career path and therefore a secure social identity. Like the earlier embodiments of the anti-work ethic, they represent the wistful yearning for flight from the work world, and they are generally – and usually unironically – presented as morally superior to the adult sellouts. But unlike the Depression-era escapees, who seem congenitally and ingenuously indisposed to work, these characters have a self-conscious, self-righteous edge. Unemployment is still glorified as preferable to wage slavery, but there is a new sense of weary resignation to the Hobson's choice between career ambition and job stagnation. Many of the slacker characters lack the courage of their anti-work convictions, so their defiant avoidance of work has the quality of a last fling or, perhaps, a stay of execution. The fantasy of escape has soured somewhat, and there is often, in these films, a looming sense of submission to the need to grow up and get a job.

Reality Bites (1994) is a typical entry in the slacker canon. The main characters are a group of newly post-college malcontents whose McJobs include convenience store clerk, chain store clerk, and underpaid, overqualified production assistant for a hopelessly middlebrow television show. For these arrested adolescents, work is emphatically not fulfilling or identity defining; rather, it is something to be endured. As the slackers go kicking and screaming into dreaded adulthood, the adult characters are characteristically irrelevant to their quest for meaning. Parents and employers are, at best, clueless fools or preening meanies. (The heroine's dad diagnoses her anomie by announcing, 'The problem with your generation is you don't have any work ethic.') The plot revolves around a romantic triangle in which the protagonist needs to declare herself by choosing between a careerist nerd and a smug slacker who telegraphs his intellectual depth by reading Sartre's *Being and Nothingness* in his spare time, of which he has plenty. Although he is, at one point, described by another character as a 'master of time suckage,' his refusal to buy into the requisites and perquisites of the work world is meant to be taken as a sign of integrity and dignity. As he tells the young woman who is at the apex of the triangle: 'I'm a bum … but I'm the only real thing that you have.'

In *Reality Bites* and its slacker cohort, the gloss has gone out of joblessness, and the rallying cry is no longer, 'Hallelujah, I'm a bum' but something closer to, 'What the hell … I'm unemployed but at least I'm not a sellout.' The self-absorption and pretensions of the slacker films notwithstanding, they are not entirely distinct from earlier equations of joblessness with righteousness. Although the milieu, tone, and intended audience may differ, the basic valuation is the same: working is bad, not working is good because it signifies release from social control. The slacker-equivalent of the beginning of the twenty-first century continues to define himself by a determined lack of ambition; he is often intermittently employed or underemployed (e.g., *The 40 Year Old Virgin* (2005), *Greenberg* (2010)) or working in a proudly countercultural milieu while turning his back on conventional notions of professional success (e.g., *High Fidelity* (2005)). Each generation crafts its own version of the glorification of unemployment, and collectively these movies comprise compelling diachronic evidence of a deep-seated unease with work as an indicator of self-worth and as a guarantor of the good life.[53]

In an essay analyzing that unease, titled 'Work and Its Discontents,' Daniel Bell once argued that in America, 'Dissatisfactions on the job lead[s] not to militancy, despite occasional sporadic outbursts, but to escapist fantasies....'[54] Those fantasies, which equate unemployment with leisure, creativity, and personal agency, find their realization and validation in our mass-mediated myths and narratives. By reifying the wishful thinking of a work-weary populace, the movies harbor the displacement of our collective lack of certitude about the place of work in our lives and in the formation of our individual and social identities. They perform the essential cultural task of negotiating our desires, and they function as a site for illuminating – if not resolving – the perplexity at the heart of our notions of work and success.

Conclusion

A culture's forms of escape, if they can be called escape, are as significant and revealing as its social criticism.
— Morris Dickstein, *Dancing in the Dark*

In 2008, journalist Malcolm Gladwell published another in his string of bestselling books that purport to explain diverse phenomena by identifying an overarching, one-size-fits-all analytical frame. Like his previous books, *Outliers: The Story of Success* had a simple, single, and, claimed Gladwell, broadly applicable aperçu: that success stems not solely from ambition and talent. He tried to demonstrate in his case histories that individual success is, instead, heavily reliant on chance: a convergence of fortuitously optimal circumstances that allow those with ambition and talent to thrive. He further claimed that biographical accounts of self-made success are a bit of a sham since they tend to ignore the substantial contributions of other people – parents, wives, teachers, mentors, colleagues, communities – that lie behind our stories of individuals who make good. As Gladwell explained, '[Highly successful people] are products of history and community, of opportunity and legacy. Their success is not exceptional or mysterious. It is grounded in a web of advantages and inheritances, some deserved, some not, some earned, some just plain lucky – but all critical to making them who they are.'[1]

This is hardly an epiphany. Several scholars who have written about the ethos of American individualism have pointed out that success is often attained through cultural advantages and through the indispensable involvement of a network of other people and support systems.[2] Even Horatio Alger included luck, along with assistance from benefactors and family members, as a crucial factor in the ascendancy of his characters. But Gladwell's challenge to the gospel of self-making was greeted with critical hosannas and bestseller status, as if he had just stumbled upon some heretofore hidden secret of American life. Of course, this is a secret hidden in plain view, not just in our daily experiences but in those enduring stories about success that have often comforted but sometimes also discomfited us for generations. As the foregoing chapters demonstrate, Gladwell's is far from the first treatise on individual success that is fraught with qualifications.

At around the same time that Gladwell's book was enjoying its perch at the top of *The New York Times* bestseller list, the Indian movie *Slumdog Millionaire* (2008) was packing in audiences and winning awards, most notably the Academy Award for Best Picture. This unlikely tale of an Indian street kid who, through smarts, goodness, and an array of credulity-straining coincidences, achieves his dreams tapped a vein in the American body politic. Although *Slumdog Millionaire* was produced in India and has elements of that country's indigenous Bollywood cinema, its rags-to-riches saga is firmly in the mold of the American success myth, which is among our most widespread and ideologically significant exports. Despite the movie's provenance, it clearly spoke to American audiences in an idiom that was familiar from scores of other movies. This heart-warming, life-affirming (if ridiculously far-fetched) fantasy of success told an old story in a new guise and, like Gladwell's book, it was greeted as fresh and exciting by critics and audiences alike.

These competing takes on the success myth – one embodying it in its purest form and the other challenging it for its oversimplification, one giving rise to hope and the other to skepticism – have coexisted in the American mind from the myth's beginnings. We embrace the bromides of the success myth, all the while harboring doubts about its promises. Both perspectives are strands in a densely woven, if not always logically coherent, narrative about success and American identity. This bifurcated stance toward success runs side-by-side throughout the history of Hollywood, sometimes within a single telling of the tale. Many of the movies explored in the preceding chapters trumpet up-by-one's-bootstraps individualism but also acknowledge that individual success involves many contingencies and compromises. They tap into the essential duality at the heart of our cultural rhetoric about the American idea of success; the exhilarating sense of freedom to craft our own destinies co-exists with anxiety, bafflement, and disappointment about the limitations of personal agency in fulfilling our ambitions and balancing our material and spiritual desires.

The American cinema's enduring tendency to flaunt these heterogeneous cultural elements in narrative form fulfills our collective need for a public space in which we can work through the success myth's tensions and confusions.[3] To adapt F. Scott Fitzgerald's oft-quoted maxim about the ability of a first-rate intelligence to hold two opposed ideas in mind simultaneously and still function: the success myth's ability to entertain pairs of opposed ideas at the same time is a mark of that myth's function and ability as cultural mediator. In his investigation of the rags-to-riches myth, James Catano echoes Claude Lévi-Strauss' formulation of the purpose of such mythic binaries:

> The constitution of the myth... rests on the sociocultural need to dramatize the ambivalent desires and conflicting goals that are part and parcel of personal and social growth, or, more accurately, the performing of a particular subject position.... The paradoxical power of a myth lies precisely in the fact that it engages specific psychological and social conflicts even though it cannot resolve them. Nor is this engagement an act of self-delusion, an escapist ritual that addresses ineffable mysteries beyond the reach of a culture's descriptive power. The contradictions can be unmasked and experienced as contradictions. A cultural myth is no more and no less than an effectively constructed, rhetorical enactment of the social and psychological conflicts that it embodies.[4]

In other words, it is precisely *because* the myth is so riven by contradictions that it reverberates in American culture and fires our imagination. Those stories and biographies that bear out the myth's promises bestow on us the pleasure of identifying with our aspirations rather than with our situations. They sustain our belief in the myth of self-making even if the achievements of the few do not seem to be replicable by the many. Conversely, those stories that complicate the myth's truisms allow us to process our wariness about the myth's credibility. Varied versions of the success myth continue to resonate because they gratify these contradictory needs. By alternately nurturing the myth and questioning its veracity, and by narrativizing our hesitations as well as our hopes, these movies, in aggregate, perform vital cultural work by comprising a collective rumination about the nature of success in America. They are cultural artifacts whose significance as mediators of our values accrues incrementally and cumulatively, if imperceptibly.

Lévi-Strauss pointed out that 'Myths operate in men's minds without their being aware of the fact.'[5] The success myth's vision of ambition and achievement saturates the culture and is encoded in our self-image as Americans. That vision has become common currency: part of the imaginative capital that we exchange unthinkingly. Rarely do we consciously examine the myth's assumptions or consider the extent to which we have internalized its expectations. In terms of the success myth, the point of intersection where individual lives, social norms, and cultural artifacts collide is underexplored terrain. This is partly because movies, the primary bearers of the myth in contemporary times, seem to be the most inconsequential of cultural artifacts: entertaining but hardly worth taking seriously as ideological arbiters. Nonetheless, how we think about success in our own lives is deeply conditioned by how success is defined and presented in the recurring tropes of our popular cultural narratives.

Stories matter. In Hollywood, they matter because they sell, and tried-and-true formulas such as the rags-to-riches saga make good business sense. But in the culture at large, they matter because, whether we care to admit it or not, they shape our sense of possibility and our sense of the world. They matter because they tell us what is on our minds. Contemporary cultures, as much as ancient ones, displace their social concerns onto mythic stories and those stories become the repository of our collective desires, apprehensions, and confusions. The stories that a culture repeatedly tells are the stories that it needs in order to make sense of itself. Those stories generate, validate, and mediate norms that guide our thoughts and actions. Mythic narratives are the cultural glue that binds us to one another and to our sense of ourselves as embodiments of a cultural ethos. They are part of our civic discourse, all the more compelling when conducted under cover of Hollywood movies.

One of the most pointed and persuasive recent calls to attention regarding cultural narratives is sociologist Robert Wuthnow's 2008 book *American Mythos: Why Our Best Efforts to Be a Better Nation Fall Short.*[6] Wuthnow begins by declaring that,

> The deep narratives that shape our sense of national purpose and identity are so firmly inscribed in our culture that we usually accept them without thinking much about them.... Cultural narratives and collective mythologies play such a powerful role in the shaping of social life that we must be more reflective about the assumptions that govern our lives.[7]

America is both nation and notion: an entity defined by our political system, demographics, geography, and history but also determined by the communal experience of our national mythology and the cultural narratives that channel it. Wuthnow advocates what he calls 'reflective democracy': a deliberate, contemplative engagement with cultural narratives and the values that they transmute into stories and transmit repeatedly. Such reflection necessitates an active critical unmasking that denaturalizes the pervasive norms and assumptions embedded in familiar mythic stories. It is akin to the concept that Russian formalist Viktor Shklovsky called *ostranenie:* to make the familiar strange again so as to see its devices and suppositions.[8] Shklovsky applied the term to works of art but it is equally pertinent to the intentions of hermeneutics and to the enterprise of critical engagement. In Wuthnow's formulation, we must defamiliarize the beliefs that are embedded in contemporary myths and examine them for what they can reveal about our culturally constructed credos.

This book is written in that spirit and with that intent: to tease out and make legible the insistent, but sometimes implicit, attitudes toward success that infuse our cultural narratives and that, not incidentally, also underlie our national self-image, our public discourse, and our personal choices. What we often assume to be societal consensus about the definition of and path to success seems much less consensual when cinematic versions of the success myth are held up for inspection. Americans' faith in individualism, self-making, social mobility, and the entrepreneurial spirit is intact in movies that traffic in the myth, but so is a nagging twinge of self-doubt. The cultural evidence of these paradoxical proclivities is found in the recesses of success myth stories. In a reflective democracy, it is incumbent upon us to map that imaginative sphere.

Notes

1 Top of the World: Cultural Narratives, Myths, and Movies

1. F. Scott Fitzgerald, *The Great Gatsby* (New York: Scribner, 1925), 2.
2. Benedict Anderson, *Imagined Communities: Reflections on the Origin and Spread of Nationalism* (London: Verso, 1991), 205.
3. See, for example, Homi K. Bhabha, *Nation and Narration* (London: Routledge, 1990); Ernest Gellner, *Nations and Nationalism* (Ithaca, NY: Cornell University Press, 1983); David Miller, *On Nationality* (Oxford: Clarendon Press, 1995); and Arash Abizadeh, 'Historical Truth, National Myths and Liberal Democracy: On the Coherence of Liberal Nationalism,' *Journal of Political Philosophy* 12, no. 3 (2004): 291–313.
4. Bruce Lincoln, 'Mythic Narrative and Cultural Diversity in American Society,' in *Myth and Method*, Laurie L. Patton and Wendy Doniger, eds. (Charlottesville: University Press of Virginia, 1996), 168.
5. This linkage of myth with narrative is by no means universal among myth theorists. Roland Barthes' influential book *Mythologies* (New York: Hill and Wang, 1972) speaks of myth as a language: a semiotic system of recurring associative significations. Although the definition of myth is much debated, the majority of writers still insist that myth should be understood as having a basis in narrative.
6. The term was coined in 1931 by James Truslow Adams in his book *The Epic of America*: 'The American Dream is a gay dream that dreams of a land in which life should be better and richer and fuller for everyone, with opportunity for each according to ability or achievement. It is a difficult dream for the European upper classes to interpret adequately, and too many of us ourselves have grown weary and mistrustful of it. It is not a dream of motor cars and high wages merely, but a dream of social order in which each man and each woman shall be able to attain to the fullest stature of which they are innately capable, and be recognized by others for what they are, regardless of the fortuitous circumstances of birth or position.' James Truslow Adams, *The Epic of America* (New York: Simon Publications, 2001), 32. In spite of the hopefulness of the coinage, the book was a critique of industrial capitalism that cast doubt on simplistic formulas for success. For an extended discussion of Adams' idea, see Jeffrey Louis, *Made in America: Self-Styled Success from Horatio Alger to Oprah Winfrey* (Minneapolis, MN: University of Minnesota Press, 1997).
7. Robert A. Segal, *Myth: A Very Short Introduction* (London: Oxford, 2004), 6.
8. Bronislaw Malinowski, *Myth in Primitive Psychology* (New York: Greenwood Publishing, 1979), 101.
9. Laurie L. Patton and Wendy Doniger, eds. *Myth and Method* (Charlottesville, VA: University Press of Virginia, 1996), 13.

10. Ernst Cassirer, *The Myth of the State* (New Haven, CT: Yale University Press, 1961), 296.

11. This point was made by David Bidney, 'Myth, Symbolism, and Truth,' in *Myth: A Symposium*, Thomas A. Sebeok, ed. (Bloomington, IN: Indiana University Press, 1972), 12.

12. Wendy Doniger, *The Implied Spider: Politics and Theology in Myth* (New York: Columbia University Press, 1998), 22.

13. Ibid., 80.

14. This linkage of ideology and myth is derived from Louis Althusser's definition of ideology as 'a system…of representations (images, myths, ideas, or concepts, depending on the case), endowed with a historical existence and role within a given society.' *For Marx* (London: Verso, 2006), 231.

15. In *The Sacred and the Profane: The Nature of Religion*, Mircea Eliade argues that moderns have myths and that myths are pan-human and 'ineluctable.' He goes on to claim that there has been no real secularization of myth but that, instead, religion and myth are just 'camouflaged' in contemporary forms: 'A whole volume could well be written on the myths of modern man, on the mythologies camouflaged in the plays that he enjoys, in the books that he reads. The cinema, that "dream factory," takes over and employs countless mythical motifs. The modern man succeeds in obtaining an "escape from time" comparable to the "emergence from time" effected by myths…projects him out of his personal duration and incorporates him into other rhythms, makes him live in another "history".' *The Sacred and the Profane*, trans. Willard R. Trask (New York: Harcourt, Brace, Jovanovich, 1987), 205.

16. Christopher G. Flood, *Political Myth* (London: Routledge, 2002), 42–3.

17. Ibid., 34.

18. Robert B. Ray, *A Certain Tendency of the Hollywood Cinema, 1930–1980* (Princeton, NJ: Princeton University Press, 1985). Ray was not the first to apply Lévi-Strauss' ideas to film. In an article appearing in 1973, Charles W. Eckert demonstrated how Lévi-Strauss' structural analysis of mythic oppositions could be used to illuminate the 1930s melodrama *Marked Woman* (1937). In Eckert's analysis, *Marked Woman* is structured around a central dilemma (having to do with class distinctions), and then extrapolates from that dilemma to focus on layered pairs of oppositions that radiate out from the primary pair. In writing about the proliferation and evolution of mythic oppositions, Eckert says, 'Two of Lévi-Strauss' insights are especially provocative: that a dilemma (or contradiction) stands at the heart of every living myth, and that this dilemma is expressed through layered pairs of opposites which are transformations of a primary pair. The impulse to construct the myth arises from the desire to resolve the dilemma; but the impossibility of resolving it leads to the crystal-like growth of the myth through which the dilemma is repeated, or conceived in new terms, or inverted – in short subjected to intellectual operations that might resolve it or attenuate its force.' Charles W. Eckert, 'The Anatomy of a Proletarian Film: Warner's "Marked Woman," ' *Film Quarterly* 27, no. 2 (Winter, 1973/4), 18. Other film theorists of the period whose work was informed by Lévi-Strauss include Peter Wollen, *Signs and Meaning in the Cinema* (London: Martin Secker and Warburg, 1969),

and Jim Kitses, *Horizons West* (Bloomington, IN: Indiana University Press, 1970).

19. Claude Lévi-Strauss, *Structural Anthropology*, Vol. 2 (Chicago: University of Chicago Press, 1983), 208.
20. For a provocative historical overview of American exceptionalism, see Godfrey Hodgson, *The Myth of American Exceptionalism* (New Haven: Yale University Press, 2009). Also see Seymour Martin Lipsett, *American Exceptionalism: A Double-Edged Sword* (New York: W.W. Norton, 1996).
21. Slotkin's third volume on the frontier myth in the twentieth century explicitly engages film as he analyzes several movie versions of the frontier myth. Richard Slotkin, *Gunfighter Nation: The Myth of the Frontier in Twentieth-Century America* (New York: Atheneum, 1992).
22. Richard Slotkin, *Regeneration Through Violence: The Mythology of the American Frontier, 1600–1860* (Middletown, CT: Wesleyan University Press, 1973), 23.
23. Richard Slotkin, *The Fatal Environment: The Myth of the Frontier in the Age of Industrialization, 1800–1890* (New York: Atheneum, 1985), 19.
24. Slotkin, *Gunfighter Nation*, 659.
25. Slotkin, *Fatal Environment*, 16.
26. Ibid., 24.
27. Ibid., 87.
28. This brief summary of success in American thought and culture relies on a number of detailed histories of success. For more thorough accounts of the evolution of the success myth, see Jeffrey Louis Decker, *Made in America: Self-Styled Success from Horatio Alger to Oprah Winfrey* (Minneapolis: University of Minnesota Press, 1997); Irvin G. Wyllie, *The Self-Made Man in America: The Myth of Rags to Riches* (New York: The Free Press, 1954); Rex Burns, *Success in America: The Yeoman Dream and the Industrial Revolution* (Amherst, MA: University of Massachusetts Press, 1976); Richard Weiss, *The American Myth of Success: From Horatio Alger to Norman Vincent Peale* (New York: Basic Books, 1969); John G. Cawelti, *Apostles of the Self-Made Man: Changing Concepts of Success in America* (Chicago: University of Chicago Press, 1965); Micki McGee, *Self-Help, Inc.: Makeover Culture in American Life* (Oxford: Oxford University Press, 2005); Richard M. Huber, *The American Idea of Success* (New York: Pushcart, 1987); Loren Baritz, *The Good Life: The Meaning of Success for the American Middle Class* (New York: Harper and Row, 1982); Martha Banta, *Failure and Success in America: A Literary Debate* (Princeton: Princeton University Press, 1978). Further, Moses Rischin, ed. *The American Gospel of Success: Individualism and Beyond* (Chicago: Quadrangle Books, 1965), anthologizes several primary source documents pertinent to the history of the American success myth.
29. Cotton Mather, 'A Christian and His Calling' (1701), reprinted in *The American Gospel of Success*, 23–30.
30. As Richard Weiss has written, ' "the rags-to-riches" tradition, by creating an illusion of opportunity, served as a social pacifier inimical to reform. Furthermore, by equating failure with sin and personal inadequacy, self-help popularizers obscured the objective cause of social injustice.' Weiss, *The American Myth of Success*, 7.

31. For an excellent discussion of failure in America, see Scott A. Sandage, *Born Losers: A History of Failure in America* (Cambridge, MA: Harvard University Press, 2005).
32. Benjamin Franklin, 'The Way to Wealth' (1758), reprinted in Rischen, *The American Gospel of Success*, 33–38.
33. The term itself was first used by Henry Clay on the floor of the Senate in 1832. In a defense of business enterprise, Clay declared: 'In Kentucky, almost every manufactory known to me is in the hands of enterprising and self-made men, who have acquired whatever wealth they possess by patient and diligent labor.' Calvin Colton, ed. *The Works of Henry Clay* (New York: VA.S. Barnes and Burr, 1857), V, 464.
34. *The Adams-Jefferson Letters: The Complete Correspondence between Thomas Jefferson and Abigail and John Adams*, Lester J. Cappon, ed. (Chapel Hill: NC, University of North Carolina Press, 1988), 387.
35. Self-help manuals and fictional versions of the success myth have existed side by side since the early nineteenth century. It is worth noting that whereas the self-help guides tend to simplify the formulas for success, when the myth gets rendered in fictional form, it gets more problematized and its irreconcilable values get acknowledged more consistently.
36. Ruth Miller Elson, 'American Schoolbooks and Culture in the Nineteenth Century,' in *The National Temper: Readings in American Culture and Society*, 2nd edition, Lawrence W. Levine and Robert Middlekauff, eds. (New York: Harcourt Brace, 1972), 113–131.
37. William Holmes McGuffey, *McGuffey's Newly Revised Eclectic Third Reader* (Cincinnati, OH: Winthrop B. Smith, 1843), 175.
38. Cawelti, *Apostles of the Self-Made Man*, 62. Cawelti points out that, contrary to popular belief, most of the sentimental novels of the nineteenth century, including those of Alger, suggest that success is, first and foremost, a matter of fate: 'Although the self-help books insist that individual qualities of character are the key to success, in the novels one can hardly find a single instance where industriousness, frugality, and piety are the operative factors in the hero's rise in society ... the hero's problems are solved by a kind of magic rather than by a clearly envisioned process of cause and effect.'
39. Weiss claims: 'Correctly understood, Alger is not a representative of his time but a nostalgic spokesman of a dying order. Of middle-class rural origins, he was always an alien in the industrially dominated society of his adulthood ... Alger remained a truer spokesman of the era of his birth than that of his maturity.' Weiss, *The American Myth of Success*, 49.
40. Cawelti, *Apostles of the Self-Made Man*, 169. Cawelti sees a distinct break in the success ethic in this period: 'The virtues appropriate to a society in which most men were farmers, artisans, or petty capitalists were not so evidently relevant in a society of large organizations ... the popular philosophy of self-improvement gradually changed, accommodating itself more closely to the needs of business enterprise and the large corporation. The main trend in the development of ideas of self-help was away from the earlier balance of political, moral, religious, and economic values and in the direction of an overriding emphasis on the pursuit and use of wealth.'

41. In his study of the period, Alan Trachtenberg articulates the new ethos: 'Measured against the antebellum work ethic, the robber barons seemed aggrandizers, rather than honest and frugal producers. Success literature hid this conflict in melodramatic victories over the unscrupulous capitalist, but could not eliminate it altogether. The popular image of the business world held unresolved tensions: on one hand, it seemed the field of just rewards, on the other, a realm of questionable motives and unbridled appetites.' *The Incorporation of America: Culture and Society in the Gilded Age* (New York: Hill and Wang, 1982), 80.

42. Weiss, *The American Myth of Success*, 9–10.

43. The most influential and widely cited discussion of this idea was economist and sociologist Thorstein Veblen's notion of conspicuous consumption: people consume to signal their wealth and incite social envy. *The Theory of the Leisure Class* (London: Oxford University Press, 2008). For a consideration of how Hollywood movies see consumer culture and the accumulation of commodities as the markers of success, see David Desser and Garth S. Jowett, eds. *Hollywood Goes Shopping* (Minneapolis, MN: University of Minnesota Press, 2000).

44. Decker, *Made in America*, 78.

45. Although the precise attributes and parameters of Hollywood's classical era have been a matter of ongoing debate among film scholars, one of the most lucid explanations of the term appears in David Bordwell, Janet Staiger, and Kristin Thompson, *The Classical Hollywood Cinema* (New York: Columbia University Press, 1985).

46. Lévi-Strauss, 'The Structural Study of Myth,' in *Myth: A Symposium*, Thomas A. Sebeok, ed. (Bloomington, IN: Indiana Unversity Press, 1968), 105.

47. Not incidentally, it also coincided with rapid urbanization and immigration. A number of film historians have written about the role of movies in acculturating new Americans and instilling them with an understanding of what it means to be American. See, for example, Steven J. Ross, *Working Class Hollywood: Silent Film and the Shaping of Class in America* (Princeton, NJ: Princeton University Press, 1998).

48. Anderson, *Imagined Communities*, 24.

49. Slotkin, *Regeneration Through Violence*, 19–20.

50. Slotkin, *The Fatal Environment*, 19.

51. For extended discussions of the strategies of Hollywood endings and narrative closure, see Richard Neupert, *The End: Narration and Closure in the Cinema* (Detroit: Wayne State University Press, 1995). For a basic taxonomy of types of closure, see, for example, David Bordwell, *Making Meaning: Inference and Rhetoric in the Interpretation of Cinema* (Cambridge, MA: Harvard University Press, 1989). Also in his classic work *Narration in the Fiction Film*, Bordwell discusses the inadequacy and implausibility of many Hollywood endings, which he calls 'a more or less arbitrary readjustment of that world knocked awry in the previous eighty minutes.' *Narration in the Fiction Film* (Madison, WI: University of Wisconsin Press, 1985).

52. Fredric Jameson, *The Political Unconscious: Narrative as a Socially Symbolic Act* (Ithaca, NY: Cornell University Press, 1982), 53.

2 Moving Up and Moving On: Mobility and the American Success Myth

1. Chuck Kleinhans, 'Working-Class Film Heroes: Junior Johnson, Evel Knieval and the Film Audience,' in *Jump Cut: Hollywood, Politics and Counter Cinema*, Peter Steven, ed. (New York: Praeger, 1985), 66.
2. http://www.boxofficemojo.com/movies/?id=pursuitofhappyness.htm
3. The precise on-screen claim is that the movie is 'inspired by a true story.' The biography of the man who inspired it varies significantly from what we see in the film. A few of the movie's reviewers noted this discrepancy and pointed out how Hollywood movies based on true stories play fast and loose with facts to suit their ideologies and narrative agendas: http://www.chasingthefrog.com/reelfaces/pursuitofhappyness.php
4. These 'two faces of capitalism' in film were noted by Robin Wood, 'Ideology, Genre, Auteur,' in *Film Genre Reader II*, Barry Keith Grant, ed. (Austin, TX: University of Texas Press, 2003), 65.
5. James V. Catano, *Ragged Dicks: Masculinity, Steel, and the Rhetoric of the Self-Made Man* (Carbondale, IL: University of Illinois Press, 2001), 158.
6. See Martha P. Nochimson, *Dying to Belong: Gangster Movies in Hollywood and Hong Kong* (Malden, MA: Blackwell Publishing, 2007), for a trenchant discussion of performativity and the fragmentation and discontinuity of identity in gangster films.
7. Leslie Fiedler, *Love and Death in the American Novel* (New York: Stein and Day, 1966).
8. Catano, *Ragged Dicks*, 9.
9. Catano goes on to define masculinity as 'a willful struggle to separate, leave origins behind, and move toward the places and goods whose possession denotes a place at society's top rather than its bottom,' 158.
10. Manohla Dargis, 'Climbing Out of the Gutter with a Five-Year-Old in Tow,' *The New York Times*, 15 December 2006, arts section.
11. *The Pursuit of Happyness* is an obvious echo of an earlier film about an unemployed father who trolls the streets with his son. According to the website *Cineuropa*, Gabriele Muccino, the Italian director of *The Pursuit of Happyness* sent Will Smith a DVD of the Italian neo-realist classic *The Bicycle Thief*, directed by Vittorio de Sica, before they began shooting the film. So both director and actor were seemingly aware of de Sica's film as an antecedent. But whereas *The Bicycle Thief* acknowledges the desperation that results from dire poverty, this movie acknowledges it only to insist that it can be overcome by doggedness. The contrast between the two films' final scenes – one ends with the central character shamed and at a dead end while the other ends with its character triumphantly beginning new life – encapsulates the variance in the films' visions and intentions. http://cineuropa.org/newsdetail.aspx?lang=en&documentID=72032
12. In his article, 'Ideology, Genre, Auteur,' Robin Wood claims that success and wealth comprise 'a value of which Hollywood ideology is…deeply ashamed, so that, while hundreds of films play on its allure, very few can allow themselves openly to extol it.' So many films contain what Wood calls the 'ideological shadow' of cheery success myth stories. 'Ideology, Genre, Auteur,' *Film Comment* 13, no. 1 (January–February 1977): 46–51.

13. In his 1974 article, Kleinhans identified 'two stages of bourgeois ideology dealing with success,' and differentiated between what he called 'the naïve success myth' and 'the sophisticated or ironic success myth.' But stories that complicate or qualify the basic assumptions of the success myth are often neither particularly ironic nor narrationally or ideationally sophisticated. Many of the most trenchant critiques of the myth's assumptions appear in canonical Hollywood movies that, in their formal and narrative properties, hew to familiar conventions. Kleinhans, 'Working-Class Film Heroes,' 14.

14. Barbara Klinger, ' "Cinema/Ideology/Criticism" Revisited: The Progressive Genre,' in *Film Genre Reader II*, Barry Keith Grant, ed. (Austin, TX: University of Texas Press, 1995), 79.

15. Three of the most detailed and insightful analyses of the film were written in the 1970s and 1980s when close analysis of classic Hollywood films was hitting its stride. See Robert B. Ray, *A Certain Tendency of the Hollywood Cinema, 1930–1980* (Princeton, NJ: Princeton University Press, 1985); Robin Wood, 'Ideology, Genre, Auteur,' *Film Comment* 13, no. 1 (1977): 46–51; and Ray Carney, *American Vision: The Films of Frank Capra* (West Nyack, NY: Cambridge University Press, 1986).

16. James Agee, *The Nation*, February 15, 1947.

17. The movie is structured as a frame tale, with the story of George's life contained in the inner narrative. Since the outer frame is precipitated by George's suicide attempt, the audience is aware, from the outset, that something has gone awry in his life story. Therefore, our interest in his unfolding biography is focused not just on what happened to him but how he got to the point of suicide.

18. In *Restless Nation: Starting Over in America* (Chicago, IL: University of Chicago Press, 2000), James M. Jasper makes the point that the infrastructure of America, with its vast system of roads, is itself a symbol of progress and possibility.

19. For a good introduction to the significance of the road in American film, see David Laderman, *Driving Visions: Exploring the Road Movie* (Austin, TX: University of Texas Press, 2002).

20. Ray, *A Certain Tendency of the Hollywood Cinema*, p. 189.

21. Carney, *American Vision*, 39.

22. Ibid., 410–12.

23. Ibid., 424.

24. As Kleinhans writes in his article on working-class heroes, 'When members of the working class find their aspirations impossible to achieve yet still accept the prevailing ideology of individualism, the result is self-blame,' 66.

25. Jasper, *Restless Nation*, 7. He goes on to discuss how the geographical hugeness, lack of population density, and plentiful natural resources encouraged movement and equated mobility with opportunity.

26. Ray, *A Certain Tendency of the Hollywood Cinema*, 182.

27. Wood, 'Ideology, Genre, Auteur,' 66–8.

28. Ray, *A Certain Tendency of the Hollywood Cinema*, 212.

29. Ibid., 202.

30. Ibid., 192.

31. Peter Stead, in *Film and the Working Class: The Feature Film in British and American Society* (Oxford: Routledge, 1991), identifies popular culture's

'vague belief in the common man and a moral if politically neutral criticism of the abuse of wealth.' He goes on to note 'how easy it was to tell stories that would be sympathetic to the common man, that would condemn all truly evil men and their agencies, and yet at the same time would do nothing other than confirm existing social values,' 22.

32. Peter Roffman, *The Hollywood Social Program Film: Madness, Despair, and Politics from the Depression to the Fifties* (Bloomington IN: Indiana University Press, 1981).
33. Gwendolyn Audrey Foster, *Class-Passing: Social Mobility in Film and Popular Culture* (Carbondale, IL: Southern Illinois University Press, 2005), 17–18.
34. Jack Boozer calls this recurring pattern 'rise-and-fall overreacher narratives' and focuses his discussion on promotional hucksterism in films of the 1950s. Jack Boozer, *Career Movies: American Business and the Success Mystique* (Austin, TX: University of Texas Press, 2002), 165.
35. More often than not, success sagas in which the protagonist is beyond youth depict a character who is weary, defeated, and past his prime as a mover and shaker. The many movies that consider success at advanced age come in a variety of modes: comic (e.g., *In Good Company* (1984)), melodramatic (e.g., *Save the Tiger* (1973)), and tragic (e.g., *Death of a Salesman* (1951 and remade several times for television)).
36. A thorough list of biopics up until the early 1990s can be found in Eileen Karsten, *From Real Life to Reel Life: A Filmography of Biographical Film* (Metuchen, NJ: Scarecrow Press, 1993). For analytical considerations of the genre, see Dennis Bingham, *Whose Lives Are They Anyway?: The Biopic As Contemporary Film Genre* (New Brunswick, NJ: Rutgers University Press, 2010) and George Custen, *Bio/Pics: How Hollywood Constructed Public History* (New Brunswick, NJ: Rutgers University Press, 1992).
37. The two film biographies of composer/lyricist Cole Porter provide a case in point of the tendency of contemporary biopics to foreground the wages of sin and success in a way that earlier films did not. See *Night and Day* (1946) and *De-Lovely* (2004).
38. Showbiz biopics have had a resurgence in the past few decades. Among the many titles that traffic in the rise-and-fall pattern are *Lady Sings the Blues* (1972), *Lenny* (1974), *The Buddy Holly Story* (1978), *Coal Miner's Daughter* (1980), *Mommy Dearest* (1981), *Frances* (1982), *Sweet Dreams* (1985), *Sid and Nancy* (1986), *Bird* (1988), *Great Balls of Fire* (1989), *What's Love Got to Do with It* (1993), *Ray* (2004), *Beyond the Sea* (2004), *De-Lovely* (2004), *Walk the Line* (2005), and *Cadillac Records* (2008).
39. The film's basis in and faithfulness to the life of newspaper baron William Randolph Hearst has been investigated by many writers, including Laura Mulvey, *Citizen Kane* (London: BFI Publishing, 1992), and Simon Callow, *Orson Welles: The Road to Xanadu* (New York: Penguin, 1995).
40. For an introduction to scholarship about the alliance between cinema and consumer culture, see David Desser and Garth S. Jowett, eds. *Hollywood Goes Shopping* (Minneapolis, MN: University of Minnesota Press, 2000).
41. Throughout Hollywood history, story after story preaches the ascendancy of spiritual over material values while image after image presents us with a veritable department store of goods to lust after. In a sense, this is a shrewd ploy. We leave the movies feeling both ennobled by our identification with

characters who choose the right – if financially unrewarding – path and simultaneously titillated by the vision of goods which can only be acquired and enjoyed through financial expenditure. These movies are, at once, a renunciation and a celebration of materialism.

42. Robert Warshow, 'The Gangster As a Tragic Hero,' in *The Immediate Experience: Movies, Comics, Theatre and Other Aspects of Popular Culture* (New York: Atheneum, 1974), 131.

43. Ibid., 132.

44. Ibid., 133.

45. Thomas Schatz, *Hollywood Genres: Formulas, Filmmaking, and the Studio System* (New York: McGraw Hill, 1981), 85.

46. For an extended discussion of gangster ethnicity, see Rachel Rubin and Jeffrey Melnick, *Immigrants and Popular Culture* (New York: New York University Press, 2007).

47. The inventory of movies that chart the immigrant experience in America is a long one. Notable selections that touch on the success myth include *They Knew What They Wanted* (1940), *The Glass Key* (1942), *An American Romance* (1944), *My Girl Tisa* (1948), *I Remember Mama* (1948), *Give Us This Day* (1949), *West Side Story* (1961), *America, America* (1963), *The New Land* (1972), *Hester Street* (1975), *Ragtime* (1981), *El Norte* (1983), *Moscow on the Hudson* (1984), *Dim Sun* (1984), *Avalon* (1990), *Pushing Hands* (1994), *In America* (2002), *Gangs of New York* (2002), *Goodbye Solo* (2008), *Sugar* (2008). See James A. Clapp, 'Immigrants in the City and in Cinema,' *Visual Anthropology*, 22: 1–19 for a discussion of the urban immigrant experience on film.

48. For a discussion of the loss of ethnic identity in immigrant sagas, see Mark Winokur, *American Laughter: Immigrants, Ethnicity, and 1930s Hollywood Film Comedy* (New York: St. Martin's Press, 1996). Winokur points out: 'The price of assimilation is the individual's renunciation of his old family and the conscious and so necessarily incomplete identification with a new family whose signs of communality are based on affluence rather than on shared historical referents. For those born wealthy, affluence is a shared culture, and success is a return to the parents... For those born poor and ethnic, success is traumatic, a renunciation of the consensual reality one knows in favor of an alternative, alienating reality that nevertheless must be life sustaining. The New-World plot, in which success may be chosen without consequences, is a fantasy of an acculturation that has already taken place without its concomitant identity-suicide,' 62.

49. Rubin and Melnick discuss the 1930s gangster film as an acknowledgement of the influx of urban immigrants and as a means of coming to terms with immigrant ethnicity: symbolic means for Americans to ponder, publicly and collectively, the status of immigrants that Robert Orsi and others have called 'inbetweenness,' 26.

50. *Public Enemies* (2009), a self-aware pastiche of earlier gangster motifs, puts the gangster's credo in the mouth of its protagonist, the notorious John Dillinger. When asked what he wants, he replies: 'Everything, right now.' In another invocation from the gangster's gospel he declares: 'Where people come from ain't as important as where somebody's going.' And in a moment overtly reflexive of the genre's history, Dillinger tells his girlfriend that they are 'on top of the world.'

51. There is an echo of this at the end of *The Godfather Part II* when the oldest brother Sonny, who is cut from the same mold as the early gangsters, yells at his younger, Ivy League-educated brother, 'Why did ya go to college – to get stupid? You're really stupid.' As a proud graduate of the School of Hard Knocks, the classic gangster has only scorn for the idea of bettering oneself through education or other conventional routes to success.

52. Jonathan Munby, *Public Enemies, Public Heroes: Screening the Gangster from 'Little Caesar' to 'Touch of Evil'*. (Chicago, IL: University of Chicago Press, 1999), 48–9.

53. Munby points out that many of these endings seem tacked-on in that they contradict or undercut the foregoing character development and narrative: 'As such, these films all turn the gangster's death into a question rather than a solution.' These endings reinvoke, rather than resolve, the tensions that define the genre. Munby, *Public Enemies, Public Heroes*, p. 64.

54. In discussing Michael, Nochimson points out the instability of the hyphenated American's identity: 'What seems to be a solid self turns out to be a highly fragile All-American patina.' She goes on to claim that 'Michael is aware that he is creating a performance....' The self-styled gangster wears the mask of the mythical American self-made man; when he falls, he confronts what Nochimson (invoking the gangster in *Public Enemy's* dying realization) calls 'the old "I ain't so tough" shock of recognition.' Nochimson, *Dying to Belong*, 56–8.

55. See the essays in Nick Browne, *Francis Ford Coppola's Godfather Trilogy* (Cambridge: Cambridge University Press, 1999).

56. In an interview with William Murray, Coppola called Michael 'the perfect metaphor for the new land.' Reprinted in Browne, *Francis Ford Coppola's Godfather Trilogy*, 180.

57. Barbara Ehrenreich, *Fear of Falling: The Inner Life of the Middle Class* (New York: Pantheon Books, 1989).

58. One of the best books on how American movies represent and speak to class is Steven J. Ross, *Working-Class Hollywood: Silent Film and the Shaping of Class in America* (Princeton, NJ: Princeton University Press, 1998).

59. Robert N. Bellah's landmark sociological study *Habits of the Heart: Individualism and Commitment in American Life* (Berkeley, CA: University of California Press, 1985) remains a seminal study of American thought regarding the two strains of individualism and the ongoing tension between individualist and communal commitments and traditions in American life.

60. Winokur offers an extended analysis of *My Man Godfrey*.

61. For an extended discussion of marriage in 'the women's film,' see the chapter on marriage in Jeanine Basinger, *A Women's View: How Hollywood Spoke to Women 1930–1960* (New York: Alfred A. Knopf, 1993).

62. For discussions of the film's improbable ending, see Jeanine Basinger, *A Women's View: How Hollywood Spoke to Women 1930–1960* (New York: Alfred A. Knopf, 1993); Gwendolyn Audrey Foster, *Class-Passing: Social Mobility in Film and Popular Culture* (Carbondale, IL: Southern Illinois University Press, 2005); Thomas Doherty, *Pre-Code Hollywood: Sex, Immorality, and Insurrection in American Cinema, 1930–1934* (New York: Columbia University Press, 1999).

63. Director Douglas Sirk once called such endings 'emergency exits': improbable, last-minute resolutions of the vexing issues that have informed the preceding narrative. For Sirk's astute musings on the resolutions of melodramas, see Douglas Sirk, *Sirk on Sirk: Interviews with Jon Halliday* (London: BFI Publishing, 1971).
64. See Christine Gledhill, ed. *Home is Where the Heart Is: Studies in Melodrama and the Women's Film* (London: BFI Publishing, 1987), one of the first (and still one of the best) considerations of melodrama on film. Also Marcia Landy, *Imitations of Life: A Reader of Film and Television Melodrama* (Detroit, MI: Wayne State University Press, 1991); John Mercer and Martin Shinger, *Melodrama: Genre, Style, and Sensibility* (London: Wallflower Press, 2004).
65. Roland Barthes, *Mythologies*, trans. Annette Lavers (New York: Hill and Wang, 1972), 129.
66. William McNeil, 'Make Mine Myth,' *The New York Times*, December 28, 1981, 19.

3   Work and Its Discontents: The Corporate Workplace Film

1. For a sociological/economic overview of the American cult of work, see Juliet B. Schor, *The Overworked American: The Unexpected Decline of Leisure* (New York: Basic Books, 1991).
2. The Protestant work ethic and the divine incentive for it was codified by Max Weber in his classic work, *The Protestant Ethic and the Spirit of Capitalism*, trans. Talcott Parsons (London: Routledge, 1998). In *Religion and the Rise of Capitalism* (New York: Harcourt, Brace and Company, 1926). R.H. Tawney also considered the gospel of work and its centrality in everyday life as deriving from a religiously inspired sense of ethical duty and asceticism.
3. John Kenneth Galbraith, *The Affluent Society*, 3rd edition (Boston, MA: Houghton Mifflin, 1976), 261.
4. Until recently, conventional success myth heroes were always male. Although in the late 1980s there began to be films about women in the corporate world, including *Baby Boom* (1987), *Broadcast News* (1987), and *Working Girl* (1988), their essential storyline and their view of the corporate workplace hews closely to classic success myth narratives. For a discussion of the relation between gender and success in 1980s movies, see Elizabeth Traube, *Dreaming Identities: Class, Gender, and Generation in 1980s Hollywood Movies* (Boulder, CO: Westview Press, 1992),.
5. Just as the cowboy hero can't settle into civilization because its collective values would interfere with his untrammeled free will, the hero of corporate dramas and comedies needs to exit the corporate sphere in order to assert his individuality and morality.
6. Several movies, including *The Rainmaker* (1997), *A Civil Action* (1998), *The Insider* (1999), and *Erin Brockovich* (2000) suggest that only those situated outside of the corporative structure can effect change, thereby endowing

their work with the sense of mission and importance lacking in corporate toil. But, as Phillip Lopate has pointed out:

Anticorporate films are only seemingly subversive. In fact, they enshrine the capitalist principles of individualism and hard work. The old American ethos declared that if you worked hard you might become a millionaire; the new one says, if you pound the pavements and scan the computer records long enough, you might nail a millionaire. And maybe become one in the process, as shown by the having-your-cake-and-eating-it ending of *Erin Brockovich*.

Phillip Lopate, 'The Corporation as Fantasy Villain,' *The New York Times* April 9, 2000: 24.

7. Barbara Ehrenreich, *Fear of Falling: The Inner Life of the Middle Class*. (New York: Pantheon Books, 1989), 4.
8. Chuck Kleinhans claims that Hollywood movies rarely examine working-class life except in the context of the success myth, which purports to offer its protagonists a rise in class status. This suggests that there is a universal, vocationally, and materially determined definition of success. Chuck Kleinhans, 'Contemporary Working Class Film Heroes,' *Jump Cut: Hollywood, Politics and Counter Cinema*, Peter Steven, ed. (New York: Praeger Publishers, 1985), 64.
9. Vidor himself discussed environmental conditioning in *The Crowd* in His autobiography *A Tree is a Tree* (New York: Harcourt, Brace, 1952) and again in his *King Vidor on Filmmaking* (Philadelphia, PA: David McKay, 1972).
10. Vidor, who went on to have a long career in sound films, once explained, 'In silent films, where we didn't have all the words to explain everything, we thought in terms of symbols, graphic arrangements, or possibilities. We were trained in these terms. When you had to explain something, you didn't think "What's the exact word for this? The exact phrase of sentence?" You just thought, "What's the picture, the symbol?" ' Quoted in Eric Sherman, *Directing the Film: Directors on Their Art* (Boston, MA: Little, Brown, 1976), 201.
11. The later scene, when the family escapes to Coney Island, reinforces this point. The camera initially shows only the family foursome and then, in a sort of visual joke, shows them surrounded by a crowd of weekenders who are likewise intent on getting away from it all. In scene after scene, there is no escaping the crowd.
12. In an unpublished letter to Dartmouth College, Vidor reveals that the forced perspective of this scene was accomplished using a ten-foot miniature model of the building lying flat on the floor with the camera operator suspended over it on a moveable bridge. King Vidor, Letter to Dartmouth College. May 14, 1974.
13. Charlie Chaplin, in *Modern Times* (1935), likewise has the factory in the film produce a generic product as a way of suggesting that the salient point about the assembly line is that it produces generic workers.
14. Christian Marclay's *The Clock*, a twenty-four-hour *tour de force* montage that edits together movie scenes featuring clocks synchronized to the time of the screening, provides vivid demonstration of how many films with workplace scenes have included insert shots showing the clock about to strike the hour when the workers are released.

15. In a letter to Dartmouth College, Vidor acknowledges that he was 'greatly influenced' by the German expressionist films of Lang and Murnau. Although *Sunrise*, Murnau's American masterpiece and a film that also uses expressionist visuals to present city life as, at once, bustling, exciting, and terrifying, makes an interesting analogue to *The Crowd*, it was released four months before *The Crowd*, so it is unlikely that that film had much influence on Vidor's vision of the city. But Murnau's *The Last Laugh* (1924), Fritz Lang's *Metropolis* (1926) and Karl Grune's *The Street* (1923) all relied on a mix of realist and expressionist techniques similar to that in *The Crowd*.

16. Loren Baritz, *The Culture of the Twenties* (Indianapolis, IN: Bobbs-Merrill, 1970), 231.

17. Bruce Barton, *The Man Nobody Knows: A Discovery of the Real Jesus* (Indianapolis, IN: Bobbs-Merrill, 1925).

18. *The Crowd* was far from alone in its ambivalence about modern urban life and its toll. Published five years before *The Crowd* was released, Sinclair Lewis' *Babbitt* (New York: Grosset & Dunlap, 1922) satirically took aim at business ambition and cultural complacency.

19. Released in 1928, *The Crowd* grossed a then healthy $500,000 in the United States and went on to screen widely in Europe. Herbert G. Luft, 'King Vidor: A Career that Spans Half a Century,' *Film Journal* Summer (1971): 34.

20. The number of corporate critiques published in the late 1990s and early 2000s, for example, seems to bear this out. Among them are *White Collage Blues* (New York: Basic Books, 1995); Daniel S. Levine, *Disgruntled: The Darker Side of the World of Work* (New York: Putnam, 1998); Joanne B. Ciulla, *The Working Life: The Promise and Betrayal of Modern Work* (New York: Times Books, 2000); Jill Andresky Fraser, *White-Collar Sweatshop: The Deterioration of Work and Its Rewards in Corporate America* (New York: W.W. Norton, 2001); Charles Heckscher, *White Collar* (New York: Basic Books, 1995); and Robert Reich, *The Future of Success* (New York: Knopf, 2001).

21. For example, although such screwball comedies such as *Meet John Doe* (1941) *You Can't Take It with You* (1938), and *The Magnificent Dope* (1941) are not primarily set in the workplace, their soulless tycoons, repressed workers, and contented dropouts are stock figures that are used to comment obliquely on the impersonality of corporate life.

22. The post-war decades were marked by economic growth, job security, and corporate prosperity. Between 1945 and 1960, the gross national product rose by 52 percent. Mansel G. Blackford and K. Austin Kerr, 'The Company in the Postwar World,' in *History of the U.S. Economy Since World War II*, Harold G. Vatter and John F. Walker, eds. (Armonk, NY: M.E. Sharpe, 1996), 129.

23. Adolf A. Berle, Jr., and Gardiner C. Means' *The Modern Corporation and Private Property* (New York: Macmillan, 1933) is considered the classic early work dealing with the incursion of corporations into the American business landscape. The authors discuss the growing presence and influence of public corporations as well as the significance of the corporate separation of management and ownership. C. Wright Mills' chapter, 'The Chief Executives,' in *The Power Elite*, C. Wright Mills, 2nd edition (Oxford: Oxford University Press, 2000 (1956)) is likewise a useful introduction to the corporation at mid-century and to the men at the top.

24. C. Wright Mills, *White Collar: The American Middle Classes* (New York: Oxford University Press, 1956); David Reisman, *The Lonely Crowd: A Study of the*

Changing American Character (New Haven, CT: Yale University Press, 1950); William H. Whyte, Jr., *The Organization Man* (New York: Simon and Schuster, 1956).

25. Whyte, *The Organization Man*, 3.
26. Ibid., 7.
27. Ibid., 435.
28. Mills, *White Collar*, 106.
29. Mills' pithy phrase for the new gospel of work was 'agility rather than ability.' Mills, *White Collar*, 263.
30. Ibid., 262–3.
31. Ibid., 259.
32. Whyte, *The Organization Man*, 272. In *Nickel and Dimed: On (Not) Getting by in America* (New York: Henry Holt, 2001). Barbara Ehrenreich describes a Walmart survey given to prospective employees. She discovers that, according to Walmart, the correct response to the statement, 'There is room in every corporation for a nonconformist,' is 'totally disagree,' 135.
33. In Vance Packard's popular sociology tract *The Status Seekers*, published one year before the release of *The Apartment*, he details the intricate semiotics of mid-century corporate success in a chapter titled 'Pecking Orders in the Corporate Barnyards.' Among the signifiers of executive status (many of which serve their symbolic purpose in films of the era) are the corner office with view, mahogany desks (which outrank walnut and oak), wall-to-wall carpeting, access to the private washroom and the executive dining room. Vance Packard, *The Status Seekers* (New York: David McKay, 1959), 114–27.
34. Ethnicity is often posed as a marker of authenticity in Hollywood movies, but although Dr. Dreyfuss is clearly the moral center of the film, his exaggerated Yiddishkeit persona marks him as an unlikely role model in the *echt* WASP world of 1950s corporate workplace movies.
35. For a discussion of the possibility of 'open' endings that allow for a consideration of the lingering issues raised by the film, see Neupert, *The End.*
36. In *Seeing Is Believing: How Hollywood Taught Us to Stop Worrying and Love the Fifties* (New York: Pantheon, 1983), Peter Biskind talks about what he calls 'antisuccess' films, several of which appeared in the late 1940s. He says that 'In these films, men who were ambitious, attractive, and talented turned out to be heels. When they succeeded in clawing, kicking, and gouging their way up the ladder of success, they were likely to find that winning wasn't much different from losing. They found success, but lost themselves,' 254. Bud, conversely, loses his shot at success but finds himself.
37. Significantly, Shaw is the only one of the film's major characters whose personal life is never shown. The other characters have homes, wives, and mistresses, but Shaw seems to live at the office and lust only after power.
38. For instance, see Robert Ray, *A Certain Tendency of the Hollywood Cinema, 1930–1980* (Princeton, NJ: Princeton University Press, 1985), 64–6.
39. Leslie A. Fiedler, *Love and Death in the American Novel* (New York: Stein and Day, 1966), 355.
40. Whyte, *The Organization Man*, 276–91.
41. In *Running Time: Films of the Cold War* (New York: Dial Press, 1978), Nora Sayre makes a similar point: 'But while these movies show that success in "the chromium jungle" is extremely dangerous to respiration or circulation,

and very damaging to home life, they hardly criticize the system. Severe problems at the office are usually caused by one very unpleasant individual; when his schemes are defeated, all will be well...the issues are reduced to the level of personal conflict or behavior. Yet the passions that these films display belie the optimistic endings: despite the colleagues' congratulations and the beaming wife, we sense that heart attacks await those who are full of brave resolve to improve the company or its performance,' 140.

42. Serling later amplified his critique of corporate America in his television series *The Twilight Zone* and *Night Gallery*. The shows 'Walking Distance,' 'A Stop at Willoughby,' and 'They're Tearing Down Tim Reilly's Bar' likewise revealed the heartlessness and greed of corporate capitalism and the emotional toll exacted from the corporate rank and file.

43. In *A Certain Tendency of the Hollywood Cinema, 1930–1980*, Ray discusses at length American movies' denial of the necessity for choice. Endings such as this one offer a sort of mass wish fulfillment that suggests we can have it both ways without sacrificing either our principles or our livelihood.

44. In a typical assessment of the atmosphere of the 1950s corporation, economist Robert Reich claims that, 'The executive suite of the large-scale American enterprise at mid-century was a quietly distinguished place...in which men went about their work with no particular urgency. The stability that characterized large-scale production bestowed a quiescence and certitude upon those who were in charge.' Reich, *The Future of Success*, 71.

45. The corporate executive and his travails are dealt with directly in such films as *How to Succeed in Business Without Really Trying* (1967) and *Save the Tiger* (1973) and indirectly in, for example, *The Graduate* (1967), where 'plastics' became a code word for the late 1960s perspective on the corporation. But these films lack the concentrated verve of the 1950s corporate-based movies. In the 1970s, the critique of over-organized apparatuses of power seemed to shift from corporate workplace movies to such government exposes as *Chinatown* (1974), *All the President's Men* (1976), and *The China Syndrome* (1979). *The Godfather* (1972) is arguably the most trenchant 1970s movie about American corporate work structures, even though it comments on them obliquely. As the *Godfather* trilogy charts the watering down of the generations, it sets the entrepreneurial enterprise of the *paterfamilias* Don Corleone against the increasingly bureaucratized business apparatus of his descendents. The patriarchal boss is viewed with acute nostalgia when compared to the soulless businessmen that succeed him. For a discussion of *The Godfather* as a critique of corporate institutions, see Michael Ryan and Douglas Kellner, *Camera Politica: The Politics and Ideology of Contemporary Hollywood Film* (Bloomington, IN: Indiana University Press, 1988), 66.

46. Although several of these titles were released after the stock market crash of October 1987, they were all in production before that date.

47. Ray, *A Certain Tendency of the Hollywood Cinema, 1930–1980*, 55–69.

48. In *Dreaming Identities*, Elizabeth G. Traube says that 'such appeal as the film has emanates from the supposedly negative dimension of capitalism personified in Michael Douglas's Gordon Gekko...Douglas' performance (which won the film's only major Oscar), overpowers the plot,' 105.

49. Many film scholars have made note of the commodity fetishism of American movies. For example, in his book *Power and Paranoia: History, Narrative and*

the American Cinema, 1940–1950 (New York: Columbia University Press, 1986), Dana Polan talks about the 'visual richness' and 'the promise of the product' (294) that are part of the discourse of many American films. In *Wall Street*, what Polan calls 'display for the sake of display' (294) overwhelms the moralistic message of the narrative. See also David Desser and Garth S. Jowett, eds. *Hollywood Goes Shopping* (Minneapolis, MN: University of Minnesota Press, 2000).

50. Traube, *Dreaming Identities*, 106.
51. A discussion of classic comic form and comic endings is found in Northrup Frye, 'The Mythos of Spring: Comedy,' *Anatomy of Criticism: Four Essays* (Princeton, NJ: Princeton University Press, 1973), 158–86.
52. The term, referring to corporate, multinational, consumer capitalism (as opposed to the putatively more benign mom-and-pop variety) derives from Ernest Mandel, *Late Capitalism* (New York: Verso, 1978). Fredric Jameson takes it up in his seminal article, 'Postmodernism, or the Cultural Logic of Late Capitalism,' *New Left Review* 146 (July–August 1984), 53–92.
53. This vision of the corporation as expressionist hellhole was previewed in Terry Gilliam's *Brazil* (1985). There, however, the dystopian workplace is a government office where workers are surrounded by labyrinthine, wheezing pipes and ducts, and a single desk is shared (or, rather, wrestled over), by two workers on opposite sides of a wall.
54. The widely syndicated comic strip *Dilbert* has a similarly satirical – and cynical – view of the absurdities of office life. By the end of the twentieth century, the knowing smirk seemed to have replaced the tendentious screed of 1950s corporate critiques.
55. For an extended consideration of American films centered around characters who exemplify the entrepreneurial spirit, see the chapter 'The Entrepreneurial Impulse,' in *Career Movies: American Business and the Success Mystique*, Jack Boozer (Austin, TX: University of Texas Press, 2002).
56. It is significant that these films, as well as a few other entrepreneur-focused movies, are set in the automobile industry, the longtime symbol of American inventiveness, business ingenuity, and technological prowess. Here and elsewhere, the corporatization of the auto industry is synecdoche for the decline of the visionary American entrepreneurial spirit.

4   Success Reassessed: Ambitious Women/Midlife Men

1. See Carolyn Galerstein, *Working Women on the Hollywood Screen: A Filmography* (New York: Garland, 1989).
2. Non-white or non-middle-class women fare even worse, often appearing as maids, farm workers, or prostitutes. Haskell and the other early analysts of the representation of women in film paid scant attention to women in auxiliary roles, focusing, instead, on middle-class women.
3. Molly Haskell, *From Reverence to Rape: The Treatment of Women in the Movies*, 2nd edition (Chicago, IL: University of Chicago Press, 1987), 142.
4. Ibid., 144. Of course, the question of whether there is validity to the very idea of 'female natures' has been at the center of feminist discourse since the time when Haskell wrote.

5. Ibid., 150.
6. Brandon French has pointed out that the screen's treatment of 'the wholesale female retreat to the home' and the insistence on woman as homemaker was, contrary to popular belief, not mirrored in the culture at large. She cites sources that claim that by 1955, women represented a proportionately larger segment of the workforce than at any time during the war. *On the Verge of Revolt: Women in American Film of the Fifties* (New York: Frederick Unger, 1978), xiv.
7. Ibid., 130.
8. See Marjorie Rosen, *Popcorn Venus* (New York: Coward, McCann, and Geoghegan, 1973) and Joan Mellen, *Women and Their Sexuality in the New Film* (New York: Horizon Press, 1973).
9. Many film theorists have written about Hollywood's realist aesthetic and, taking their cues from Louis Althusser, about the unconscious way dominant ideology infiltrates everyday life. For an introductory consideration of realist film, see David Bordwell, *Narration in the Fiction Film*.
10. Claire Johnston, 'Women's Cinema as Counter-Cinema,' in *Notes on Women's Cinema*, Claire Johnston, ed. (London: Society for Education in Film and Television, 1973), 25.
11. The former position, first articulated by the writers who became known as 'the Frankfurt school,' is found in Max Horkheimer and Theodor W. Adorno, 'The Culture Industry: Enlightenment As Mass Deception,' *Dialectic of Enlightenment* (New York: Herder & Herder, 1972), 20–67.
12. E. Ann Kaplan, 'The Case of the Missing Mother: Maternal Issues in Vidor's *Stella Dallas*,' *Heresies* 16 (1983): 81–85 and Linda Williams, ' "Something Else Besides a Mother": *Stella Dallas* and the Maternal Melodrama,' *Cinema Journal* 24, no. 2 (1985): 22–43.
13. See, for instance, Pam Cook, 'Duplicity in *Mildred Pierce*,' in *Women and Film Noir*, 3rd edition, E. Ann Kaplan, ed. (London: British Film Institute, 1998); Annette Kuhn, *Women's Pictures: Feminism and Cinema* (New York: Verso, 1994); and Lucy Fisher, ed. *Imitation of Life* (New Brunswick, NJ: Rutgers University Press, 1991).
14. Diana Carson, 'To Be Seen But Not Heard: *The Awful Truth*,' in *Multiple Voices in Feminist Film Criticism*, Diane Carson, Linda Dittmar and Janice R. Welsch, eds. (Minneapolis, MN: University of Minnesota Press, 1994), 214.
15. Jeanine Basinger, *A Women's View: How Hollywood Spoke to Women* (New York: Knopf, 1993), 23.
16. Ibid., 25.
17. Ibid., 452.
18. Ibid., 31.
19. In 1950, the number of working women totaled 18.4 million; by the mid-1980s, that number had leapt to over 45 million (www.womensbusinessresearch.org). The most significant influx of women in the workplace occurred during the late 1970s. The labor force participation rate for women in the mid-1960s was 40 percent; by the late 1980s, it had risen to over 58 percent (www.bls.gov). Further, an increasing number of older women were working. In 1950, women aged 16–24 claimed the highest labor force participation rate (43.9 percent); by the late 1980s, women aged 35–44 had the highest rate (85.1 percent) (www.bls.gov.). The types of jobs held by

women also saw significant change. From 1900 to 1970, female workers were concentrated in occupations that were predominantly female. In 1970, half of all women workers were employed in only 17 occupations (as opposed to 63 occupations in which half of employed men worked). By the 1980s, women were beginning to ascend to the professional heights in managerial roles. See Rosabeth Kanter, *Men and Women of the Corporation*, 2nd edition (New York: Basic Books, 1993).

20. Stuart Hall, 'Notes on Deconstructing "the Popular",' in *People's History and Socialist Theory*, Raphael Samuel, ed. (London: Routledge, 1981), 232–33.
21. Traube, *Dreaming Identities*, 25.
22. Susan Faludi, *Backlash: The Undeclared War Against America's Women* (New York: Crown, 1991), 126.
23. Mike Nichol's 1988 film is one of three movies to play on the punning implications of that title. The others are Dorothy Arzner's *Working Girls* (1931) and Lizzie Borden's 1986 independent film of the same name. Writing about the Arzner film, Judith Mayne discusses the double meaning of the title: its literal sense of women with jobs and its suggestion that women who work are prostituting themselves and are somehow morally suspect. Judith Mayne, *Directed by Dorothy Arzner* (Bloomington, IN: Indiana University Press, 1994). Yvonne Tasker also adopted it as the title of her exploration of gender and sexuality in film. Yvonne Tasker, *Working Girls: Gender and Sexuality in Popular Cinema* (New York: Routledge, 1998).
24. Yvonne Tasker refers to Tess' successive costume changes as a sort of cross-dressing: transgressing classes rather than genders. Tasker goes on to discuss the working woman's uniform as a sort of masquerade/costume: 'If anarchic men dress as women to learn about self-control whilst enjoying the evident pleasures of transformation, narratives and images of women cross-dressing relate to opportunity and achievement in different, though related ways. Both gendered and class cross-dressing is explicitly presented as allowing female protagonists an opportunity and a *freedom* (of both physical movement and behavior) that they would not otherwise achieve... the development of a wardrobe for working women continues to involve the negotiation of images and ideologies of gender and class. Women's entry into previously restricted areas of work in the 1980s (re)produced a "new" stereotype (that of the independent woman) and a "new" look – crystallized in the phrase "power dressing." The shoulder pad (and shoulder pad build-up) was to become a symbol and symptom of women's attempts to carve out a space for themselves in the world of work,' 35.
25. See Northrup Frye, 'Archetypal Criticism: The Theory of Myths,' in *The Anatomy of Criticism: Four Essays* (Princeton, NJ: Princeton University Press, 2000).
26. Tasker, *Working Girls*, 17.
27. Ibid., 135.
28. Working women in the movies tend to be either de-eroticized, as is the case with the lifetime professional women cited earlier, or over-eroticized vagina dentatas in business suits. Either way, their sexuality serves as a metaphor for the threat that they pose, either to themselves, in the former case, or to the men in the film and the social order, in the latter.
29. Tasker, *Working Girls*, 126.

30. Susan Jeffords, *The Remasculinization of America: Gender and the Vietnam War* (Bloomington, IN: Indiana University Press, 1989) and *Hard Bodies: Hollywood Masculinity in the Reagan Era* (Brunswick, NJ: Rutgers University Press, 1994).
31. In addition to Jefford's books, see Steven Cohan and Ina Rae Hark, *Screening the Male: Exploring Masculinities in Hollywood Cinema* (New York: Routledge: 1993), Mike Chopra-Gant, *Hollywood Genres and Postwar America: Masculinity, Family and Nation in Popular Movies and Film Noir* (London: I.B. Tauris, 2006) and Peter Lehman, ed. *Masculinity: Bodies, Movies, Culture* (New York: Routledge. 2001).
32. Tania Modleski, *Feminism Without Women: Culture and Criticism in a 'Post-Feminist' Age* (London: Routledge, 1991), 7.
33. That confusion is not new in this period and conflicted masculinity certainly predates these movies. Steve Cohan and Stella Bruzzi, among others, have pointed out that men in post-war movies were often 'contradictory figure[s] in whom several ideals of post-war American masculinity collide but ultimately fail to homogenize.' Stella Bruzzi, *Bringing up Daddy: Fatherhood and Masculinity in Post-War Hollywood* (London: BFI Publishing, 2005), 40.
34. Susan Faludi, *Stiffed: The Betrayal of the American Man* (New York: William Morrow, 1999).
35. A number of writers have pointed out that even conventional images of masculinity during Hollywood's classical period contain contradictions and confusion. For example, see the essays in Pat Kirkham and Janet Thumim, eds. *You Tarzan: Masculinity, Movies and Men* (New York: St. Martin's Press, 1993) and the same editors' *Me Jane: Masculinity, Movies and Women* (New York: St. Martin's Press, 1995).
36. Lynn Segal, *Slow Motion: Changing Masculinities* (Brunswick, NJ: Rutgers University Press, 1990), 293.
37. The preceding chapter presented several instances of workers who rethink their devotion and relation to work. Disaffected midlife manhood is broadly represented across film genres and across the decades. For example, several westerns from the 1950s onward, ranging from *The Man Who Shot Liberty Valence* (1962) to *Unforgiven* (1992) narrativize mid-life ambivalence about having one's identity tied to accomplishment. Other films appearing in the past few years that take up the theme of professionally derived identities include *Election* (1999) and *Little Children* (2006) (both exploring precocious, early mid-life doubts about masculinity and professional attainment and both based on novels by Tom Perrotta, who has distinguished himself as a bard of male angst), *In Good Company* (2004), *Up in the Air* (2009), and *Company Men* (2010).
38. The split between wordy and laconic men is hardly new to the cinema. Indeed, the two central male archetypes of American film – the fast-talking gangster and the barely talking westerner – exhibit these poles of verbal expression. In both cases, the characters' verbal style is connected with his power. But here the characters' prolixity or terseness is not a sign of masculine action or restraint but, rather, a sign of their frustration and inability to make sense of what they feel. Both tendencies are taken to comic extreme in these films, with some of the characters unable to shut up and stop obsessively processing their careening lives and others unable to articulate. In an

article on male voice in *Me Jane: Masculinity, Movies and Women*, Christine Gledhill writes about how the garrulousness of old timers in western movies is 'coded as part of his move out of the realm of the masculine,' 45. The linkage between gender and verbal expression is one more way these films explore their characters' social positioning and identity.

39. Traube, *Dreaming Identities*, 122–4.
40. See David Laderman, *Driving Visions: Exploring the Road Movie* (Austin, TX: University of Texas Press, 2002) for an overview of the road movie as cultural critique and subversion, and for a retrospective consideration of the meaning of the flight from civilization in American cultural narratives. In these films, the conventional equation of the road with adventure and rebellion is contradicted by the characters' aimlessness and ambivalence.
41. See, for example, Lizabeth Cohen, *A Consumer's Republic: The Politics of Mass Consumption in Postwar America* (New York: Knopf, 2003); Stuart Ewen, *Captains of Consciousness* (New York: McGraw-Hill, 1976); David L. Lewis and Laurence Goldstein, eds. *The Automobile and American Culture* (Ann Arbor, MI: University of Michigan Press, 1983); and Alan Tomlinson, ed. *Consumption, Identity, & Style* (London: Comedia, 1990).
42. Several of the essays in *Me Jane* analyze the cinema's voyeuristic fascination with the iconic male body.
43. In her study of women's fiction, *Loving with a Vengeance: Mass-Produced Fantasies for Women* (London: Methuen, 1984), Tania Modleski points out that 'if self-aggrandizement has been the male mode, self-abasement has too frequently been the female mode,' 13. So these characters' indulgence in self-abasement is one more marker of their fluid gender profile.
44. Steven Cohan, *Masked Men: Masculinity and the Movies in the Fifties* (Bloomington, IN: Indiana University Press, 1997), 47.
45. Kaja Silverman, *Male Subjectivity at the Margins* (New York: Routledge, 1992), 24.
46. Ibid., 389.
47. Ibid.
48. Nina Baym, 'Melodramas of Beset Manhood: How Theories of American Fiction Exclude Women Authors,' in *Locating American Studies: The Evolution of a Discipline*, Lucy Maddox, ed. (Baltimore, MD: Johns Hopkins University Press, 1998), 215.
49. Modleski, *Feminism Without Women*, 10.
50. Interestingly, the director shot several scenes of Bingham feathering his nest once he has decided he wants a life with Alex. In these outtakes, the character buys and decorates a condo, purchases a car, and readies himself for a settled, domestic, shared life. Although those scenes did not make the final cut, they can be viewed on the DVD of *Up in the Air*.
51. Basinger, *A Women's View*, 4.

5 Hallelujah, I'm a Bum: The Glorification of Unemployment

1. In *Doing Nothing: A History of Loafers, Loungers, Slackers, and Bums in America* (New York: Farrar, Straus, and Giroux, 2006), his cross-century history of

characters who embrace idleness as a personal philosophy, Tom Luntz points out that the anti-work stance of these slackers is significant because it homes in on an enduring cultural tension surrounding work and leisure: 'What is important is not the utopian dream of a work-free world, but the cultural give-and-take such dreams engender... slack subcultures have performed an important emotional function, expressing and adding to our culture's repertoire of feelings about work,' 53. Later, he again points to the contradictory quality and double function of such fictional figures: 'Slackers represent our fondest fantasies and our deepest fears,' 102.

2. Among the most moving presentations of the humiliations and deprivations of unemployment during the depression are *I Am a fugitive from a Chain Gang* (1932), *Wild Boys of the Road* (1933), *Man's Castle* (1933), *Our Daily Bread* (1934), *Dead End* (1937), *The Grapes of Wrath* (1940), and *Sullivan's Travels* (1941).

3. Northrup Frye, *Anatomy of Criticism: Four Essays* (Princeton, NJ: Princeton University Press, 2000), 170.

4. Ibid., 167.

5. There are movies in which characters move in the opposite direction as well, playing at unemployment and lower class status in their search for an authentic self. *My Man Godfrey* (1936) is one of the best examples of a character disguising himself downward.

6. Johan Huizinga, *Homo Ludens* (New York: Beacon Press, 1971).

7. Barbara Ehrenreich, *Fear of Falling: The Inner Life of the Middle Class* (New York: Pantheon, 1989), 85.

8. Among the many books about screwball comedies that discuss the centrality of play are: Ed Sikov, *Screwball!: Hollywood's Madcap Romantic Comedies* (New York: Crown, 1989) and Stanley Cavell, *Pursuits of Happiness: The Hollywood Comedy of Remarriage* (Cambridge, MA: Harvard University Press, 2004).

9. One of the best discussions of comedy and transgression is found in William Paul, *Laughing Screaming: Modern Hollywood Horror and Comedy* (New York: Columbia University Press, 1994).

10. Geoff King, *Film Comedy* (London: Wallflower Press, 2002), 78.

11. Victor Turner, *The Forest of Symbols: Aspects of Ndembu Ritual* (Ithaca, NY: Cornell University Press, 1970), 97.

12. Victor Turner, *The Ritual Process: Structure and Anti-Structure* (Ithaca, NY: Cornell University Press, 1969), 95.

13. Mikhail Bakhtin, *Rabelais and His World* (Bloomington, IN: Indiana University Press, 1984), 177, 15. For a discussion of Bakhtin's applicability to film, see Robert Stam, *Subversive Pleasures: Bakhtin, Cultural Criticism, and Film* (Baltimore, MD: Johns Hopkins University Press, 1989).

14. Karl Marx's son-in-law, Paul Lafargue, penned a popular manifesto titled *Le Droit à la paresse* (*The Right to Be Lazy*), which was a paean to leisure as the essence of life (New York: Charles H. Kerr, 1989). A half century later, in *The Arcades Project*, Walter Benjamin wrote about the *flâneur*'s aimless stroll as a sort of street theater that demonstrated disapproval of the post-industrial division of labor (Cambridge, MA: Belknap Press, 2002). Benjamin's insistence that 'the act of ambling is an act of revolt' was echoed by Michel Foucault who saw sloth as 'the absolute form of rebellion,' *Madness and*

Civilization: A History of Insanity in the Age of Reason (New York: Vintage, 1988), 56. And in Bertrand Russell's essay, 'In Praise of Idleness,' written in the midst of the Depression, Russell saw leisure as a refuge from labor and bemoaned the 'immense harm [that] is caused by the belief that work is virtuous,' *In Praise of Idleness and Other Essays* (New York: Routledge, 2004), 9. As objections to the systematic enshrinement of work and productivity, such endorsements of the non-working life comprise a compelling doctrine of leisure.

15. Joanne B. Ciulla, *The Working Life: The Promise and Betrayal of Modern Work* (New York: Three Rivers Press, 2001), 6.
16. Russell's 1932 essay, 'In Praise of Idleness,' suggests that devotion to work has historically been a method for the ruling classes to convince the working classes to serve the status quo. The essay endorses the democratization of leisure and suggests that technological progress should enable a broad swath of people to indulge in idleness.
17. Anson Rabinbach, *The Human Motor: Energy, Fatigue, and the Origins of Modernity* (New York: Basic Books, 1990), 28. Rabinbach's book is a sprawling intellectual history of cultural perspectives on labor.
18. Robert Warshow, 'The Gangster as a Tragic Hero,' *The Immediate Experience* (Cambridge, MA: Harvard University Press, 2002). Warshow's essay on the cowboy, in this same volume, also discusses the American archetype of the maverick loner who needs to isolate himself in order to be himself.
19. For a listing of movies about labor, see Tom Zaniello, *Working Stiffs, Union Maids, Reds and Riffraff: An Expanded Guide to Films about Labor* (Ithaca, NY: Cornell University Press, 2003). For an analysis of labor movies, see John Bodnar, *Blue-Collar Hollywood: Liberalism, Democracy, and Working People in American Film* (Baltimore, MD: Johns Hopkins University Press, 2003) and the chapter 'The Good, the Bad, and the Violent: Class Conflict and Labor-Capital Genre,' in *Working-Class Hollywood: Silent Film and the Shaping of Class in America*, Steven J. Ross (Princeton, NJ: Princeton University Press, 1998).
20. Ray's book is particularly incisive about this as is Jim Purdy's and Peter Roffman's *The Hollywood Social Problem Film: Madness, Despair, and Politics from the Depression to the Fifties* (Bloomington, IN: Indiana University Press, 1981).
21. Ray, *A Certain Tendency of the Hollywood Cinema, 1930–1980*, 11.
22. Ibid., 57.
23. King, *Film Comedy*, 67.
24. Ibid., 71.
25. The term 'workaholic' was coined by theologian Wayne C. Oates in the late 1960s.
26. Unemployment as an antidote to the dehumanization of work is certainly not a uniquely American idea. During this same period, films such as Rene Clair's *À nous la liberté* (1931) and Jean Renoir's *Boudu sauvé des eaux* (1932) also focus on the opposition between a free-spirited protagonist and a work world that requires conformity. When *Modern Times* was released, Chaplin was sued for plagiarism by Clair's distribution company but Clair distanced himself from the legal action and claimed that he was flattered by the resemblance between the films. The suit was eventually settled.

27. Purdy and Roffman, *The Hollywood Social Problem Film*, 103.
28. The film proved to be something of a swan song for Jolson's career. Jolson never recovered from the failure of the film and his status as a screen icon diminished in his remaining films. Langdon was already past his prime as a film comic although, like Jolson, he, too, made films into the 1940s.
29. Acorn is one in a long line of African-American sidekicks in Hollywood movies whose primary function seems to be to aid the protagonist in fulfilling his desires. *Hallelujah, I'm a Bum* is one of the few Jolson films of the era in which the star did not appear in his famous (later to become infamous) blackface guise. In the film's vision of a bum's paradise, there seems to be a willful effort to ignore race, gender, class, or age. The bums are simply a congenial cohort of like-minded refuseniks. This utopian community in which social categories of identity and political alignments are irrelevant is, of course, simplistic, but given the racism of Jolson's blackface routines, it comes as something of a relief.
30. See Charles Musser, 'Work, Ideology, and Chaplin's Tramp,' in *Resisting Images: Essays on Cinema and History*, Robert Sklar and Charles Musser, eds. (Philadelphia, PA: Temple University Press, 1990) for a discussion of the tramp's persona and the ideology of work in Chaplin's two-reelers. Musser also discusses the resonance of Chaplin's outlook on work for working-class audiences of the time.
31. An ongoing debate in interpretations of Chaplin's films involves whether the tramp is an outcast or a rebel: whether he *can't* or *won't* conform. Is his inability to hold a job a conscious, conscience-driven rejection of work and its attendant drudgery or is it simply an inability to measure up to what's required? The persistent appearance in American films of a protagonist who bails out of the work force in an act of opposition to its oppressions suggests the former interpretation. See, for instance, Donald W. McCaffrey, *Focus on Chaplin* (Englewood Cliffs, NJ: Prentice-Hall, 1971).
32. Several authors have written about why Chaplin was intent on making essentially silent films well into the sound era. See, for instance, Walter Kerr, *The Silent Clowns* (New York: Knopf, 1975).
33. Gerald Weals, *Canned Goods as Caviar: American Film Comedy of the 1930s* (Chicago, IL: University of Chicago, 1985), 26.
34. It is significant that we don't even find out what the factory makes. The sign on the factory declares simply, 'Electro Steel Corporation.'
35. When the tramp takes a bathroom break and tries to steal a moment for a cigarette and a stretch, the boss appears on a big brother screen and orders him back to work. During the lunch break, Charlie is once again denied his break time when he is enlisted to demonstrate the feeding machine.
36. In his book on immigrants and film comedy, Mark Winokur suggests that these and other ambiguities are at the crux of Chaplin's appeal: '[Chaplin's] tramp becomes culturally attractive because of the contradictions he contains: he is simultaneously hard-working and lazy, gallant and lecherous, generous and greedy. These contradictions help define the tramp as an epistemological contradiction: he contains the hegemonic representation of the assimilated, as well as various immigrant versions of accommodation.' *American Laughter: Immigrants, Ethnicity, and 1930s Hollywood Film Comedy* (New York: St. Martin's, 1996), 91.

37. One of the best extended discussions of Capra's films is Ray Carney's *American Vision: The Films of Frank Capra* (Hanover, NH: Wesleyan University Press, 1986).
38. Sikov locates the film in a collection of what he calls crazy family comedies of the period. Sikov, *Screwball!*, 143.
39. The story was wildly popular and clearly hit a nerve with the public. *You Can't Take It with You* is one of the few plays that were still running to full houses on Broadway when the film opened.
40. When Mr. Poppins, one of the characters who Grandpa Vanderhof inspires to leave his job and join the household's shenanigans, asks how the family lives and who takes care of them, Grandpa looks heavenward and replies, 'Same one that takes care of the lilies of the field.' Whenever Grandpa leads the family in saying grace, he addresses God as 'Sir' and says, 'we are certainly much obliged... all we ask is just to go along as we are... as far as anything else is concerned we leave that up to you.' In his autobiography, *The Name above the Title* (New York: Macmillan, 1971), Capra confesses his quasi-theological intentions: 'Hidden in *You Can't Take It with You* was a golden opportunity to dramatize Love Thy Neighbor in living drama. What the world's churches were preaching to apathetic congregations, my universal language of film might say more entertainingly to movie audiences, *if* it could prove, in theatrical conflict, that Christ's spiritual law can be the most powerful sustaining force in anyone's life,' 267–8. See Carney for a discussion of more overt religious symbolism and sensibility in other Capra films including *Meet John Doe* (1941) and *It's a Wonderful Life* (1946).
41. Frye, *Anatomy of Criticism*, 170.
42. In his autobiography, Capra discusses how he altered the play to focus on the eventual kinship of Grandpa and Mr. Kirby. Capra, *The Name above the Title*, 268.
43. Cavell and Ray both discuss the cult of childhood in American movies.
44. Leslie A. Fiedler, *Love and Death in the American Novel* (Normal, IL: Dalkey Archive Press, 1988).
45. Both John Locke and Karl Marx discuss *homo faber* as a type. The title and type is also featured in Max Frisch's 1959 novel by that name, about a technocrat who lacks passion and artistic sensibility.
46. Pauline Kael, *Kiss Kiss Bang Bang* (Boston, MA: Little, Brown, 1968), 29.
47. David Sterritt, *Mad to Be Saved: The Beats, the 50s, and Film* (Carbondale, IL: Southern Illinois University Press, 1998), 168–9.
48. Carl Jung, *Four Archetypes: Mother, Rebirth, Spirit, Trickster* (Princeton, NJ: Princeton University Press, 1970).
49. Janice Morgan, 'From Clochards to Cappuccinos: Renoir's Boudu is "Down and Out" in Beverly Hills,' *Cinema Journal* 29, no. 2 (Winter, 1990): 23–35.
50. Ibid., 29.
51. Tom Lutz locates the first use of the term 'slacker' in its contemporary meaning as far back as 1898 Oxford English Dictionary. Lutz, *Doing Nothing*, 13.
52. Explorations of teen archetypes in American movies can be found in Thomas Doherty's *Teenagers and Teenpics: The Juvenilization of American Movies in the 1950s* (Philadelphia, PA: Temple University Press, 2002); Timothy Shary, *Generation Multiplex: The Image of Youth in Contemporary American Cinema*

(Austin, TX: University of Texas Press, 2002); and Timothy Shary, *Teen Movies: American Youth on Screen* (New York: Wallflower, 2006).

53. Lutz comments on the endurance of diametrically opposed cultural attitudes toward work as follows:

> The two ways of understanding may goad each other into more extreme positions, but the two together form, through their opposing pressures, the way we feel about work. They do so in part by deflating two of our culture's prime motivating fantasies: the dreams of a perfectly realized calling on the one hand and of a life of guilt-free leisure on the other. By challenging such fantasies, the work and slacker ethics can help us revise our understanding of our own work lives, a process that, as those lives continuously change, is repeatedly necessary.
>
> (306)

54. Daniel Bell, 'Work and Its Discontents,' in *The End of Ideology*, Daniel Bell (Cambridge, MA: Harvard University Press, 1988), 255.

Conclusion

1. Malcolm Gladwell, *Outliers: The Story of Success* (New York: Little, Brown, 2008), 285.
2. For two particularly compelling demonstrations of the generally unacknowledged role of women in the success of men, see Micki McGee, *Self-Help, Inc: Makeover Culture in American Life* (New York: Oxford University Press, 2005) and Scott A. Sandage. *Born Losers: A History of Failure in America* (Cambridge, MA: Harvard University Press, 2005).
3. John Bodnar has written, 'Ultimately the movies were – and still are – what Michel Foucault might call "heterotopias," or sites where many of the most powerful ideas in a culture could be represented at the same time. They merged attitudes that were rational and emotional, moral and immoral, angry and sentimental. A typical film story generally contained contrasting images of common people and tended to integrate numerous points of view... into one feature that often rendered any one view or image "less potent".' *Blue Collar Hollywood: Liberalism, Democracy, and Working People in American Film* (Baltimore, MD: Johns Hopkins University Press, 2003), xviii.
4. James. V. Catano, *Ragged Dicks: Masculinity, Steel, and the Rhetoric of the Self-Made Man* (Carbondale, IL: Southern Illinois University Press, 2001), 14.
5. Claude Lévi-Strauss, *The Raw and The Cooked: Introduction to a Science of Mythology, Vol. 1*, trans. John Weightman and Doreen Weightman (New York: Harper and Row, 1969).
6. Robert Wuthnow, *American Mythos: Why Our Best Efforts to Be a Better Nation Fall Short* (Princeton, NJ: Princeton University Press, 2006).
7. Ibid., 1, 3.
8. See Shklovsky's 'Art as Technique,' in *Literary Theory: An Anthology*, Julie Rivkin and Michael Ryan, eds. (Malden, MA: Blackwell Publishing, 2004).

Bibliography

Adams, James Truslow. *The Epic of America*. New York: Simon Publications, 2001.
Adorno, Theodor W. 'Culture Industry Reconsidered.' *New German Critique* 6 (Fall 1975): 12–19.
Althusser, Louis. 'The Piccolo Teatro: Bertollazi and Brecht.' In *For Marx*, trans. Ben Brewster. London: New Left Books, 1977, 129–51.
Anderson, Benedict. *Imagined Communities: Reflections on the Origin and Spread of Nationalism*. London: Verso, 1991.
Andresky Fraser, Jill. *White-Collar Sweatshop: The Deterioration of Work and Its Rewards in Corporate America*. New York: W.W. Norton, 2001.
Aronowitz, Stanley. *How Class Works: Power and Social Movement*. New Haven, CT: Yale University Press, 2003.
Bakhtin, Mikhail. *Rabelais and His World*. Bloomington, IN: Indiana University Press, 1984.
Banta, Martha. *Failure and Success in America: A Literary Debate*. Princeton, NJ: Princeton University Press, 1978.
Baritz, Loren. *The Culture of the Twenties*. Indianapolis, IN: Bobbs-Merrill, 1970.
———. *The Good Life: The Meaning of Success for the American Middle Class*. New York: Harper and Row, 1982.
Barthes, Roland. *Mythologies*. New York: Hill and Wang, 1972.
Barton, Bruce. *The Man Nobody Knows: A Discovery of the Real Jesus*. Indianapolis, IN: Bobbs-Merrill, 1925.
Basinger, Jeanine. *A Women's View: How Hollywood Spoke to Women 1930–1960*. New York: Alfred A. Knopf, 1993.
Baym, Nina. 'Melodramas of Beset Manhood: How Theories of American Fiction Exclude Women Authors.' In *Locating American Studies: The Evolution of a Discipline*, Lucy Maddox (ed.). Baltimore, MD: Johns Hopkins University Press, 1998. 215–34.
Bell, Daniel. *The Cultural Contradictions of Capitalism*. New York: Basic Books, 1976.
———. *The End of Ideology: On the Exhaustion of Political Ideas in the Fifties*. Cambridge, MA: Harvard University Press, 2000.
———. 'Work and Its Discontents.' In *The End of Ideology: On the Exhaustion of Political Ideas in the Fifties*, Daniel Bell. Cambridge, MA: Harvard University Press, 1988. 227–72.
Bellah, Robert N. *Habits of the Heart: Individualism and Commitment in American Life*. Berkeley, CA: University of California Press, 1985.
Beller, Manfred and Joep Leerseen (eds.). *Imagology: The Cultural Construction and Literary Representation of National Characters: A Critical Survey*. Amsterdam: Rodopi, 2007.
Benjamin, Walter. *The Arcades Project*. Cambridge, MA: Belknap Press, 2002.
Bennett, Amanda. *The Death of the Organization Man*. New York: William Morrow, 1990.

Bergman, Andrew. *We're in the Money: Depression American and Its Films*. New York: New York University Press, 1971.

Bhabha, Homi K. *Nation and Narration*. London: Routledge, 1990.

Bidney, David. 'Myth, Symbolism, and Truth.' In *Myth: A Symposium*, Thomas A. Sebeok (ed.). Bloomington, IN: Indiana University Press, 1972.

Bingham, Dennis. *Whose Lives Are They Anyway?: The Biopic as Contemporary Film Genre*. New Brunswick, NJ: Rutgers University Press, 2010.

Biskind, Peter. *Seeing Is Believing: How Hollywood Taught Us to Stop Worrying and Love the Fifties*. New York: Pantheon, 1983.

Bodnar, John. *Blue-Collar Hollywood: Liberalism, Democracy, and Working People in American Film*. Baltimore, MD: Johns Hopkins University Press, 2003.

Boozer, Jack. *Career Movies: American Business and the Success Mystique*. Austin, TX: University of Texas Press, 2002.

Bordwell, David. *Making Meaning: Inference and Rhetoric in the Interpretation of Cinema*. Cambridge, MA: Harvard University Press, 1989.

———. *Narration in the Fiction Film*. New York: Routledge, 1987.

Bordwell, David, Janet Staigerand Kristin Thompson. *The Classical Hollywood Cinema*. New York: Columbia University Press, 1985.

Browne, Nick. *Francis Ford Coppola's Godfather Trilogy*. Cambridge: Cambridge University Press, 1999.

Bruzzi, Stella. *Bringing up Daddy: Fatherhood and Masculinity in Post-War Hollywood*. London: British Film Institute, 2005.

Burns, Rex. *Success in America: The Yeoman Dream and the Industrial Revolution*. Amherst, MA: University of Massachusetts Press, 1976.

Butler, Judith. *Gender Trouble: Feminism and the Subversion of Identity*. New York: Routledge, 1998.

Capra, Frank. *The Name above the Title*. New York: Macmillan, 1971.

Carney, Ray. *American Vision: The Films of Frank Capra*. West Nyak, NY: Cambridge University Press, 1986.

Carson, Diane. 'To Be Seen but Not Heard: The Awful Truth.' In *Multiple Voices in Feminist Film Criticism*, Diane Carson, Linda Dittmar and Janice R. Welsch (eds.). Minneapolis, MN: University of Minnesota Press, 1994. 213–25.

Cassirer, Ernst. *The Myth of the State*. New Haven, CT: Yale University Press, 1961.

Catano, James V. *Ragged Dicks: Masculinity, Steel, and the Rhetoric of the Self-Made Man*. Carbondale, IL: University of Illinois Press, 2001.

Cavell, Stanley. *Pursuits of Happiness: The Hollywood Comedy of Remarriage*. Cambridge, MA: Harvard University Press, 2004.

Cawelti, John G. *Apostles of the Self-Made Man: Changing Concepts of Success in America*. Chicago, IL: University of Chicago Press, 1965.

ChasingtheFrog.com, CTF Media. *Christ Gardner Stock Broker – Pursuit of Happyness True Story*. http://chasingthefrog.com/reelfaces/pursuitofhappyness.php.

Chopra-Gant, Mike. *Hollywood Genres and Postwar America: Masculinity, Family and Nation in Popular Movies and Film Noir*. London: I.B. Tauris, 2006.

Ciulla, Joanne B. *The Working Life: The Promise and Betrayal of Modern Work*. New York: Three Rivers Press, 2001.

Clapp, James A. 'Immigrants in the City and in Cinema.' *Visual Anthropology* 22, no. 1 (January 2009): 1–19.

Cohan, Steven. *Masked Men: Masculinity and the Movies in the Fifties*. Bloomington, IN: Indiana University Press, 1997.

Cohen, Lizabeth. *A Consumer's Republic: The Politics of Mass Consumption in Postwar America*. New York: Knopf, 2003.

Cook, Pam. 'Duplicity in Mildred Pierce.' In *Women and Film Noir*, E. Ann Kaplan (ed.). London: British Film Institute, 1998.

Cullen, Jim. *The American Dream: A History of an Idea that Shaped a Nation*. Oxford: Oxford University Press, 2003.

Custen, George. *Bio/Pics: How Hollywood Constructed Public History*. New Brunswick, NJ: Rutgers University Press, 1992.

Dargis, Manohla. 'Climbing Out of the Gutter with a Five-Year-Old in Tow.' *The New York Times*, 15 December 2006: Arts Section.

de Marco, Camillo. *Muccino and The Pursuit of Happyness*. 11 January 2007. http://cineuropa.org/newsdetail.aspx?lang=en&documentID=72032.

de Tocqueville, Alexis. *Democracy in America*, Henry Reeve (ed.) Vol. II. New York: American Classics Library, 1990.

Decker, Jeffrey Louis. *Made in America: Self-Styled Success from Horatio Alger to Oprah Winfrey*. Minneapolis, MN: University of Minnesota Press, 1997.

Desser, David and Garth S. Jowett (eds.). *Hollywood Goes Shopping*. Minneapolis, MN: University of Minnesota Press, 2000.

Dickstein, Morris. *Dancing in the Dark: A Cultural History of the Great Depression*. New York: W.W. Norton, 2009.

Doherty, Thomas. *Pre-Code Hollywood: Sex, Immortality, and Insurrection in American Cinema, 1930–1934*. New York: Columbia University Press, 1999.

————. *Teenagers and Teenpics: The Juvenilization of American Movies in the 1950s*. Philadelphia, PA: Temple University Press, 2002.

Doniger, Wendy. *The Implied Spider: Politics and Theology in Myth*. New York: Columbia University Press, 1998.

Donkin, Richard. *Blood Sweat and Tears: The Evolution of Work*. New York: Texere, 2001.

Doty, William G. *Mythography: The Study of Myths and Rituals* 2nd Edition. Tuscaloosa, AL: University of Alabama Press, 2000.

Dyer, Richard. *The Matter of Images: Essays on Representation* 2nd Edition. London: Routledge, 2002.

Easthope, Anthony. *What a Man's Gotta Do: The Masculine Myth in Popular Culture*. Winchester, MA: Union Hyman, 1990.

Eckert, Charles W. 'The Anatomy of a Proletarian Film: Warner's "Marked Woman"' *Film Quarterly* 27, no. 2 (Winter 1973–1974): 18.

Ehrenreich, Barbara. *Fear of Falling: The Inner Life of the Middle Class*. New York: Pantheon Books, 1989.

Eliade, Mircea. *The Sacred and the Profane*, trans. Willard R. Trask. New York: Harcourt, Brace, Jovanovich, 1987.

Elson, Ruth Miller. 'American Schoolbooks and Culture in the Nineteenth Century.' In *The National Temper: Readings in American Culture and Society* 2nd Edition. Lawrence W. Levine and Robert Middlekauff (eds.). New York: Harcourt Brace, 1972.

Ewen, Stuart. *Captains of Consciousness: Advertising and the Social Roots of the Consumer Culture*. New York: McGraw-Hill, 1976.

Faludi, Susan. *Backlash: The Undeclared War against America's Women*. New York: Crown, 1991.

———. *Stiffed: The Betrayal of the American Man*. New York: Harper Perennial, 2000.

Fiedler, Leslie. *A Fiedler Reader*. New York: Stein and Day, 1977.

———. *Love and Death in the American Novel*. New York: Stein and Day, 1966.

Fitzgerald, F. Scott. *The Great Gatsby*. New York: Scribner, 1925.

Flood, Christopher G. *Political Myth*. London: Routledge, 2002.

———. 'Myth and Ideology.' In *Thinking Through Myths: Philosophical Perspectives*, Kevin Schilbrack (ed.). London: Routledge, 2002.

Foster, Gwendolyn Audrey. *Class-Passing: Social Mobility in Film and Popular Culture*. Carbondale, IL: Southern Illinois University Press, 2005.

Franklin, Benjamin 'The Way to Wealth (1758).' In *The American Gospel of Success: Individualism and Beyond*, Moses Rischen (ed.). Chicago, IL: Quadrangle Books, 1965. 33–8.

French, Brandon. *On the Verge of Revolt: Women in American Film of the Fifties*. New York: Frederick Unger, 1978.

Frye, Northrup 'The Mythos of Spring: Comedy.' In *Anatomy of Criticism: Four Essays*, Northrup Frye. Princeton, NJ: Princeton University Press, 2000, 158–86.

Galbraith, John Kenneth. *The Affluent Society* 3rd Edition. Boston, MA: Houghton Mifflin, 1976.

Galerstein, Carolyn. *Working Women on the Hollywood Screen: A Filmography*. New York: Garland, 1989.

Gellner, Ernest. *Nations and Nationalism*. Ithaca, NY: Cornell University Press, 1983.

Gini, Al. *The Importance of Being Lazy: In Praise of Play, Leisure, and Vacations*. New York: Routledge, 2003.

Gladwell, Malcolm. *Outliers: The Story of Success*. New York: Little, Brown, 2008.

Gledhill, Christine. (ed.). *Home Is Where the Heart Is: Studies in Melodrama and the Womens Film*. London: BFI Publishing, 1987.

Goldstein, Laurence and David L. Lewis. *The Automobile and American Culture*. Ann Arbor, MI: University of Michigan Press, 1983.

Hall, Stuart. 'Notes on Deconstructing "the Popular".' In *People's History and Socialist Theory*, Raphael Samuel (ed.). London: Routledge, 1981. 232–3.

Hark, Steven Cohan and Ina Rae. *Screening the Male: Exploring Masculinities in Hollywood Cinema*. New York: Routledge, 1993.

Haskell, Molly. *From Reverence to Rape: The Treatment of Women in the Movies* 2nd Edition. Chicago, IL: University of Chicago Press, 1987.

Heckscher, Charles. *White Collar*. New York: Basic Books, 1995.

Hodgkinson, Tom. *How to Be Idle*. New York: Harper Collins, 2005.

Hodgson, Godfrey. *The Myth of American Exceptionalism*. New Haven, CT: Yale University Press, 2009.

Huber, Richard M. *The American Idea of Success*. New York: Pushcart, 1987.

Huizinga, Johan. *Homo Ludens*. New York: Beacon Press, 1989.

IMDb.com, Inc. *The Pursuit of Happyness (2006)*. http://boxofficemojo.com/movies/?id=pursuitofhappyness.htm.

Israel, Betsy. *Bachelor Girl: The Secret History of Single Women in the Twentieth Century*. New York: HarperCollins, 2002.

Jameson, Fredric. 'Postmodernism, or the Cultural Logic of Late Capitalism.' *New Left Review*, 146 (July–August 1984): 53–92.

Jasper, James M. *Restless Nation: Starting over in America*. Chicago, IL: University of Chicago Press, 2000.

Jeffords, Susan. *Hard Bodies: Hollywood Masculinity and the Reagan Era*. Brunswick, NJ: Rutgers University Press, 1994.

———. *The Remasculinization of America: Gender and the Vietnam War*. Bloomington, IN: Indiana University Press, 1989.

Jillson, Cal. *Pursuing the American Dream: Opportunity and Exclusion over Four Centuries*. Lawrence, KA: University Press of Kansas, 2004.

Johnston, Claire. 'Women's Cinema as Counter-Cinema.' In *Notes on Women's Cinema*, Claire Johnston (ed.). London: Society for Education in Film and Television, 1973. 31–40.

Jordan, Chris. *Movies and the Reagan Presidency: Success and Ethics*. Westport, CT: Praeger, 2003.

Kael, Pauline. *Kiss Kiss Bang Bang*. Boston, MA: Little Brown, 1968.

Kanter, Rosabeth. *Men and Women of the Corporation* 2nd Edition. New York: Basic Books, 1993.

Kaplan, E. Ann. 'The Case of the Missing Mother: Maternal Issues in Vidor's Stella Dallas.' *Heresis* 16 (1983): 81–5.

Karsten, Eileen. *From Real Life to Reel Life: A Filmography of Biographical Film*. Metuchen, NJ: Scarecrow Press, 1993.

Kellner, Douglas and MichaelRyan. *Camera Politica: The Politics and Ideology of Contemporary Hollywood Film*. Bloomington, IN: Indiana University Press, 1988.

Kerr, K. Austin and Blackford, Mansel G. 'The Company in the Postwar World.' In *History of the U.S. Economy Since World War II*, Harold G. Vatter and John F. Walker (eds.). Armonk, NY: M.E. Sharpe, 1996.

Kerr, Walter. *The Silent Clowns*. New York: Knopf, 1975.

Kilmer, Paulette D. *The Fear of Sinking: The American Success Formula in the Gilded Age*. Knoxville, TN: University of Tennessee Press, 1996.

King, Geoff. *Film Comedy*. London: Wallflower Press, 2002.

Kleinhans, Chuck. 'Working-Class Film Heroes: Junior Johnson, Evel Knievel and the Film Audience.' In *Jump Cup: Hollywood, Politics and Counter Cinema*, Peter Steven (ed.). New York: Praeger Publishers, 1985.

Klinger, Barbara. ' "Cinema/Ideology/Criticism." Revisited: The Progressive Genre.' In *Film Genre Reader II*, Barry Keith Grant (ed.). Austin, TX: University of Texas Press, 1995. 74–90.

Kuhn, Annette. *Women's Pictures: Feminism and Cinema*. New York: Verso, 1994.

Laderman, David. *Driving Visions: Exploring the Road Movie*. Austin, TX: University of Texas Press, 2002.

Lafrague, Paul. *Le Droit a La Pareses [The Right to Be Lazy]*. New York: Charles H. Kerr, 1989.

Lehman, Peter. *Between Men: Masculinity: Bodies, Movies, Culture*. New York: Routledge, 2001.

Levine, Daniel S. *Disgruntled: The Darker Side of the World of Work*. New York: Times Books, 1998.

Lévi-Strauss, Claude. *The Raw and the Cooked: Introduction to a Science of Mythology*, Vol. 1, trans. John Weightman and Doreen Weightman. New York: Harper and Row, 1969.

———. *Structural Anthropology*, Vol. 2. Chicago, IL: University of Chicago Press, 1983.

————. 'The Structural Study of Myth.' In *Myth: A Symposium*, Thomas A. Sebeok (ed.). Bloomington, IN: Indiana University Press, 1968.

Lincoln, Bruce. 'Mythic Narrative and Cultural Diversity in American Society.' In *Myth and Method*, Laurie L. Patton and Wendy Doniger. Charlottesville, VA: University Press of Virginia, 1996.

————. *Theorizing Myth: Narrative, Ideology, Scholarship*. Chicago, IL: University of Chicago Press, 1999.

Lipset, Seymour Martin. *American Exceptionalism: A Double-Edged Sword*. New York: WW. Norton and Co, 1996.

Lopate, Phillip. 'The Corporation as Fantasy Villain.' *The New York Times* (9 April 2009), 24.

Luft, Herbert G. 'King Vidor: A Career that Spans Half a Century.' *Film Journal* (Summer 1971), 34.

Lutz, Tom. *Doing Nothing: A History of Loafers, Slackers, and Bums in America*. New York: Farrar, Straus, and Giroux, 2006.

Malinowski, Bronislaw. *Myth in Primitive Psychology*. New York: Greenwood Publishing, 1979.

Mandel, Ernest. *Late Capitalism*. New York: Verso, 1978.

Mather, Cotton. 'A Christian and His Calling (1701).' In *The American Gospel of Success: Individualism and Beyond*, Moses Rischen (ed.). Chicago, IL: Quadrangle Books, 1965. 23–30.

May, Larry. *The Big Tomorrow: Hollywood and the Politics of the American Way*. Chicago, IL: University of Chicago Press, 2000.

Mayne, Judith. *Directed by Dorothy Arzner*. Bloomington, IN: Indiana University Press, 1994.

McCaffrey, Donald W. *Focus on Chaplin*. Englewood Cliffs, NJ: Prentice-Hall, 1971.

McGee, Micki. *Self-Help, Inc.: Makeover Culture in American Life*. Oxford: Oxford University Press, 2005.

McGuffey, William Holmes. *McGuffey's Newly Revised Eclectic Third Reader*. Cincinnati, OH: Winthrop B. Smith, 1843.

McNeil, William. 'Make Mine Myth.' *The New York Times* (28 December 1981): 19.

Mellen, Joan. *Women and Their Sexuality in the New Film*. New York: Horizon Press, 1973.

Mercer, John and Shinger, Martin. *Melodrama: Genre, Style, and Sensibility*. London: Wallflower Press, 2004.

Miller, Perry. 'The Shaping of the American Character.' *New England Quarterly* 28, no. 4 (December 1955): 435–54.

Mills, C. Wright. 'The Chief Executives.' In *The Power Elite*, C. Wright Mills. Oxford: Oxford University Press, 2000.

————. *White Collar: The American Middle Classes*. New York: Oxford University Press, 1956.

Modleski, Tania. *Feminism Without Women: Culture and Criticism in a "Postfeminist" Age*. New York: Routledge, 1991.

————. *Loving with a Vengeance: Mass-Produced Fantasies for Women*. London: Methuen, 1984.

Morgan, Janice. 'From Clochards to Cappuccinos: Renoir's Boudu Is "Down and Out" in Beverly Hills.' *Cinema Journal* 29, no. 2 (1990): 23–5.

Munby, Jonathan. *Public Enemies, Public Heroes: Screen the Gangster from Little Caesar to Touch of Evil*. Chicago, IL: University of Chicago Press, 1999.

Musser, Charles. 'Work, Ideology, and Chaplin's "Tramp".' In *Resisting Images: Essays on Cinema and History*, Robert Sklar and Charles Musser (eds.). Philadelphia, PA: Temple University Press, 1990.

Neal, Steve. 'Questions of Genre.' In *Film and Theory: An Analogy*, Robert Stam and Toby Miller (eds.). Malden, MA: Blackwell Publishing, 2000. 157–78.

Neupert, Richard. *The End: Narration and Closure in the Cinema*. Detroit, MI: Wayne State University Press, 1995.

Nochimson, Martha P. *Dying to Belong: Gangster Movies in Hollywood and Hong Kong*. Malden, MA: Blackwell Publishing, 2007.

Packard, Vance. *The Status Seekers*. New York: David McKay, 1959.

Patton, Laurie L. and Wendy Doniger (eds.). *Myth and Method*. Charlottesville, VA: University Press of Virginia, 1996.

Paul, William. *Laughing Screaming: Modern Hollywood Horror and Comedy*. New York: Columbia University Press, 1994.

Pells, Richard H. *Radical Visions and American Dreams*. New York: Harper and Row, 1973.

Polan, Dana. *Power and Paranoia: History Narrative and the American Cinema*. New York: Columbia University Press, 1986.

Purdy, Jim and Peter Roffman. *The Hollywood Social Problem Film: Madness, Despair, and Politics from the Depression to the Fifties*. Bloomington, IN: Indiana University Press, 1981.

Rabinbach, Anson. *The Human Motor: Energy, Fatigue, and the Origins of Modernity*. New York: Basic Books, 1990.

Ray, Robert B. *A Certain Tendency of the Hollywood Cinema, 1930–1980*. Princeton, NJ: Princeton University Press, 1985.

Reich, Robert and Charles Heckschert. *The Future of Success*. New York: Knopf, 2001.

Reisman, David. *The Lonely Crowd: A Study of the Changing American Character*. New Haven, CT: Yale University Press, 1950.

Rischin, Moses (ed.). *The American Gospel of Success: Individualism and Beyond*. Chicago, IL: Quadrangle Books, 1965.

Roffman, Peter. *The Hollywood Social Program Film: Madness, Despair, and Politics from the Depression to the Fifties*. Bloomington, IN: Indiana University Press, 1981.

Rosen, Marjorie. *Popcorn Venus*. New York: Coward, McCann, and Geoghegan, 1973.

Ross, Steven J. *Working Class Hollywood: Silent Film and the Shaping of Class in America*. Princeton, NJ: Princeton University Press, 1998.

Rubin, Rachel and Jeffrey Melnick. *Immigrants and Popular Culture*. New York: New York University Press, 2007.

Russell, Bertrand. *In Praise of Idleness and Other Essays*. New York: Routledge, 2004.

Rybczynski, Witold. *Waiting for the Weekend*. New York: Penguin, 1991.

Sandage, Scott A. *Born Losers: A History of Failure in America*. Cambridge, MA: Harvard University Press, 2005.

Sayre, Nora. *Running Time: Films of the Cold War*. New York: Dial Press, 1978.

Schatz, Thomas. *Hollywood Genres: Formulas, Filmmaking, and the Studio System*. New York: McGraw Hill, 1981.

Segal, Lynn. *Slow Motion: Changing Masculinities*. New Brunswick, NJ: Rutgers University Press, 1990.

Segal, Robert A. *Myth: A Very Short Introduction.* London: Oxford, 2004.

Sennett, Richard. *The Corrosion of Character: The Personal Consequences of Work in the New Capitalism.* New York: W.W. Norton, 1998.

Shary, Timothy. *Generation Multiplex: The Image of Youth in Contemporary American Cinema.* Austin, TX: University of Texas Press, 2002.

———. *Teen Movies: American Youth on Screen.* New York: Wallflower Press, 2006.

Sherman, Eric. *Directing the Film: Directors on Their Art.* Boston, MA: Little, Brown, 1976.

Sikov, Ed. *Screwball!: Hollywood's Madcap Romantic Comedies.* New York: Crown Press, 1989.

Silverman, Kaja. *Male Subjectivity at the Margins.* New York: Routledge, 1992.

Sirk, Douglas, interview by Jon Halliday. *Sirk on Sirk: Interviews with Jon Halliday.* London: BFI, 1971.

Slotkin, Richard. *Gunfighter Nation: The Myth of the Frontier in Twentieth-Century America.* New York: Atheneum, 1992.

———. *The Fatal Environment: The Myth of the Frontier in the Age of Industrialization, 1800–1890.* New York: Atheneum, 1985.

———. *Regeneration Through Violence: The Mythology of the American Frontier 1600–1860.* Middletown, CT: Wesleyan University Press, 1973.

Stam, Robert. *Subversive Pleasures: Bakhtin, Cultural Criticism, and Film.* Baltimore, MD: Johns Hopkins University Press, 1989.

Stead, Peter. *Film and the Working Class: The Feature Film in British and American Society.* Oxford: Routledge, 1991.

Sterritt, David. *Mad to Be Saved: The Beats, the 50s, and Film.* Carbondale, IL: Southern Illinois University Press, 1998.

Tasker, Yvonne. *Working Girls: Gender and Sexuality in Popular Cinema.* New York: Routledge, 1998.

Tawney, R.H. *Religion and the Rise of Capitalism.* New York: Harcourt, Brace and Company, 1926.

Taylor, Ella. 'All in the Work-Family: Television Families in the Workplace Settings.' In *Prime-Time Families: Television Culture in Postwar America*, Ella Taylor. Berkeley, CA: University of California Press, 1989.

Thumim, Janet and Kirkham, Pat. *Me Jane: Masculinity, Movies and Women.* New York: St. Martin's Press, 1995.

———. *You Tarzan: Masculinity, Movies and Men.* New York: St. Martin's Press, 1993.

Tomlinson, Alan. *Consumption, Identity, & Style.* London: Comedia Publishing, 1990.

Trachtenberg, Alan. *The Incorporation of America: Culture and Society in the Gilded Age.* New York: Hill and Wang, 1982.

Traube, Elizabeth G. *Dreaming Identities: Class, Gender, and Generation in 1980s Hollywood Movies.* Boulder, CO: Westview Press, 1992.

Turner, Victor. *The Forest of Symbols: Aspects of Ndembu Ritual.* Ithaca, NY: Cornell University Press, 1970.

———. *The Ritual Process: Structure and Anti-Structure.* Ithaca, NY: Cornell University Press, 1969.

Veblen, Thorstein. *The Theory of the Leisure Class.* London: Oxford University Press, 2008.

Vidor, King. *A Tree Is a Tree.* New York: Harcourt, Brace and Company, 1952.

————. *King Vidor on Filmmaking*. Philadelphia, PA: David McKay, 1972.

————. 'Letter to Dartmouth College.' 14 May 1974.

Warshow, Robert. 'The Gangster as a Tragic Hero.' In *The Immediate Experience: Movies, Comics, Theatre and Other Aspects of Popular Culture*, Robert Warshow. New York: Atheneum, 1974.

Weals, Gerald. *Canned Goods as Caviar: American Film Comedy of the 1930s*. Chicago, IL: University of Chicago Press, 1985.

Weber, Max. *The Protestant Ethic and the Spirit of Capitalism*, trans. Talcott Parsons. London: Routledge, 1998 [1905].

Weiss, Richard. *The American Myth of Success: From Horatio Alger to Norman Vincent Peale*. New York: Basic Books, 1969.

Whyte, Jr. William, H. *The Organization Man*. New York: Simon and Schuster, 1956.

Williams, Linda. ' "Something Else Besides a Mother": Stella Dallas and the Maternal Melodrama.' *Cinema Journal* 2, no. 24 (1985): 22–43.

Winokur, Mark. *American Laughter: Immigrants, Ethnicity, and 1930s Hollywood Film Comedy*. New York: St. Martin's Press, 1996.

Wondra, Janet. 'Marx in a Texas Love Triangle: "Marrying up" and the Classed Gaze in *Days of Heaven*.' *Journal of Film and Video* 57, no. 4 (Winter 2005): 3–17.

Wood, Robin. 'Ideology, Genre, Auteur.' *Film Comment* 13, no. 1 (1977): 46–51.

Wuthnow, Robert. *American Mythos: Why Our Best Efforts to Be a Better Nation Fall Short*. Princeton, NJ: Princeton University Press, 2006.

————. *Poor Richard's Principle: Recovering the American Dream Through the Moral Dimension of Work, Business, and Money*. Princeton, NJ: Princeton University Press, 1996.

Wyllie, Irvin G. *The Self-Made Man in America: The Myth of Rags to Riches*. New York: The Free Press, 1954.

Zaniello, Tom. *Working Stiffs, Union Maids, Reds and Riffraff: An Expanded Guide to Films about Labor*. Ithaca, NY: Cornell University Press, 2003.

Filmography

A Face in the Crowd. Director: Elia Kazan. 1957.
À nous la liberté. Director: René Clair. 1931.
A Place in the Sun. Director: George Stevens. 1951.
A Thousand Clowns. Director: Fred Coe. 1965.
About Schmidt. Director: Alexander Payne. 2002.
Adam's Rib. Director: George Cukor. 1949.
Adaptation. Director: Spike Jonze. 2002.
Alice Adams. Director: George Stevens. 1935.
All About Eve. Director: Joseph L. Mankiewicz. 1950.
All Quiet on the Western Front. Director: Lewis Milestone. 1930.
American Beauty. Director: Sam Mendes. 1999.
An American Tragedy. Director: Josef von Sternberg. 1931.
Baby Boom. Director: Charles Shyer. 1987.
Baby Face. Director: Alfred E. Green. 1933.
Boiler Room. Director: Ben Younger. 2000.
Boudu sauvé des eaux. Director: Jean Renoir. 1932.
Broadcast News. Director: James L. Brooks. 1987.
Broken Flowers. Director: Jim Jarmusch. 2005.
Caught. Director: Max Ophüls. 1949.
Citizen Kane. Director: Orson Welles. 1941.
City Lights. Director: Charles Chaplin. 1931.
Clerks. Director: Kevin Smith. 1994.
Clockwatchers. Director: Jill Sprecher. 1997.
Days of Heaven. Director: Terrence Malick. 1978.
Dazed and Confused. Director: Richard Linklater. 1993.
Dead End. Director: William Wyler. 1937.
Disclosure. Director: Barry Levinson. 1994.
Down and Out in Beverly Hills. Director: Paul Mazursky. 1986.
Easy Rider. Director: Dennis Hopper. 1969.
Easy Street. Director: Charles Chaplin. 1917.
Edison the Man. Director: Clarence Brown. 1940.
Employees' Entrance. Director: Roy del Ruth. 1933.
Everything Must Go. Director: Dan Rush. 2010.
Executive Suite. Director: Robert Wise. 1954.
Fatal Attraction. Director: Adrian Lyne. 1987.
Female. Director: Michael Curtiz. 1933.
Five Easy Pieces. Director: Bob Rafelson. 1970.
Flash of Genius. Director: Marc Abraham. 2008
Gentleman Prefer Blondes. Director: Howard Hawks. 1953.
Glengarry Glen Ross. Director: James Foley. 1992.
Greenberg. Director: Noah Baumbach. 2010.
Hallelujah I'm a Bum. Director: Lewis Milestone. 1933.

High Fidelity. Director: Stephen Frears. 2000.
His Girl Friday. Director: Howard Hawks. 1940.
His New Job. Director: Charles Chaplin. 1915.
His New Profession. Director: Charles Chaplin. 1914.
Holiday. Director: George Cukor. 1938.
How to Marry a Millionaire. Director: Jean Negulesco. 1953.
If You Could Only Cook. Director: William A. Seiter. 1935.
Imitation of Life. Director: Douglas Sirk. 1959.
It. Director: Clarence G. Badger. 1927.
It's a Wonderful Life. Director: Frank Capra. 1946.
It's Always Fair Weather. Director: Stanley Donen. 1955.
Judicial Consent. Director: William Bindley. 1994.
Kicking and Screaming. Director: Jesse Dylan. 2005.
Kramer vs. Kramer. Director: Robert Benton. 1979.
Little Caesar. Director: Mervyn LeRoy. 1931.
Little Children. Director: Todd Field. 2006.
Local Hero. Director: Bill Forsyth. 1983.
Look Who's Talking. Director: Amy Heckerling. 1989.
Lost in America. Director: Albert Brooks. 1985.
Lost in Translation. Director: Sofia Coppola. 2003.
Making a Living. Director: Henry Lehrman. 1914.
Mallrats. Director: Kevin Smith. 1995.
Manhattan Melodrama. Director: W.S. Van Dyke. 1934.
Mary Stevens, M.D. Director: Lloyd Bacon. 1933.
Mildred Pierce. Director: Michael Curtiz. 1945.
Modern Times. Director: Charles Chaplin. 1936.
Mr. Mom. Director: Stan Dragoti. 1983.
Mrs. Doubtfire. Director: Chris Columbus. 1993.
My Man Godfrey. Director: Gregory La Cava. 1936.
Nine to Five. Director: Colin Higgins. 1980.
No Reservations. Director: Scott Hicks. 2007.
Norma Rae. Director: Martin Ritt. 1979.
Nothing in Common. Director: Garry Marshall. 1986.
Office Space. Director: Mike Judge. 1999.
Patterns. Director: Fielder Cook. 1956.
Pay Day. Director: Charles Chaplin. 1922.
Possessed. Director: Clarence Brown. 1931.
Presumed Innocent. Director: Alan J. Pakula. 1990.
Rain. Director: Lewis Milestone. 1932.
Rambo: First Blood. Director: Ted Kotcheff. 1982.
Reality Bites. Director: Ben Stiller. 1994.
Red-Headed Woman. Director: Jack Conway. 1932.
Robocop. Director: Paul Verhoeven. 1987.
Ruby Gentry. Director: King Vidor. 1954.
Sadie McKee. Director: Clarence Brown. 1934.
Scarface. Director: Howard Hawks. 1932.
Sideways. Director: Alexander Payne. 2004.
Skyscraper Souls. Director: Edgar Selwyn. 1932.
Slackers. Director: Dewey Nicks. 2002.

Slumdog Millionaire. Director: Danny Boyle. 2008.
Stella Dallas. Director: King Vidor. 1937.
Stranger Than Paradise. Director: Jim Jarmusch. 1984.
Sullivan's Travels. Director: Preston Sturges. 1941.
Take a Letter, Darling. Director: Mitchell Leisen. 1942.
Tell It to the Judge. Director: Norman Foster. 1949.
Thank You for Smoking. Director: Jason Reitman. 2005.
The 40 Year Old Virgin. Director: Judd Apatow. 2005
The Apartment. Director: Billy Wilder. 1960.
The Best of Everything. Director: Jean Negulesco. 1959.
The Company Men. Director: John Wells.2010.
The Crowd. Director: King Vidor. 1928.
The Devil Wears Prada. Director: David Frankel. 2006.
The Front Page. Director: Lewis Milestone. 1931.
The Godfather. Director: Francis Ford Coppola. 1972, 1974, 1990.
The Gold Rush. Director: Charles Chaplin. 1925.
The Graduate. Director: Mike Nichols. 1967.
The Hudsucker Proxy. Director: Joel Coen. 1994
The Idle Class. Director: Charles Chaplin. 1921.
The Kid. Director: Charles Chaplin. 1921.
The Lady Eve. Director: Preston Sturges. 1941.
The Last Seduction. Director: John Dahl. 1994.
The Magnificent Dope. Director: Walter Lang. 1942.
The Man in the Gray Flannel Suit. Director: Nunnally Johnson. 1956
The Match King. Directors: Howard Bretherton and William Keighley. 1932.
The Public Enemy. Director: William A. Wellman. 1931.
The Pursuit of Happyness. Director: Gabriele Muccino. 2006.
The Secret of My Success. Director: Herbert Ross. 1987.
The Social Network. Director: David Fincher. 2010.
The Story of Alexander Graham Bell. Director: Irving Cummings. 1939.
The Weather Man. Director: Gore Verbinski. 2005.
They All Kissed the Bride. Director: Alexander Hall. 1942.
Three Men and a Baby. Director: Leonard Nimoy. 1987.
To Die For. Director: Gus van Sant. 1995.
To Each His Own. Director: Mitchell Leisen. 1946.
Trading Places. Director: John Landis. 1983.
Tucker: The Man and His Dream. Director: Frances Ford Coppola. 1988
Up in the Air. Director: Jason Reitman. 2009.
Wall Street. Director: Oliver Stone. 1987.
White Heat. Director: Raoul Walsh. 1949.
Woman Chases Man. Director: John G. Blystone. 1937.
Woman of the Year. Director: George Stevens. 1942.
Wonder Boys. Director: Curtis Hanson. 2000.
Work. Director: Charles Chaplin. 1915.
Working Girl. Director: Mike Nichols. 1988.
You Can't Take It with You. Director: Frank Capra. 1938.

Index